DIVIDED OVER
THAKSIN

DIVIDED OVER
THAKSIN
Thailand's Coup and Problematic Transition

EDITED BY
John Funston

SILKWORM BOOKS
Thailand

ISEAS

Institute of Southeast Asian Studies
Singapore

First published in Singapore in 2009 by
Institute of Southeast Asian Studies
30 Heng Mui Keng Terrace
Pasir Panjang
Singapore 119614
E-mail: publish@iseas.edu.sg
Website: <http://bookshop.iseas.edu.sg>

Co-published for distribution in Thailand only by Silkworm Books
6 Sukkasem Road, Suthep, Chiang Mai 50200
E-mail: info@silkwormbooks.com
Website: <www.silkwormbooks.com>

The responsibility for facts and opinions in this publication rests exclusively with the editor and contributors and their interpretations do not necessarily reflect the views or the policy of the publishers or their supporters.

ISEAS Library Cataloguing-in-Publication Data

Funston, John.
   Divided over Thaksin : Thailand's coup and problematic transition.
   1.   Thaksin Chinnawat, 1949-
   2.   Thailand—Politics and government.
   3.   Thailand—History—Coup d'état, 2006.
   I.   Title.
DS578.32 T32F98   2009

ISBN 978-981-230-961-7 (hard cover)
ISBN 978-981-230-962-4 (PDF)

Cover photo © Agron Dragaj 2008.

Typeset by International Typesetters Pte Ltd
Printed in Singapore by Chung Printing

Contents

List of Tables and Figures

List of Contributors

Bhanupong Nidhiprabha is Associate Professor in the Faculty of Economics, Thammasat University.

Chairat Charoensin-o-larn is Associate Professor in the Faculty of Political Science, Thammasat University.

Chaiwat Satha-Anand, Professor in the Faculty of Political Science, Thammasat University, is Director of the Peace Information Center, Foundation for Democracy and Development Studies, and Senior Research Scholar with the Thailand Research Fund.

Michael K. **Connors** teaches in the Department of Asian and International Studies, City University of Hong Kong.

John **Funston** is a Visiting Fellow, Faculty of Asian Studies, Australian National University.

Gothom Arya is Chairman of the National Economic and Social Advisory Council and Director of the Mahidol University Research Centre for Peace Building.

Joseph Chinyong **Liow** is Associate Professor and Head of Research at the Institute of Defence and Strategic Studies (IDSS), Singapore.

Michael J. **Montesano** is a Visiting Research Fellow at the Institute of Southeast Asian Studies, Singapore.

Glen **Robinson** is Executive Director of the ASEAN Focus Group.

Suchit Bunbongkarn is Senior Fellow at the Institute of Security and International Studies (ISIS Thailand), Emeritus Professor at the Faculty of Political Science, Chulalongkorn University, and was a member of the appointed National Legislative Assembly (2006–07).

Thitinan Pongsudhirak is Director of the Institute of Security and International Studies, Faculty of Political Science, Chulalongkorn University.

Vitit Muntarbhorn is Professor in the Law Faculty, Chulalongkorn University and currently serving the United Nations as Special Rapporteur on the situation of human rights in the Democratic People's Republic of Korea.

Peter **Warr** is the John Crawford Professor of Agricultural Economics and Director, Poverty Research Centre, Division of Economics, Research School of Pacific and Asian Studies at the Australian National University.

Preface

Thailand's recent political turbulence was closely monitored by the National Thai Studies Centre (NTSC) in a series of seminars and annual Thailand Update Conferences in 2006 (held only ten days after the 19 September military coup) and 2007. This volume includes selected presentations from these events.

The 2006 and 2007 Updates were held at the Australian National University on 29 September and 31 August respectively. The NTSC is most grateful for assistance in presenting these conferences. The Australia-Thailand Institute (ATI) provided generous support, both for administrative costs and assistance with travel funds for keynote speakers. It also provided funding for seminars on governance in Thailand, which enabled visits by Professors Vitit Muntarbhorn and Chaiwat Satha-Anand in August 2007 just prior to the Update. The Centre for Democratic Institutions at ANU, and Thammasat University funded travel for Thailand-based speakers in 2006 and 2007 respectively.

The NTSC is most grateful for all this support, and additional assistance provided during this time by the Royal Thai Embassy in Canberra. Without this, and ongoing support from ANU, it would not have been possible to maintain Centre activities.

Political unrest in Thailand made this time exceptionally busy for the NTSC. This volume reflects only a part of that, and reports of other events may be found on the website <www.anu.edu/thaionline>. I was at that time executive director of the centre, and as usual received invaluable assistance from numerous colleagues. NTSC staff members Jason Hall, Elizabeth Nunrom and David Hunter all made major contributions. Julian Kusa provided valuable editorial advice. Ajarn Chintana Sandilands was, as always, tireless in her contribution to NTSC activities. A special thank you to Sarah Bishop who had the main burden of preparing this manuscript, and provided skilled editorial assistance.

Roslina Johari provided helpful advice on the book cover, and Agron Dragaj was most generous in making photographs available for this.

Finally, a warm thanks to all contributors. The NTSC is most grateful for their outstanding expertise, and generosity in contributing to the centre's seminars and updates.

John Funston
Visiting Fellow
Faculty of Asian Studies
Australian National University

Introduction

John Funston

In August 2006, former Prime Minister Anand Panyarachun warned that Thailand risked becoming a failed state: "If Thai society is ... divided and there is so much hate, and the environment is conducive to prolonging this hate, and to sustaining conflict, it is frightening, very frightening." If allowed to continue, the government would be unable to administer the country.[1] On 19 September the military staged a coup which promised to resolve these problems and return Thailand to democratic rule. Yet by late 2008 Anand's prediction appeared close to realization. In November, opponents of former Prime Minister Thaksin Shinawatra had blockaded and shut down Bangkok's two airports for more than a week, causing chaos to international travellers and immobilizing government. Wearing yellow shirts as a symbol of their loyalty to the monarchy, the People's Alliance for Democracy (PAD), clashed intermittently with red-shirted members of the United Front of Democracy Against Dictatorship (UDD) aligned to Thaksin. The deadlock was broken only by a court decision banning the ruling party and removing Prime Minister Somchai Wongsawat from office.

The airport blockade was the culmination of a turbulent year in Thai politics. The first elections after the 2006 coup were held in December 2007, and gave an overwhelming victory to the Thaksin-aligned People Power Party (PPP). It won 233 of 480 seats in its own right, and five closely allied parties won 82 seats. A coalition government of all parties was soon established, minus the Democrat Party which won only 165 seats and remained in opposition.

The PPP government, led by controversial veteran Samak Sundaravej, was soon besieged by street protests. In May 2008 a revived PAD, whose continued protests against the Thaksin administration during 2006 paved the way for the coup, protested against mooted constitutional changes. Those changes were aimed at removing from the charter provisions intended to weaken Thaksin and his allies. Soon the PAD demanded that the government give up power, and when Samak refused, stormed and occupied Government House on 26 August. In September Samak was forced to relinquish power when the Constitutional Court ruled against him, finding that by hosting two commercial television cooking shows he had violated constitutional provisions against conflicts of interest. A new PPP-dominated government, headed by Somchai (Thaksin's brother-in-law) took power and the PAD escalated its campaign. In October the PAD blockaded parliament to try and prevent Somchai from presenting the new government's policy statement. Police moved against them on 7 October, and in the ensuing conflict two were killed and hundreds injured. The PAD then took over Bangkok's airports in a bid to prevent Somchai returning from an overseas trip. On 2 December the Constitutional Court dissolved the PPP (and two coalition allies) and disqualified all party executive members for electoral fraud — invoking Article 237 of the constitution which provides for the dissolution of a party if an executive member is found guilty of violating the election law and the party is found to be complicit in the offence.

Later in December the defection of a group from the PPP replacement, Puea Thai, saw the emergence of a Democrat-led coalition government, headed by Abhisit Vejjajiva. It began tentatively, with several cabinet members facing accusations of conflict of interest, and coming under similar pressures from the UDD as its predecessors had from the PAD.[2]

While the breakaway of a Puea Thai faction might reflect a weakening of Thaksin's influence, this was not clear cut. Thaksin had returned to an enthusiastic Bangkok welcome in February 2008, declaring himself ready to clear his name by contesting legal cases brought against him. On 31 July, however, his wife was found guilty of tax evasion and sentenced to three years jail. The next day Thaksin left the country, and ten days later declared he would remain in exile. On 21 October Thaksin was found guilty of abuse of power and conflict of interest for helping his wife purchase land in Bangkok from a state agency in 2003, and sentenced to two years jail in absentia. Yet even in exile Thaksin kept in constant contact with PPP and Peau Thai leaders, receiving regular delegations at a variety of overseas destinations. He guided the tactics of these parties, and appeared at mass rallies through satellite connections or recorded messages. Mass support in Thailand showed no signs of diminishing — around 30,000 turning out for a rally at the end of January 2009.

By early 2009, rather than returning to democracy as coup leaders had promised, Thai society remained polarized between pro-Thaksin forces on the one hand — comprising remnants of the Thai Rak Thai and other right-wing parties, mass supporters in the north, northeast and some in Bangkok (organized in the UDD), and democrats resolutely opposed to changing government by military putsch — and a more diverse coalition of anti-Thaksin forces. Ranged against Thaksin were members of Bangkok's middle class opposed to Thaksin's alleged corruption, blatant disregard for media freedom, human rights, and the rule of law, and sometimes prickly approach towards the monarchy (supporters of the PAD), Thailand's oldest political party, the Democrats, groups close to the royal family, and the military. The judiciary was also arguably aligned with this group, handing down a series of decisions that went against Thaksin and his followers. Rather than moving towards democracy, Thailand found itself divided between two coalitions committed to destroying the other, by force if necessary, and with a constitution that remained contested and unable to provide a framework for conflict resolution.

How did Thailand reach this point? Why had the September 2006 coup, and the new constitution that resulted from this, failed to heal social divisions and return the country to democracy? The period between 2005 and 2007 is critical — the immediate months leading up to the September coup, the coup itself, and post-coup attempts to forge a new constitution and political framework. That is the focus of this volume.

Thaksin Shinawatra came to office in 2001 during a moment of national optimism, winning elections convincingly under a new "people's constitution" approved in 1997. The constitution was the most democratic ever, including important guarantees of civil rights and an array of independent institutions to enforce these, though at the same time strengthening executive powers to reduce instability associated with weak coalition governments and factional conflicts. Thaksin's Thai Rak Thai (TRT — Thais Love Thais) campaigned under the slogan of "new thoughts, new actions", promising more reform to protect the interests of the rural poor, strengthened economic dynamism (still constrained by fallout from the 1997 Asian economic crisis) and expanded democratic opportunities.

During his first term in office Thaksin entrenched his position. His populist economic policies, particularly a universal health scheme and village credit, were wildly popular with the electorate. Some in the middle class became worried about Thaksin's apparent tolerance of corruption and disregard for democracy ("Democracy", he once said, "is just a tool, not our goal."[3]). Still, the TRT won an even stronger mandate at elections in 2005.[4]

But at the height of his power and popularity, Thaksin's fortunes began to change. *Michael J. Montesano* argues that government closure of Sondhi Limthongkul's weekly current affairs programme on government-owned television in September 2005 was a critical turning point. Sondhi, a media magnate and former associate of Thaksin turned critic, responded by launching a mass movement, which gained further momentum following the controversial sale of the Thaksin family company Shin Corporation to the Singapore government-controlled Temasek in January 2006. The parameters of debate for the rest of the year were set during this period. Sondhi and his supporters criticized Thaksin for not respecting democratic norms such as freedom of speech and the rule of law; Thaksin responded by invoking the 19 million who had voted for him in the 2005 elections. Sondhi and supporters also requested royal intervention, taking this to a new level with a formal petition to the king. Thaksin sought to overcome opposition by seeking a fresh electoral mandate only a year into his second administration.

Between March and June 2006 conflict intensified, with royal intervention increasingly becoming a reality. Elections were boycotted by the Democrats and other opposition parties, and showed less support than in 2005, but Thaksin was quick to declare victory. However, as Montesano notes, following a "meeting with the king from which he apparently emerged stunned, Thaksin announced that he would not become prime minister when the newly elected parliament sat." On 25 April the king told newly appointed judges that the one-party election had not been democratic, ruled out direct royal intervention in the absence of a parliament, and called on the judiciary to find a way out of the "mess". That was soon followed by judicial annulment of the elections. Thaksin hit back by alleging a threat to democracy from a "charismatic individual outside the constitution", a reference either to the royal institution or someone closely associated with it.

From July the battle lines sharpened even further. Individuals close to the king, including former prime minister and head of the king's Privy Council, Prem Tinsulanonda, and Anand Panyarachun, made repeated criticisms of Thaksin. The military, estranged by Thaksin's attempts to install his own favourites in top army positions, was increasingly drawn into the conflict. As hope that the situation might be resolved by the disintegration of the ruling Thai Rak Thai or judicial intervention faded, the military intervened.

Montesano notes that a "perfect storm" of factors highlighted the growing role of the monarchy in political developments. The sixtieth anniversary of the king's accession to the throne was celebrated with elaborate pomp and circumstance and enthusiastic public acclaim. The publication of Paul Handley's *The King Never Smiles* and a seminal article on "network monarchy" by Duncan McCargo attracted widespread academic interest (and followed the 2005 publishing sensation of Pramual Rujanaseri's *Phra Ratcha-amnat,* or "*Royal Powers*" — arguing that the king retained residual power to intervene in political affairs). Finally, during the prolonged political crisis, the monarchy was repeatedly urged to intervene.

The 1997 constitution had a central role in these developments. *Thitinan Pongsudhirak* outlines the background to this charter, linking it to dramatic events associated with the 1991 military coup and mass demonstrations against military rule the following year. A movement for constitutional reform began in 1993, and eventually formed into a Constitutional Drafting Assembly, which toured the countryside listening to public opinion before finalizing a draft in 1997.

Out of this emerged consensus over the need for an elected prime minister (General Prem never faced the electorate during his rule from 1980 to 1988), and for provisions that would address problems such as electoral fraud, vote-buying and money politics. A number of key provisions specifically addressed these concerns, including compulsory voting, a party-list system for 100 of the 500 members of the Lower House, and single-member constituencies. Candidates had to have a bachelor's degree — intended to keep out provincial "mafia" figures. A number of special courts and independent institutions were set up to guard the public interest, including the Constitutional and Administrative Courts, the Electoral Commission (EC), the National Counter Corruption Commission (NCCC) and the National Economic and Social Advisory Council (NESAC). (The role of the NESAC, both prior to and immediately after the coup, is examined separately by current chairman, *Gothom Arya.*) The charter also promoted a strong executive, particularly the premiership with parliamentary censure requiring support from 40 per cent of the Lower House.

The constitution was initially very popular, and institutions such as the EC and NCCC scored some notable successes, particularly the latter's conviction of Deputy Prime Minister Sanan Kachornprasart for failing to disclose assets. Then, however, Thaksin came to power, and the Constitutional Court failed a critical test when it found the prime minister not guilty of asset concealment, by a narrow 8:7 margin. This, Thitinan sees as the beginning of Thaksin's unravelling. Emboldened by success, Thaksin then moved to exert control over the Constitutional Court and other independent institutions, including the EC and NCCC, ignoring critics who opposed this, and other restrictions on democratic accountability. This provoked a strong reaction, including by many who had supported Thaksin during his court case.

An additional factor that contributed to the coup was the tragic resumption of armed conflict in the predominantly Muslim provinces in the south, which has claimed over 3,000 lives since 2004. Montesano notes that army chief General Sonthi Boonyaratglin raised the possibility of opening talks with the southern insurgents — a proposal that put him sharply at odds with Thaksin, and was identified by several in the international media as directly linked to the coup. Media analysis probably overstates the significance of the Thaksin-Sonthi disagreement — few of the leaders referred to this in coup announcements, and only limited attempts were made to shift policy afterwards. However several articles in this volume argue Thaksin's inability to contain this conflict did undermine the prime minister's authority.

Broader aspects of the southern conflict are addressed in four chapters. *Chaiwat Satha-Anand* provides an overview of the conflict, focusing particularly on why the conflict has been so difficult to resolve — highlighting official vested interests in its continuation, conflicting perceptions on conflict origins, and Thai society's unwillingness to recognize Bangkok policies towards Malay Muslims as constituting a form of internal colonialism. *Michael K. Connors* argues that there is a stateless "nation" in the south, describing Malays there as a language and ethnic community in the process of re-mobilization and regeneration. Recognition of another nation ("in whatever political form") should be the starting point for peace-building. *John Funston* argues that decentralization, as proposed by southern Thai academic and activist Wan Kadir Che Wan (based on provisions for decentralization set out in Chapter 9 of the 1997 constitution) and in the government appointed National Reconciliation Commission report (building on existing institutions that constitute a *de facto* form of decentralization), could help alleviate conflict. *Joseph Chinyong Liow* examines aspects of Islamic education in the south, in particular the role of controversial educator Ismail Lutfi Japakiya, and argues that a more nuanced understanding of his teachings is warranted.

Did economic factors contribute to the coup? *Peter Warr* does not argue for such an interpretation, though he does note that economic recovery under Thaksin was only moderate, averaging around 5 per cent per annum. Like neighbouring countries, Thailand failed to do better because it failed to stimulate private investment. More controversially, Warr rejects the view that Thaksin's policies successfully addressed the needs of the poor. There were, he agrees, some benefits, including the 30 baht (US$0.83) universal health scheme, the freeze on repayment of loans by farmers, and the village credit scheme. But in general the results were unremarkable. Poverty reduction, which made large gains during the high growth periods of the 1980s and early 1990s, was "below the long-term average" under Thaksin.

Turning to the immediate aftermath of the coup, *Chairat Charoensin-o-larn* notes a sharply divided society. Included among opponents were an educated elite who opposed coups in principle, and lower income people who feared losing the economic benefits Thaksin had extended. Supporters included members of royalty, the old elite, armed forces, the middle class and urban intellectuals. Many among this group saw the coup as a "last resort" after all other measures had failed. As members of Bangkok's public came out to garland soldiers in tanks, some saw it as a "special" coup with a human face.

However a year after the coup, Chairat argues, the proclaimed goal of healing divisions in Thai society had made no progress. The military had proven themselves unable to govern. The economy had declined. Civil liberties were curtailed, and the coup group was unable to provide a democratic alternative to Thaksin's authoritarianism.

Until May 2007 coup leaders remained uncertain about how they would deal with the Thaksin legacy. They set institutions in place to address this, appointing new members to the NCCC, modifying the Constitutional Court (and renaming it the Constitutional Tribunal), and establishing an Assets Scrutiny Commission (ASC) as the main body to investigate alleged instances of corruption. On 30 May a second period began when the Constitutional Tribunal controversially dissolved the ruling Thai Rak Thai, and imposed a five-year political ban on 111 of its executives. Less than two weeks later the ASC froze 52 billion baht of Thaksin's assets (later increased by a further 20 billion baht), and laid a series of charges against the former premier. Even so, Thaksin's continuing influence was shown by the strong vote against the constitution during the referendum on 19 August 2007 — a majority of voters in the north and northeast opposed it, and overall the government fell well short of its desired 70 per cent majority.

Chairat agrees that the 2007 constitution does give additional power to the people in some areas, but overall its main focus is on controlling the government and little else. The military still regards itself as the "guardian" of democracy, and will be able to use this constitution — together with the new Internal Security Bill passed in December 2007 — to ensure the reimposition of a security state and bureaucratic polity.

Vitit Muntarbhorn examines the 2007 constitution in more detail, and comes to similar conclusions. There are, he agrees, some notable innovations compared to 1997, including strengthened controls over the executive, stronger provisions for protecting human rights, and greater powers to the courts, independent institutions and the general public. There are, however, many "grey areas" in a constitution drafted by a small elite, without public participation. The military was "the unwritten power behind the constitutional process", and stood to gain from a constitutional amnesty extended to their putsch, along with other moves to consolidate their influence. The judiciary had been enhanced, changing its relationship with the legislature, and executive. The constitution reveals a deep distrust of politicians, resulting in an electoral system that will favour weaker parties and enhance the prospect of unstable coalition governments. The partly appointed Senate (74 of 150) is likely to come under government influence, and human rights and civil society provisions will prove difficult to implement in practice.

Suchit Bunbongkarn is more optimistic. He argues that the 2007 constitution expands civil and political rights, while restricting the power of politicians and ensuring more effective checks and balances. In retrospect, he argues, the 1997 constitution went too far in entrenching the executive. The new constitution makes the executive more dependent on parliament. Contrary to other analysts, Suchit argues against the military continuing to play a major role. Since the coup, the military had demonstrated that it could seize power but it could not rule. The constitution placed strict limits on military involvement in politics, and it would have no option but to withdraw from the political arena.

The other post-coup issue discussed in this volume is the economy. *Bhanupong Nidhiprabha* sees the coup and post-coup government as extremely detrimental to economic growth and a threat to the long-term future. Unlike earlier coups, this one destroyed the confidence of the business sector and consumers. Political uncertainty and policy blunders made the Thai economy the regional laggard, and its 4.5 per cent growth rate was even below the world average (5.1 per cent).

Slow growth was not related to a lack of foreign demand or supply constraints. Like Warr, Bhanupong attributes slow growth to shortfalls in investment, along with a decline in consumption. A series of policy changes deterred foreign investors — including attempts to amend the alien business law, and above all an ill-fated attempt to impose capital controls in December 2006. Although capital controls were quickly relaxed, the action damaged confidence in Thailand's open-door policy.

Government changes adversely affected particularly the poor. Slow growth has limited capacity to reduce poverty, and an increase in defence spending has diverted resources away from more productive economic sectors. The poor made known their objections by voting against the military-imposed constitution and subsequently supporting the PPP when it promised to act as a successor to the TRT.

Glen Robinson, a businessman, however finds differences between "perceptions" of what happened in Thailand during a period of political uncertainty, and the reality. Media reports, he noted, suggested that FDI had dried up, foreign business was withdrawing from Thailand, and international tourists were giving Thailand the cold shoulder. Statistics, he argues, did not bear this out — FDI was steady, investment applications to the Board of Investment increased, and Australian tourists arrived in increasing numbers.

But if foreign business was not overly concerned by an uncertain political environment, Thais were unimpressed. Why appointed Finance Minister MR Pridiyathorn Devakula, a noted technocrat and former governor of the Bank of Thailand, should stumble over currency controls and a Foreign Business Act remains a mystery, but it contributed to an impression of a government that was out of its depth. In addition, the attempt to replace Thaksin's populism with the king's proposal for a "sufficiency economy" met little enthusiasm. While this arguably led to limited change in practice, many suspected that it would eventually mean a reduction in benefits extended under Thaksin.

Nonetheless it was political shortcomings of the military-installed interim government under Prime Minister Surayud Chulanont that made transition to a promised new democracy so problematic. It proved unable to convince the broad public that allegations against Thaksin — particularly those relating to corruption — had substance. It made no progress in addressing the violence in the south. It presided over the drafting of a new constitution that few were happy with. And it left Thai society even more polarized than when the coup was conducted. That contributed to the continuing political crisis since elections in 2007, and presents an enormous challenge to future governments.

NOTES

1. "Thailand 'at Risk of becoming Failed State'", *Bangkok Post*, 31 August 2006.
2. Civil unrest flared anew in April 2009, when UDD demonstrations aborted an ASEAN-East Asia summit meeting in Pattaya, and was followed by armed confrontation between the UDD and army in Bangkok. Dispersal of demonstrators in Bangkok bought the Abhisit government time, but the UDD remains a force to be reckoned with.
3. "PM's Declaration: 'Democracy is Not My Goal'", *The Nation*, 11 December 2003.
4. For discussion of politics at this time, see John Funston, ed., *Thaksin's Thailand: Populism and Polarisation* (Bangkok: Institute of Strategic and International Studies; Canberra: National Thai Studies Centre, 2009).

1

Political Contests in the Advent of Bangkok's 19 September Putsch

Michael J. Montesano

INTRODUCTION

For more than three decades, since Thailand's emergence from naked military dictatorship in the early 1970s, both academic and journalistic observers have tended to view its politics as a work in progress. Extreme cynics, some historians, and a few remaining crude "cultural" determinists have resisted this Whig view of Thai developments. But its appeal has otherwise proved strong and general. A resolve to craft some sort of stable, putatively modern and democratic, idealized political order numbered among the main influences on the drafters of Thailand's 1997 constitution.[1] The subsequent, widespread hope that the constitution would undermine money politics and see to the emergence of a collection of independent oversight bodies testified even more directly to the appeal of the idea of progress in Thai politics. Thaksin Shinawatra put paid to that hope after becoming premier in 2001. Then, the evening of 19 September 2006 brought the dismal spectacle of a twenty-first-century military seizure of state power in Bangkok and the abrogation of the 1997 constitution.

On one level, the conduct of the Thaksin government and the putsch that removed Thaksin from the political arena might each seem to vindicate the cynics, historians, and the crude culturalists in their scepticism about progress in Thai politics. On a more fundamental level, however, what defined that politics during the year preceding Thaksin's ouster was a contest between two visions of where political progress should lead. Far from deadening the appeal of such visions, the year confirmed their continued relevance. Likewise, the tanks that appeared on the streets of Bangkok on 19 September in no way ended that contest. It has resumed, and, not least now that the reign of King Bhumiphol has passed the sixty-two-year mark, there is every reason to believe that that contest will only intensify in the months and years ahead.

The 19 September 2006 putsch in Bangkok came at the end of a year of endlessly confusing turns, twists, advances, and reverses on the Thai political scene. Nevertheless, these developments came in three discernible phases: September 2005–February 2006, March–June 2006, and July–September 2006. These distinct phases notwithstanding, a number of factors proved important throughout the entire period. These factors included the opposition to Thaksin, the monarchy and its network, the Thai courts, the place of Bangkok-Singapore ties in Thailand's long crisis of 2006, and the continuing insurgency in the country's far south. Similarly, at least preliminary scrutiny of the putsch itself has considerable value to an understanding of the contest between visions for the Thai political order that defined the year preceding the military's seizure of state power.

PHASES IN THE CRISIS

September 2005–February 2006

On 16 September 2005, the Thaksin government took idiosyncratic media entrepreneur Sondhi Limthongkul's weekly current-events programme Mueang Thai Raisapda off the Mass Communication Organization of Thailand's Channel 9 television station. Sondhi had begun to use the programme to mount criticisms of the prime minister, his former business associate.[2] Just a few days more than five months later, the mass movement that Sondhi launched in response to being taken off the air forced Thaksin to dissolve parliament and seek a fresh electoral mandate.

This Sondhi episode was hardly the first in which Thaksin used his control of the airwaves to shut down a critic. What differed this time was, first, Sondhi's ingenuity in putting up a fight and, second and more important, the willingness of some Bangkokians, at least, to side with him in his contest with Thaksin. Thaksin's February 2005 landslide election victory notwithstanding, some better-educated residents of the capital had moved away from the admiration with which they had long regarded their premier. They had begun to heed those critics who harped on his authoritarian manner and his naked use of the levers of government to benefit his family's business concerns and those of some of his closest associates. Some numbers of these Bangkokians turned out consistently to hear Sondhi's string of charges against the Thaksin government, after he took his programme live, to Thammasat University and then to the open-air setting of Lumphini Park.

Whether Sondhi's anti-Thaksin drive would have gained momentum or petered out, if not for the announcement on 23 January 2006 that the Singaporean state investment company Temasek Holdings would purchase Shin Corporation, must remain a hypothetical question. The sale hardly came as a surprise. Not only were Thaksin's warm relations with Singapore's People's Action Party (PAP) government and his habit of mixing Thailand's foreign relations with his personal business activities well known, but cash-rich Temasek had begun increasingly and deliberately to invest outside Singapore, and not least in the region. Further, Thaksin made a New Year's trip to Singapore, amid widespread rumour that the sale of Shin to Temasek's listed Singapore Telecom subsidiary was imminent.[3]

Of course, if Thaksin indeed used that trip or any other meeting to take an active role in this transaction, he was violating provisions of the 1997 constitution banning cabinet ministers from most business activity.[4] By January 2005, however, such abuses on his part had become so persistent as to be taken virtually for granted. More noteworthy was the question of why Thaksin finally opted to sell. He himself claimed that he wanted to put to rest allegations of conflict of interest between his government and his family's business once and for all. Other often cited theories related to the future prospects of the telecommunications business in Thailand and to the introduction of "third-generation" or "3G" mobile-phone technology.[5] However, neither seemed a particularly convincing explanation of the Shin sale.

In one respect at least, the timing of the Shin-Temasek deal presented no mystery. It came directly after legislation raising the limit on foreign ownership of telecommunications firms from 25 to 49 per cent and thus proved one more case of the "policy corruption" that had typified Thaksin's administration. Too, the last-minute transfer of a large block of his family's shares from a previously unknown holding company in the British Virgin Islands allowed Thaksin and his family to sell their entire Shin stake on the Thai stock exchange. This manoeuvre freed them of any tax liability on a 73 billion baht (US$2 billion) transaction.[6]

Other aspects of the transaction, above all the role and control of holding companies created by Temasek in a fairly transparent attempt to dodge foreign-ownership regulations in Thailand, also aroused comment and outrage. Shin's operations in sectors — telecommunications, television, civil aviation — in which income streams depended on concessions awarded by the Thai state only sharpened the effect of the firm's sale to foreign interests. These reactions presented a boost to Sondhi's movement, one on which he very quickly capitalized. His 4 February rally in Bangkok's Royal Plaza drew some 50,000 people. Having spent the previous half-year claiming that his movement was a fight for the king,[7] he took his attempt to draw the monarchy into his campaign to oust Thaksin to a new level by invoking the historical practice of directly petitioning the monarch. He delivered his petition, calling on the king to replace the prime minister, to the residence of former prime minister and incumbent Privy Council president General Prem Tinsulanonda and to the office of the king's principal private secretary. In reaction to all this, Thaksin invoked the 19 million Thais who had supported him in the 2005 general election, but acknowledged that, should he receive a whisper from the king telling him that it was time to go, he would resign.[8]

Very quickly, then, the terms of debate that would define Thai politics right up to 19 September 2006 had been set. While Thaksin stressed his electoral mandate, his antagonists invoked a more normative understanding of democratic government in their effort to oust him. Somewhere in the resultant contest, both sides seemed to agree, was a role for Thailand's prestigious royal institution.

Sondhi's movement soon expanded into a new People's Alliance for Democracy (PAD), whose collective leadership came to include Chamlong Srimuang — leader of the bloody 1992 street protests that drove General Suchinda Kraprayoon from power, a secretary-general to General Prem when the latter served as premier during the 1980s, and the man who had brought Thaksin into politics in the early 1990s by recruiting him into his Phalang Tham Party. Chamlong's decision to join the PAD and to bring to its rallies the members of his "Dharma Army" contributed substantially to its heft.[9] At the same time, formation of the PAD broadened the range both of the speakers at anti-Thaksin rallies and of topics addressed. Student leaders seemed poised, if only for a moment, to make their first significant appearance on the national political scene since 1992; opponents of the proposed Thai-U.S. free trade agreement became fixtures at PAD events.

Not all efforts to resolve the political crisis to which the Shin-Temasek deal had given new intensity unfolded on the streets. A group of senators petitioned the Constitutional Court to impeach Thaksin, only to meet with rejection. Thaksin proposed a joint meeting of the Assembly and the Senate, only to find himself rebuffed by opposition parties. Finally, on 23 February 2007, Thaksin called on Privy Council president Prem. The following day, accusing his opponents of foisting "mob rule" on the country, the premier dissolved Parliament and called for new elections. The voters, following formal democratic procedures, would be allowed to decide his fate. Almost immediately, the Chart Thai, Democrat, and Mahachon parties announced their plans to boycott these polls. They argued, justifiably, that formal scrutiny by regulators or the courts rather than what amounted to a plebiscite was the appropriate means of addressing the allegations against Thaksin.[10] Tactical considerations aside, their electoral boycott thus emphasized a vision of democratic legitimacy whose basis lay in the functioning of institutions and the rule of law. Ironically, it was to end the conflict between that vision and one stressing the ballot box and the ballot box alone that the Thai Army would claim to intervene in late September.

March–June 2006

Of course, the conflict was never so straightforward, as the camp that in principle favoured correct processes rather than mere electoral tallies at the same time sought to force Thaksin's ouster through the extra-institutional means of mounting as large public rallies as possible. Its protests would continue during the second phase of the year's crisis.

Privy Council president Prem's apparent role in triggering Thaksin's decision to dissolve parliament prefigured another aspect of this phase: almost total focus among many of the premier's opponents on calls for royal intervention to effect Thaksin's ouster. These calls for a premier directly appointed by the king centred on the putative applicability of Article 7 of the 1997 constitution. They culminated in a rally of some 300,000 people along Ratchadamnoen Nok Avenue on the night of 25 March, at which the PAD presented another petition calling for the invocation of that article to end the impasse. While such a direct renewed appeal and correspondingly naked attempt to involve the king in the politics of the move against Thaksin were controversial, three factors made clear that it was not just the PAD that sought to involve the palace in the crisis.

One was, quite simply, the density of royal-jubilee-year yellow shirts and head-bands at PAD demonstrations. Not only the PAD's leaders but also evidently much of its base of attentive, educated Bangkok residents had placed hope in the king. Second was the unprecedented prominence of the president of the Privy Council in the events of the period. Of course, General Prem's stature and renown were independent of the body that he headed, a low-profile institution about which few Thais knew much.[11] All the same, Prem did not function as respected former prime minister and elder statesman but as holder of a formal office that gave him regular, direct, generally acknowledged access to the king. Finally, in a bizarre occurrence, Thai television showed on the evening of 12 March footage of the king's 20 May 1992 meeting with Generals Suchinda and Chamlong.[12] That crisis-ending intervention was the one clearly on the minds of most now calling for the monarch to appoint a prime minister in 2006.

In the event, the palace did not move before the parliamentary elections of 2 April. Boycotted by all serious opposition, those polls resulted in 16 million party-list votes for Thaksin's Thai Rak Thai Party (TRT), as against 10 million of the so-called "no votes" indicating preference for no party and presumed to reflect anti-Thaksin sentiment.[13] In 27 of Bangkok's 36 constituencies, "no votes" actually outnumbered ballots cast for TRT.[14] In 36 southern constituencies where TRT candidates ran unopposed, they did not win the constitutionally required 20 per cent of total possible votes needed to secure their seats. These issues notwithstanding, Thaksin appeared on television the day after the elections confidently, even arrogantly, to proclaim victory. One day later, following a late-afternoon meeting with the king from which he apparently emerged stunned, Thaksin announced that he would not become prime minister when the newly elected parliament sat. On 5 April, he began a constitutionally anomalous leave of absence from the premiership pending formation of a new government, with Deputy Prime Minister Police General Chitchai Wannasathit to serve in his stead.

The failure of a second round of voting to deliver a complete parliament and continued protests focused on the elimination of the "Thaksin regime" rather than just Thaksin himself overshadowed the 19 April elections for the Senate. To those who paused to consider, the contrast with the interest that had attended races for and the installation of Thailand's first elected upper house six years earlier underlined the unfulfilled promise of the 1997 constitution. The Senate elected in April would never be seated.

On 25 April, the king used relatively routine audiences with newly appointed members of the Administrative and Supreme Courts to make his long-awaited intervention. Declaring the current situation a "mess",[15] he aligned himself far more unambiguously than in May 1992 with "democracy", stated that elections contested by a single party were not democratic, and dismissed the propriety of using Article 7 to justify appointing a premier at a time when no parliament existed. Finally, he instructed the judges of the Administrative and Supreme Courts and the justices of the Constitutional Court to come together to work on a way out of the mess.[16]

The three courts promptly met. They immediately cancelled a planned third round of parliamentary elections. Within two weeks the Constitutional Court annulled the 2 April elections. It based its decision on the fairly remarkable grounds that the layout of polling places had deprived voters of their right to confidentiality and that the poll had come too soon after Thaksin's dissolution of parliament.[17] These matters had hardly been secret at the time of the elections. However, that they now took on such significance gave them the appearance of shabby pretexts cooked up in response to the king's injunction. The three courts also asked the Electoral Commission to step down. And the attorney-general followed with a case filed before the Constitutional Court accusing TRT of hiring minor parties to contest the earlier polls in some constituencies (and thus relieve its candidates of the need to win 20 per cent of votes) and the Democrats of illegally boycotting the polls and improperly calling for a royally appointed premier.

Seven weeks after Thaksin's self-authorized leave began, he brought it to an end in time to return as caretaker premier for the king's sixtieth jubilee celebrations. Soon, however, he suffered the resignations of two of his government's top legal advisers, the respected Cabinet Secretary-General Bawonsak Uwanno and Deputy Prime Minister Wissanu Kruea-ngam. These resignations and further pressure led the prime minister to allege that his authority and Thai democracy were threatened by *phu mi barami nok ratthathammanun*, a "charismatic individual outside the constitution". In its blunt reference either to the royal institution or to a figure closely associated with it, Thaksin's outburst re-drew the openly acknowledged lines of the year's political conflict dramatically and unambiguously.

July–September 2006

In the third and final phase of the year's politics, charisma responded to Thaksin in kind. In addresses at the Chulachomklao military academy in Nakhon Nayok and the Thai naval academy in Samut Prakan and at Chulalongkorn University, Privy Council president Prem argued that the military's allegiance belonged to king and country rather than to the government of the day, that leaders must be moral and ethical people, and that wealth — especially if gained through improper means — was an inappropriate basis for political power.[18] Anand Panyarachun, whom the National Peace-Keeping Council junta of 1991–92 installed as premier with royal endorsement following its own February 1991 putsch, also chimed in. He voiced concern that Thailand risked becoming a "failed state". Rebutting the caretaker prime minister directly, Anand argued that democracy meant more than elections, that it required a free press and genuine political participation. Anticipating the rhetoric of the junta that would seize state power on 19 September, Anand decried the social division that had overtaken Thailand.[19] Dr Prawet Wasi also spoke publicly in a similar vein.

These astonishing outbursts proved the opening shots in a final, determined attempt to resolve the Thai political crisis of 2006. The attempt accelerated in the second half of July, with the king signing a decree calling for parliamentary elections, the conviction for negligence and brief imprisonment of the three members of the Electoral Commission who had refused to resign, and the transfer of some 120 mid-ranking military officers in key positions under the command of senior officers close to Thaksin.[20]

Having so remarkably weathered sustained efforts to oust him, both on the streets of Bangkok and on the part of powerful members of the Thai establishment, Thaksin seemed to remain unbowed. His supporters in the caretaker Senate succeeded in placing a number of men seen as his allies on the new Electoral Commission. He confirmed that he would lead TRT into the coming election. And no one in Thailand had any illusion about the outcome of such an election: yet another impressive TRT victory. With Thaksin still not convicted of any crime or formally found guilty of any wrongdoing, it was clear by early September that his opponents had to "stop" him before he could win the elections likely to take place within the next several months. They placed their hopes in a number of complementary approaches.

One was the collapse of TRT or at least Thaksin's departure from its leadership, an eventuality about which observers had speculated ever since the announcement of the Shin-Temasek deal in January. A reported dinner meeting at a well-known Italian restaurant in central Bangkok among leading members of the caretaker cabinet fuelled hopes of serious dissent over Thaksin's leadership of the party.[21] Ongoing reports of a rift between Thaksin and the serious, well regarded Deputy Prime Minister and Commerce Minister Somkhit Chatusiphitak further contributed to such hopes.

A second was the hope that Thaksin's antagonists, for all their activities on the streets and calls for royal intervention, still placed in the procedural dimensions of democratic governance about which they spoke so often. Numerous pending cases — from the perjury case against Thaksin, pressed by American cable-television operator and former Thaksin business partner William Monson, to the case against TRT for hiring minor parties to contest the April election, to many others — might serve the purpose of removing Thaksin from the Thai political scene. Notably, however, hope in such means of removal flew in the face of Thaksin's half-decade-long success in not allowing legal or procedural niceties of any sort to stand in the way of his goals. Such hope rested, in other words, on the idea that the changed climate that had seen the emergence of widespread opposition to the premier had likewise renewed the judicial system.

A third approach, perhaps, was a more dramatic move to rid the kingdom of Thaksin through the use of violence or intimidation. The alleged bomb plot against the prime minister in late August remains a very murky affair. Was it a genuine assassination attempt? Rumours that such a plot was in the works had surfaced in July. Was it an attempt to scare Thaksin into giving up politics and going into exile? Or did, as many believed, Thaksin stage the whole incident in a peculiar attempt to win support and sympathy?

In the event, of course, none of these approaches bore fruit. TRT did not collapse. Thaksin was not murdered or scared into fleeing. And legal means to remove him were not given the required time. Instead, on 19 September the Thai army, navy, air force and police seized state power under the leadership of army commander General Sonthi Boonyaratglin.

THAKSIN'S OPPONENTS

Four oddities marked the open opposition to Thaksin during the year leading up to the 19 September putsch.

First was the identity of the man who got the ball rolling in the first place: Sondhi Limthongkul. A veteran media entrepreneur whose *Phu Chatkan* or "Manager" stable of publications has contributed greatly to Thailand's quality press in the past two decades, Sondhi brought characteristic acumen to his campaign against Thaksin. Not least, his association of his movement with a "fight for the king" demonstrated that acumen. All the same, Sondhi's previous business relationship with the prime minister and previous lack of involvement either in national politics or in the Thai democratic movement made him the unlikely leader of a mass campaign.

Ultimately, the broadening of the open anti-Thaksin movement into the PAD increased its rallies' resemblance to Thai protests of the past. It also made them more impressive. The range and calibre of speakers and the engagement of the crowds that gathered to listen to them put contemporary urban, middle and upper-middle-class Thai political culture in their best possible light.[22]

Second, as time wore on and it became clear that the PAD considered its best card an appeal for royal intervention to appoint a prime minister under Article 7 of the constitution, unmistakable disillusionment and unease arose among some in the anti-Thaksin movement. The royalist songs and yellow shirts that marked the PAD's rallies notwithstanding, some critics of Thaksin wondered if all of Thailand's putative progress toward a more solid democratic order across three decades or more had really still left it dependent on an institution like hereditary monarchy. These sentiments precipitated bitter debate among Thai intellectuals and their avid public, to the point that the chief forum for such debate — the Web-board on the Midnight University site — had to be closed down and restructured for fear of straying dangerously far into *lèse majesté*. Among those Thaksin opponents uneasy with the prospect of recourse to Article 7, their country's long failure to confront the events of 6 October 1976 often weighed heavily.

Third and equally astonishing, many of Thaksin's opponents displayed a sociological ignorance that bordered on bigotry. This ignorance proved the flip-side of the contemporary Thai political culture so impressively displayed at PAD rallies. So strong was the hatred that motivated their opposition to the premier's very real abuses of power, his cynicism, and his greed that it led otherwise savvy critics to dismiss his support among Thailand's increasingly disadvantaged majority as the consequence of lack of information among members of that majority. If only they understood, if only they did not just sell their votes, well, these people would not vote for TRT. Or so it was argued. The possibility that the pro-TRT poor did indeed understand the objective conditions that they themselves faced, that they saw in Thaksin's party the most appropriate recipient of their vote, seemed not to dawn on the majority of the prime minister's Bangkok enemies. To the degree the Thai capital Bangkok remains the Lao city under *luk chin*[23] occupation that it has been for six decades or more, and that its affluent had around them every day fellow voters who could explain their support for Thaksin clearly and cogently, the anti-Thaksin movement's sociological blinders remained hard to comprehend.

These blinders did have at least two important consequences, however. One was the persistent charge — taken up by the 19 September junta itself — that Thaksin brought divisiveness to Thai society. This led one to wonder why those who levelled it did not try looking in the mirror. The other was rooted in a thoroughgoing lack of appreciation that much support for TRT was due to a continuing skew of the Thai party-political spectrum to the right and to a resultant lack of progressive alternatives for voters. It meant that the year made clear Thailand's continuing need for a credible party of the left, one that might have done battle with TRT where that party had done best at the polls.

Fourth, it is only a slight exaggeration to say that, had the chief opposition Democrat Party gone out of existence following its defeat in the April 2005 polls, the anti-Thaksin movement would have been none the worse. As said, this is an exaggeration. After all, the Democrats' decision to boycott the 2 April polls proved a political master-stroke. Further, in Aphirak Kosayothin, the party gave the Bangkok Metropolitan Administration capable leadership and its own appeal to the voters of the capital a renewed foundation. Another newcomer to the party, Korn Chatikawanit, a British-educated veteran investment banker, took a leading role in investigating the intricacies of the Shin-Temasek deal. But the success of this pair only highlighted the party's weakness in two other areas.

One was its leader, the Old Etonian Aphisit Vejjajiva, himself. Keen observers of the party remarked during the year that his ineffectual leadership meant that such figures as Aphirak and Korn must be very careful not to upstage him. Fourteen years after he first entered parliament, continued discussion of Aphisit's youth raised the clear spectre of a Peter Pan problem. It was widely believed in Bangkok that the decision to boycott the April polls was the idea of the tough, wily former Democrat secretary-general and subsequent Mahachon Party founder Sanan Kachonprasat, and that he and Aphisit's predecessor as Democrat leader Banyat Banthatthan, had to overcome Aphisit's initial resistance to the idea.

The other Democrat weakness was the party's failure effectively to compete in the most vote-rich regions of Thailand. It seemed sometimes that Aphisit failed to understand that, had there been no Sanan, there would have been no Democrat-led Chuan Likphai governments during the 1990s. While the platform that the party unveiled from late April onward demonstrated a determination to appeal to voters in the rural north and northeast, its release threatened only to underline its leader's far greater talents in the area of policy than of politics as the latter is played in most of Thailand.

HIS MAJESTY THE KING

The year 2006 was meant to be the king's year, devoted to celebration of his long record of six full decades on the Thai throne. The jubilee celebrations did come off in early June with great success. Yellow shirts remained ubiquitous across the kingdom. But they also emerged as an unofficial uniform of the anti-Thaksin forces at the rallies of the PAD. And the king did feel compelled to intervene directly and openly in the political process, to abandon his alleged position of distance from the fray, with his injunction to the courts to help solve the country's mess. That intervention had two noteworthy aspects. One was the king's bald use of the term "democracy"[24] in some contrast to his May 1992 usage, *thi khao riak wa prachathippatai*.[25] A second was the suggestion in his words to the judges on 25 April that they act as responsible men and women, as well as servants of the law and constitution, in helping the country. Indeed, the three-court "judicial summit"[26] in which the king's intervention resulted was a body for which neither law nor constitution provided. It was, rather, a gathering of the putatively capable, responsible, and good.

The jubilee celebrations in early June also had their noteworthy aspects. One was the range of monarchies represented, ranging from Lesotho and Tonga to Spain and Great Britain.[27] That the Sultan of Brunei served as the senior visiting sovereign[28] proved a splendid ASEAN touch. One can only imagine the reaction to the event of Queen Sofia of Spain, who was present at the jubilee in King Juan Carlos's absence. She is, after all, not only sister of the deposed King Constantine of what is now the Hellenic Republic but also consort to a Bourbon monarch placed on the Spanish throne after a decades-long interval of fascistic rule during which, rather as in Thailand between 1932 and 1957, monarchy was of much diminished relevance to the life of the nation.[29] Did she consider the house of Chakkri luckier than the royal house into which she was born? Analogous to the one into which she had married? Both? Neither? Answers to these questions must, perhaps pending Queen Sofia's memoirs, remain unclear.

The composition of the June gathering of sovereigns in Bangkok did make clear the strong continuities between the post-1957 restoration of monarchy to a central position in Thai affairs and its pre-1910 or pre-1932 aspect. Maurizio Peleggi has argued that "[t]he new self-perception of the House of Chakri [*sic*] as members of the fraternal order of world royalty was a distinctive trait of the modernizing project of the Fifth Reign".[30] That fraternity linked King Chulalongkorn to the rulers of powerful European nation-states and of the few other non-European polities, like Meiji Japan, that could also win admission. The organizers of King Bhumiphol's sixtieth jubilee celebrations re-affirmed the linkage forged during his grandfather's time. Monarchies represented at the event reigned over independent nation-states on the nineteenth-century European model.

The historical fluke of the Brunei sultanate's persistence as an independent nation-state on that model made possible its monarch's role at the jubilee. His fellow Malay-Muslim monarch, the Raja of Perlis — a polity with deep historical ties to Bangkok — attended not as sovereign of that state but rather as incumbent of independent Malaysia's unique, fifty-year-old, invented and inventive rotating national monarchy. The sultans of Terengganu, Kelantan, and Kedah — states that also share long relationships with Bangkok — did not make the event. Neither, for all his significance within Indonesia, did the sultan of Yogyakarta. Representatives of the former *chao mueang* of such Tai centres besides Bangkok as Nakhon Si Thammarat, Chiang Mai, Kengtung, or Luang Prabang and of the Patani royal line were also absent. The ties of these latter monarchies to Bangkok were, after all, but relics of the older, very different state system on which Siam largely turned its back during the Fifth Reign. Inevitably, the honoured guests assembled for the jubilee posed with the king for their widely reproduced group photograph in Chulalongkorn's own Italianate and Italian-built Ananta Samakhom Throne Hall[31] rather than in a setting with any relation to that older state system.

Another noteworthy feature of the jubilee, in its domestic dimension, was the deeply retrospective nature of the event. In view of the king's advanced age, it was natural that Thais celebrate his achievements and sacrifices of the past, with which the jubilee proved useful in familiarizing that large segment of the population too young to remember them. In Bangkok, this group included subjects of the king with no recollection of a Thailand in which, for example, the imperative to address rural problems and foster rural development stood at the centre of the national agenda and of his work.

Unprecedented public displays of affection for the king continued in a new form shortly after the jubilee celebrations, when he entered Sirirat Hospital for a spinal procedure. People travelled from across the city and across the country to keep a vigil outside the hospital and greet younger members of the royal family as they came and went. And, especially on Mondays, jubilee-yellow shirts remained omnipresent even after the June celebrations.

THE MONARCHY'S NETWORK

The coincidence of a number of factors in the run-up to the 19 September putsch amounted to a "perfect storm" in the king's relationship to Thai politics. First, there was the jubilee, with the focus on the king and his reign that this event brought. Second came a prolonged political crisis in which the king was pressured to and finally did, after a fashion, intervene. Third, the year saw publication of two complementary works that can only shame those observers of Thailand who have long ducked asking tough questions about the role of the monarchy into changing their ways.

The first of these was an article by Duncan McCargo, "Network monarchy and legitimacy crises in Thailand", published in December 2005.[32] The article represents one of those rare fundamental contributions to Thai studies, an essay that ought to shape our thinking on the most recent thirty years of Thai history. It offers a conceptual insight into that era as stimulating as, for example, Embree's loosely structured social system, Skinner's assimilation, Riggs's bureaucratic polity, Thak's despotic paternalism, and Nidhi's early-Bangkok *watthanatham kadumphi* (or "bourgeois culture") have been for the study of earlier eras of the Thai past.[33] McCargo's concept of "network monarchy" in Thailand embodies not a conspiracy theory but rather a flexible, suggestive, useful perspective on a reality that has long been before our eyes. This reality is that, ever since his return to Thailand from Switzerland, the king has surrounded himself with a shifting collection of associates, counsellors, and factotums. Sometimes with the explicit understanding of the palace and sometimes not, these men have continuously and actively intervened to shape outcomes in Thai politics in ways that had very little to do with their formal institutional positions. This network has played a particularly central role since the 1980s. It is shame, though an understandable one, that McCargo's article remains unpublished in a Thai-language version.

The second work in question, Paul Handley's biographical *The King Never Smiles*, represents the first seriously researched biography in any language of a man who has, for at least half a century, been the most important figure in a country whose population now exceeds sixty million.[34] In short, he is hardly an odd choice of subject for a talented biographer. Handley's book offers a critical analysis of the impact of the post-1957 revival of monarchy in Thailand on the evolution of Thai democracy. The strengths and weaknesses of Handley's analysis remain matters for debate; to many in Thailand, that analysis rang far truer after the events of 19 September 2006. Less debatable is the value of his robust account of the immensely successful process of monarchical revival during the ninth Chakkri reign.

Efforts to undermine McCargo's article and Handley's book came fast. They included a remarkably aggressive attempt actually to block publication of the latter.[35] To date, despite many jabs, no critic has laid a glove on either work, though Chris Baker's critical gloss on the Handley biography in a review for the *Asia Sentinel* Web-site is very valuable.[36] Taken together, the two works represent a timely prompt to think more systematically about the functioning of the royal institution in the Thai political arena. They have provoked not just scholars but also veteran participants in Bangkok policy circles to reconsider the level of the king's active, albeit behind-the-scenes, involvement in numerous of the events of recent decades.

Both McCargo and Handley accord General Prem a uniquely significant role in those events. Indeed, the visibility of the Privy Council and above all of its president in the contests leading to the 19 September putsch had little precedent. Two decades ago, when it was widely believed that the late, great Kukrit Pramoj often spoke on behalf of the palace, the very fact that he was not a member of the Privy Council was deemed crucial to his ability to comment as tartly as he typically did. In the year to the putsch, such deniability was apparently no longer deemed necessary, possible, or either. And, as noted above, other such prominent network figures[37] as Anand Panyarachun and Prawet Wasi joined General Prem in their strong anti-Thaksin statements. The place of these three men in the year's great contest over the nature of Thai democracy was a matter of some awkwardness. Unlike Thaksin, none of them had ever deigned to face the electorate. At the same time, however, both Anand and Prawet took leading roles in the drafting of the 1997 constitution; to that degree, at least, it might be possible to credit them with some record of commitment to the procedural aspects of democratic governance.

As for General Prem, many in Thailand feel little doubt in the matter of for whom he speaks. Whether accompanied by comfort with monarchical support for efforts to counter Thaksin's authoritarian abuses or not, a corollary of this understanding of Prem's role was tacit acceptance that the crucial contest in Thai politics up to 19 September saw sovereign and popularly elected prime minister opposed. This contest then left less privileged Thais in a curious position. They wore yellow to honour the achievements of their king, achievements acclaimed during decades of the careful royal image-building chronicled by Handley, even as their political hero Thaksin struggled to survive the palace's challenge to his premiership.

Thaksin's ability to outmanoeuvre his enemies until tanks actually rolled onto the streets of Bangkok offered remarkable testimony to his still formidable political skills and, frankly, his courage. He clearly harboured no illusion about the identity of his ultimate enemy. His continual, public invocation of the democratic basis of his support as manifest in elections served to highlight the difference between that support and not only the demonstrations on the streets of Bangkok but also the palace and its network. So it is that we must understand his reference to *phu mi barami nok ratthathamanun.*

These features of the central political contest in Thailand during the past year raise a series of questions. What, for example, led the network to be so open in its opposition to Thaksin? Did this apparent recklessness reflect its position of weakness?[38] What was it about Thaksin that so irritated or alarmed the network and perhaps even the palace? Did this concern relate to Thaksin's ability to build a durable, authoritarian regime in Thailand? To the inevitable royal succession? To uncertainty about how precisely to manage a Thai economy and Thai society that have changed beyond recognition since the palace first crafted its happy accommodation with Field Marshal Sarit Thanarat in the late 1950s?[39]

Additional questions relate to the role of Sondhi Limthongkul. In choosing to cast his anti-Thaksin drive as a campaign on behalf of the king, he doubtless sought to appeal in a general sense to what the foreign press terms Thai "reverence" for the monarch. In recent years, some Thais have also come to see the king as an implicit partner in the emergence of a more democratic order,[40] and Sondhi's movement surely tapped that understanding, too. At the same time, however, one can fairly wonder whether Sondhi and the PAD operated with a nod and a wink or even a more explicit signal from the palace or its network. For all the criticism that Sondhi and his confederates faced for dragging the royal institution into politics, parties very close to that institution put up very little resistance. Or was this lack of resistance due to those parties' having long considered themselves fully engaged in politics?

THE COURTS

Despite its legal anomalousness, the collaboration among the Constitutional, Supreme, and Administrative Courts in the most constructive pre-putsch effort to resolve the 2006 political crisis pointed to one of the year's few potentially encouraging developments. One of the most perceptive analysts of Thai affairs noted that the role taken by the judiciary in addressing a number of political controversies marked a real departure for Thailand.[41] This observation did not speak to the possibility of direction from influential parties outside the judiciary on its deliberations. In the minds of some, for example, the 21 July royal decree on general elections made inevitable the Criminal Court's conviction just four days later of the three recalcitrant members of the Electoral Commission. Such suspicions notwithstanding, the bitter infighting and extreme politicization of a decade-and-a-half ago, during the era of former Supreme Court president Praman Chansue, seemed safely behind the Thai courts. In their response to the king's 25 April instructions, the judges also made an unmistakable effort to base their actions not merely on the wisdom, goodness, and competence with which he implicitly credited them but rather on the law and legal processes.

The emergent role of the Thai judiciary during the crisis went some way to compensate for Thaksin's vitiation of the independent bodies created under the 1997 constitution.[42] The increased centrality of the courts to Thai political processes showed every indication of proving a lasting consequence of the crisis. At the same time, that centrality would make far more important the safeguarding of Thai courts and their judges from political and financial pressures. As a general matter, too, these developments merited reflection on the part of those charged by the 19 September putschists with drafting the new constitution.

THE SINGAPORE FACTOR

Rage towards and fear of Thaksin among many of his opponents proved so great that Singapore escaped much of the criticism that its role in the Thai crisis of 2006 could very well have provoked. Even now, many dimensions of the Shin-Temasek deal remain poorly understood and insufficiently examined. Chief among these dimensions are its gestation period, secret undertakings that Thaksin may have offered Temasek or the Singapore government in conjunction with the deal, the participation first of the Siam Commercial Bank and later of the little-known Thai-Malaysian businessman Surin Upatkoon (Lau Khin Koon),[43] Temasek's use of nominees and multiple holding companies — in an undertaking certain to come under close scrutiny — apparently to duck Thai restrictions on foreign ownership, and the willingness of Temasek, its high-level management, and by implication the Singapore government, to enter into so suspect a transaction.

Singapore Inc's general readiness to do business with Thaksin Shinawatra and specific failure to anticipate the political fallout of a Shin-Temasek deal that left Thaksin and his family without tax obligations flew in the face of its energetically cultivated reputation for transparency, intolerance for corruption, thoroughness, and understanding of the region. The protestations about the purely commercial basis of the purchase notwithstanding, that Temasek invested assets on behalf of the Singapore government only made matters more unfortunate still. For, in effect, the Shin-Temasek deal could be taken to represent the involvement of one ASEAN member-state in the internal affairs of another, with the ultimate consequence of the fall of that latter state's government. It remains to be seen how this episode will come to figure in historical scholarship on the Association.

Further, the Shin-Temasek deal embodied but the tip of the iceberg in Singapore's large and growing interests in Thailand's economy and politics. By some reckonings, Singapore ranked as the second-largest foreign investor in Thailand, with holdings in a number of strategic sectors.[44] Liquor tycoon Charoen Siriwatthanaphakdi's making an initial public offering of his Thai Beverage concern on the Singapore Exchange in May 2006 also raised the spooky prospect of other Thai firms' turning to that bourse, thus both stunting the development of a domestic capital market and abetting what can often seem like Singapore's economic and financial colonization of Bangkok.

On the economic side, Singapore's ability to have its way in Thailand serves as a reminder of the full damage done to the Thai economy and its historic pillars in the 1997 financial crisis. On the political side however, the Thai-Singaporean fit is a tremendously awkward one: simply contrast the PAD's Bangkok rallies during the first half of the year and the sophistication of public debate in Thailand during the same period with Singapore's general skittishness about not only public protest but also serious debate over issues of political moment.[45]

Nevertheless, Thai-Singaporean links have a long, complex history. Dating to Singapore's emergence as a major node in the intra-Asian rice trade after 1819,[46] they have in the past featured substantial Singaporean investment in the Thai rice, rubber, and cassava sectors and Thai banks' significant presence in Singapore. Those relations also long benefited from the stewardship of tycoons with a wide range of connections in, and a proven feel for, the realities of both countries.[47] A number of developments have made of such figures an endangered — or in fact extinct — species: the eclipse of Singapore's old Chinese tycoons by the PAP's government-linked corporations managed by bureaucratic high-fliers with Western academic credentials but little experience of Southeast Asia, the globalization of the region's finance capitalism, and the shattering of Thailand's bank-centred business groups after 1997 and the subsequent dominance of new-money figures like Thaksin.

All the same, the scale of recent Singaporean investment in Thailand does mean that there exists in the city-state a noteworthy cadre of businessmen and businesswomen who know that neighbouring economy and its politics very well; only a pity that Temasek seemed to listen to none of them before acquiring Shin. The two countries' relationship does not permit comprehensive analysis on the basis of one year, no matter how eventful, or one transaction, no matter how hard to understand.

THE WAR IN THE SOUTH

In what has in recent decades passed for normal times, the tragic violence that continued to plague Thailand's far south during the year-long advent of the putsch would deserve the greatest emphasis. Other contributions to the present volume bring great expertise and rigourous analysis to this unfolding tragedy. For the purposes of this contribution, then, a few brief comments must suffice.

Southern violence continued and by some measure intensified during 2006. In addition to the long-routinized pattern of often fatal shootings, insurgents scored a number of dramatic, often grisly, successes. These events included beating a schoolteacher in Narathiwat to the point of brain death, staging up to 100 bombings and acts of arson or sabotage across the region in a single day, setting off bombs simultaneously in more than twenty Yala bank branches, bombing areas of the Chinese-majority southern commercial hub of Hat Yai frequented by tourists, and shooting former Narathiwat Senator Fakhruddin Boto.

State responses to the insurgency took a variety of forms. Intelligence on the insurgents may have improved somewhat. The Thai army and regional security experts approached a shared understanding of some aspects of the insurgency's organization, even as doubts about the most important groups involved and the nature of those groups persisted.[48] Leading Thai military officers assigned to the south expressed growing awareness of political, ethnic, and religious dimensions of the crisis. Some elements close to the army criticized what they saw as the simple-minded law-and-order approach to the crisis to which the police background shared by Thaksin and Chitchai apparently inclined them. In June, the caretaker prime minister gave Thai Army Commander General Sonthi Boonyaratglin overall responsibility for security policy in the south. Though nominally replacing Police General Chitchai in this role, neither General Sonthi's actual mandate nor the effect of this change was clear. While security-driven in its response to a shooting war, in comparative perspective the stance of the Thai army proved far from hardline. For all its failure to draw on classic doctrines of "learning" in the practice of counter-insurgency, it succeeded in avoiding repetition of such earlier incidents as those at Tak Bai or the Krue Se Mosque.

June brought the long-awaited release of the National Reconciliation Commission (NRC) report on the south.[49] The NRC was, as its name implies, a reconciliation commission. Its proposals therefore properly addressed the deficiencies of the Thai state in its approach to the region and eschewed tactical advice in the practice of counter-insurgency. These proposals included the use of Patani Malay as a "working language" in the far south, the creation of a corps of unarmed peace-building units, and the improvement of dialogue and governance in the Bangkok state's interaction with southern Muslim society. For both substantive and political purposes, the report's authors made a crucial point in recognizing — as Michael Connors observed directly after its release[50] — that the crisis of governance in the Thai south represented only an extreme form of issues relevant across the country as a whole.

Reaction to the NRC report varied. Privy Council president General Prem came out, shrilly and almost instantly, against its linguistic proposals.[51] Other critics panned it for placing inordinate blame on the Thai state. More valuably, still others noted its simplistic view of southern Muslim society.[52] The increased willingness of Muslim elites to break ranks with their insurgent co-religionists and acknowledge their own worry over the course of the violence following the shooting of Senator Fakruddin highlighted the importance of the latter critique. That critique doubtless also applied below the elite level, to grass-root realities in the struggle between the Bangkok state and violent insurrectionists for local support.

Following the late-August bombings in Yala and just three weeks before his putsch, General Sonthi did raise the possibility of opening talks with the southern insurgents.[53] It was unclear whether he had in mind expanding the process or processes that both Geneva's Centre for Humanitarian Dialogue and former Malaysian prime minister Mahathir Mohamad had earlier initiated. In any case, the general response to his proposal within official Thai security circles was almost uniformly negative. Following 19 September, General Sonthi's position would have permitted him to defy the scepticism of those opposed to talks with Thailand's southern insurgents, but he showed no inclination to follow through on this possibility.

THE MILITARY AND ITS PUTSCH

In confronting its ongoing political crisis, Thailand notably avoided any trace of serious violence during the months leading to 19 September. In this regard, recourse to a military putsch — whose initial success was by definition due to its perpetrators' control of superior resources to do violence — was singularly dispiriting. So, too, was the role played by the traditional issue of tensions over military promotions in precipitating a military seizure of power.[54] Of course, one could argue that the implications of those promotions extended far beyond the Thai military caste. Had Thaksin had his way with the disputed promotions, his regime might have turned on its opponents with considerable violence, had unchallenged control of Thailand's armed forces for the foreseeable future, or both.

Intra-military tensions aside, it had by 19 September been clear for some time that significant interests needed to have Thaksin out of the way before he could win a fourth successive general election. Their willingness to countenance such extreme, anachronistic means as sending tanks onto the streets reflected both their evident position of weakness in this confrontation and Thaksin's remarkable ability to weather an onslaught of the sort that had overcome many before him. The putsch did come despite months of efforts on the part of the army publicly to distance itself from the long political crisis of 2006. Whether Thaksin or his enemies ultimately forced its hand is a question that remained unclear in the period immediately following the putsch. Had a prime minister been appointed — using the fig-leaf of Article 7 or otherwise — in March, April, or May of the year, the country could have avoided both the damage to its reputation and politics that an armed *coup d'état* in the first decade of the twenty-first century did and the waste of many months of time before beginning, somehow, to recover from the breathtaking reversal of its political development that followed the election of January 2001.

CONCLUSION: CONTESTING THE CORRECT

On the morning of 20 September 2006, video recordings of a pair of talking heads reading the first several announcements of the junta that had seized power in Bangkok the night before appeared on Thai television. That new junta would ask that it be referred to in English as "the Council for Democratic Reform under Constitutional Monarchy" (CDRM). Its Thai name was *Khana Patirup Kanpokhrong nai Rabop Prachathippatai an mi Phramahakasat Songpenpramuk*. Yet in about a third of these first few messages from the junta, the announcers offered listeners a slight variation on the name: *Khana Patirup Kanpokhrong nai Rabop Prachathippatai an mi Phramahakasat Songpenphrapramuk*. The reason for this variation is clear. While the ninth Chakri reign has witnessed an astonishing revival of *ratchasap* or archaic court language in the Thai public sphere,[55] few commoners receive proper training in its putatively correct use. They tend, therefore, to have to wing it, and one presumably safe part of that approach is erring on the side of the extra *"phra"* here and there to modify nouns related to members of the royal family. That is to say, wanton hypercorrection trumps the risk of being incorrect. What is beyond doubt, however, is that there is a standard of the correct.

The year to 19 September 2006 in Thai politics brought a contest over what was correct, over what the correct nature of "democracy" or of *thi khao riak wa prachathippatai* was, over who had the right to specify what was correct, and over what means of effecting political change might be deemed correct. It is tempting to say that even the process of constitution-drafting, on which some of the best minds in the kingdom would after the putsch — again — embark, was ultimately about the codification of correct politics. This point of course begs the question of whether constitutional tinkering and top-down political reform are fruitful or even relevant paths toward correcting Thailand's troubled politics.[56] It also ducks an ever more pressing need to take fundamental stock of Thailand's contemporary burdens and advantages, and of the resources to shoulder those burdens and maximize those advantages with which history has endowed the country. Like those burdens and advantages, these resources include the economic, social, institutional, and intellectual. But taking stock of them falls well outside the scope of the present review of political events preceding Thailand's dismaying 19 September 2006 military putsch.

NOTES

1. An invaluable discussion of the many influences that came together in the 1997 constitution is Duncan McCargo, "Alternative Meanings of Political Reform in Contemporary Thailand", *Copenhagen Journal of Asian Studies* XIII (1998): 5–30.

2. "Coup Update: Rise and Fall of Thaksin Shinawatra", *The Nation*, 21 September 2006; and Suphalak Kanchanakhundi, "Khabuankan Prachachon Kuengsamretrup" [A Semi-Realized People's Movement], *Fa Diaokan* IV, 2 (April–June 2006): 166–87, p. 170 ff. The latter article remains the indispensable account and analysis of the anti-Thaksin movement during the first half of 2006, its origins, and its implications. Similarly, the clear emergence of *Fa Diaokan* as Thailand's

pre-eminent quality journal of current affairs in itself ranks among the significant developments in the period covered here; see <www.sameskybooks.org>.

3. "Market Poised for Shin, AIS Deal", *Bangkok Post*, 10 January 2006.

4. "Politics: Conflict of Interest, Next Protest", *Bangkok Post*, 13 February 2006.

5. For example, "AIS 'assured' 3G licence", *Bangkok Post*, 26 January 2006.

6. Phinyo Traisuriyathamma et al., *25 Khamtham Bueanglang Thekowoe Chinkhop* [25 Questions: The Inside Story of the Shin Corp. Take-Over] (Bangkok: Openbooks, 2006) remains a useful, albeit very early, analysis of the transaction in its various aspects.

7. Suphalak, "Khabuankan Prachachon", p. 173 ff., considers Sondhi's proclaimed royalism in the context of other, more substantial and sophisticated, understandings of the nature of royal authority in Thailand.

8. "PM would Go only if King Tells Him", *Bangkok Post*, 5 February 2006.

9. "Thailand's Tiny Buddhist 'army'", *The Christian Science Monitor*, 9 March 2006.

10. "Opposition to Boycott Election", *Bangkok Post*, 26 February 2006.

11. A brief, perceptive history of this institution appears in James Ockey, "Monarch, Monarchy, Succession and Stability in Thailand", *Asia Pacific Viewpoint* XLVI, 2 (August 2005): 115–27.

12. "King Whispers Out", *The Nation,* 13 March 2006.

13. An overview of the Thai electoral system under the 1997 constitution and the 2006 election is available at <http://www.anu.edu.au/thaionline/Thai_Elections. pdf>.

14. "Poll: 70% in Bangkok Query Election Winners' Legitimacy", *Bangkok Post*, 4 April 2006.

15. That is, *mua.*

16. The full text of the king's comments to the judges is available in "Phraratchadamrat Nai Luang Naew Thang Kae 'Wikrit Chat'" [Royal Addresses: The Way to Solve the 'National Crisis'], *Matichon Daily*, 27 April 2005.

17. "Court Throws out April 2 Elections", *Bangkok Post*, 9 May 2006.

18. "Troops 'belong to King'", *Bangkok Post*, 15 July 2006; "Prem Slams 'Unethical Leaders'", *Bangkok Post*, 29 July 2006; and "Prem Pours Scorn on Money Politics", *Bangkok Post*, 19 August 2006.

19. "Political Division: Failed-state Danger is Real", *The Nation*, 31 August 2006; "Thailand 'at risk of becoming failed state'", *Bangkok Post*, 31 August 2006.

20. "Sondhi Stuns by Shifting PM's allies", *The Nation*, 21 July 2006.

21. "Key Ministers have Exit Plan", *The Nation*, 20 July 2006.

22. Suphalak, "Khabuankan Prachachon", casts, however, a more critical eye on this culture and its implications for Thai democracy.

23. That is, ethnic Chinese.

24. *Cf.* "Phraratchadamrat Nai Luang Naew Thang Kae 'Wikrit Chat'".

25. That is, "that which they call democracy", or even "so called democracy".

26. This apt coinage first appeared in "Judges Divided at 11th Hour", *The Nation*, 30 April 2006.

27. A roster of those present is available in Phatthanaphong Chantharanonwong, ed., *The Sixtieth Anniversary Celebrations of His Majesty's Accession to the Throne: A Pictorial Commemoration* (Bangkok: Post Publishing Company, 2006), p. 63.

28. Ibid., p. 56.

29. David K. Wyatt, *Thailand: A Short History* (New Haven: Yale University Press, 1984), p. 245.

30. Maurizio Peleggi, *Lords of Things: The Fashioning of the Siamese Monarchy's Modern Image* (Honolulu: University of Hawaii Press, 2002), p. 13.

31. *Cf.* ibid., p. 95 ff.

32. Duncan McCargo, "Network Monarchy and Legitimacy Crises in Thailand", *The Pacific Review* XVIII, 5 (December 2005): 499–519.

33. *Cf.* John F. Embree, "Thailand: A Loosely Structured Social System", *American Anthropologist* LXII, no. 2 (1950): 181–93; G. William Skinner, *Chinese Society in Thailand: An Analytical History* (Ithaca, New York: Cornell University Press, 1975); Fred W. Riggs, *Thailand: The Modernization of a Bureaucratic Polity* (Honolulu: East-West Center Press, 1966); Thak Chaloemthiarana, *Thailand: The Politics of Despotic Paternalism* (Bangkok: Social Science Association of Thailand, 1979); and Nithi Iaosiwong [Nidhi Eowseewong], *Pen and Sail: Literature and History in Early Bangkok* (English translation) (Chiang Mai: Silkworm Books, 2005).

34. Paul M. Handley, *The King Never Smiles: A Biography of Thailand's Bhumibol Adulyadej* (New Haven and London: Yale University Press, 2006).

35. A brief account of some of the many moves against Handley's book, including confirmation of the remarkable decision of Yale, its economist president, and its university press to succumb to pressure to submit the Handley manuscript to extraordinary scrutiny by the Thai government and actually to delay publication until after the royal jubilee appears in "Thais Protest Royal Biography", *Yale Alumni Magazine* LXX, 6 (September/October 2006): 22 (also available at <www.yalealumnimagazine.com/issues/2006_09/l_v.html>). Handley's own treatment of that matter is found in "Royal Maneuvers", *Asia Sentinel*, 8 September 2006 (available at <www.asiasentinel.com/index.php?option=com_content&task=view&id=153&Itemid=34>). While banned in Thailand many months before its eventual publication, *The King Never Smiles* was widely understood to be available in a rather elegant pirated edition at copy centres on or near university campuses across Bangkok within a few months of its release.

36. Chris Baker, "Revival, Renewal, and Reinvention: The Complex Life of Thailand's Monarch", *Asia Sentinel*, 8 September 2006 (available at <www.asiasentinel.com/index.php?option=com_content&task=view&id=154&Itemid=34>).

37. *Cf.* McCargo, "Network Monarchy", p. 502.

38. This weakness, particularly in the face of Thaksin's challenge, is a basic theme of McCargo, "Network Monarchy".

39. *Cf.* Kobkua Suwannathat-Pian, *Kings, Country and Constitutions: Thailand's Political Development, 1932–2000* (London and New York: Routledge Curzon, 2003), p. 155 ff.
40. *Cf.* Baker, "Revival, Renewal, and Reinvention".
41. Chris Baker, speaking on panel on "Does Thailand Need a New Government?", Foreign Correspondents' Club of Thailand, 17 August 2006.
42. For a survey, *cf.* Alex Mutebi, "Thailand's Independent Agencies under Thaksin: Relentless Gridlock and Uncertainty", in *Southeast Asian Affairs 2006*, edited by Daljit Singh and Lorraine C. Salazar (Singapore: Institute of Southeast Asian Studies, 2006), pp. 303–21.
43. "Exclusive: 'I am Not a Nominee'", *Bangkok Post*, 21 August 2006.
44. Marwaan Macan-Markar, "Anti-Thaksin, Anti-Singapore, the Swell Grows", *Asia Times Online*, 7 March 2006 (available at <http://atimes01.atimes.com/atimes/Southeast_Asia/HC07Ae02.html>).
45. On the long-term, thorough-going depoliticization of public life in the city-state, see the superb Carl A. Trocki, *Singapore: Wealth, Power and the Culture of Control* (London and New York: Routledge, 2006).
46. The future home minister of an independent Singapore, Wong Lin Ken, highlighted these links among others in his 1955 University of Malaya (then located at Singapore) Master's thesis, published as "The Trade of Singapore, 1819–1869", *The Journal of the Malayan Branch of the Royal Asiatic Society*, XXXIII, 4 (December 1960): 1–315, and recently reprinted as *The Trade of Singapore, 1819–1969* (Kuala Lumpur: MBRAS Reprint No. 23, 2003).
47. For examples from the Singapore side, see Ho Rih Hwa, *Eating Salt: An Autobiography* (Singapore and Kuala Lumpur: Times Books International, 1991), and Hsuan Owyang, *The Barefoot Boy from Songwad: The Life of Chi Owyang* (Singapore and Kuala Lumpur: Times Books International, 1996). Consecutively, Ho and then Owyang served as PAP-ruled Singapore's ambassadors to Bangkok for a period of more than two decades, through 1988. The Songwad in which Owyang grew up remains to this day the nerve-centre of Thailand's Teochew-dominated dry-goods economy; in post-war Singapore, he took a leading role in the creation of the Overseas Union Bank (OUB). Ho's Thai Wah Group, long a major player in Thai agribusiness and other sectors, made a cameo appearance in the Shin-Temasek scandal when it was alleged that four of the holding companies created to duck foreign-ownership ceilings and give a patina of legality to that byzantine transaction shared a common address in South Sathorn Road's Thai Wah Tower II; see "Shin Controversy: Direct Link to Temasek Found", *The Nation*, 12 September 2006. It is unclear whether the PAP government sought the counsel of Ho's son and heir Ho Kwon Ping, today a leading Singapore business figure in his own right and a man with extensive interests in Thailand, before entering into the Shin deal.
48. This understanding left no room for efforts to connect events in southern Thailand to patterns of international terrorism.

49. National Reconciliation Commission, *Raingan Khanakammakan Itsara Phuea Khwamsamanachan Haengchat Ao Chana Khwamrunraeng Duai Phalang Samanachan* [Report of the National Reconciliation Commission: Overcoming Violence Through the Power of Reconciliation] (Bangkok: National Reconciliation Commission, Office of the Cabinet Secretary, 2006).

50. Michael Connors, "Addressing the Southern Conflagration", *Bangkok Post*, 13 June 2006.

51. "Prem Not Happy with NRC's Idea", *The Nation*, 27 June 2006.

52. Chirawat Saengthong and Thawisak Phueaksom, "Khwamlaklai Thi Hai Pai" [Disappearing Diversity], *Fa Diaokan* IV, no. 2 (April–June 2006): 112–20.

53. "Thai General Urges Talks with Muslim Insurgents", *Financial Times*, 1 September 2006.

54. James Hookway, "Thai Coup Pre-empted Shake-up of the Military", *The Asian Wall Street Journal*, 22–24 September 2006.

55. Handley, *The King Never Smiles*, pp. 150–52.

56. On what he regards as the Thai political "disease" of "constitution-frequency", *cf.* McCargo, "Alternative Meanings", pp. 5–10.

2

The Tragedy of the 1997 Constitution

Thitinan Pongsudhirak

One of the first acts of Thailand's coup leaders after seizing power on 19 September 2006 was to abrogate the 1997 constitution. I regret to say goodbye to this constitution, which I have read in parts and in entirety time and again for almost ten years now. I harbour nowhere near the expertise of legal luminaries such as Professor Borwornsak Uwanno or Dr Wissanu Kruea-ngam, who can seemingly write constitutions overnight. Nor have I been an able practitioner in the league of Ajarn Gothom Arya, a fellow participant in this conference. Ajarn Gothom was secretary-general of the Election Commission established by the constitution, and did an excellent job in that first commission. But I did have a small part in my own way in seeing the constitution through in September 1997 when I was in London doing a Ph.D. I launched a campaign online which ended up with 3,500 signatures, mostly from people overseas, who wanted to endorse the constitution. Since then I have paid close attention to the way that constitution was implemented.[1]

BACKGROUND OF THE 1997 CONSTITUTION

Let me begin by discussing the context of the 1997 constitution. Thailand has a long history of constitution-making. There have now been sixteen constitutions in seventy-four years — many constitutions. As recently as the 1970s, it had a constitution almost every other year, in 1972, 1976, and 1978. But the 1978 constitution was important, because it lasted for several years, and provided the rules that underpinned elections in 1979, 1983 and 1986. It was also the basis through which General Prem Tinsulanonda became prime minister from 1980–88.

The constitution of 1978 emerged from the turbulent democratic interlude between 1973 and 1976, and further instability in 1977 that led to General Kriangsak Chamanand's coup. The constitution had bicameral arrangements but with an appointed Senate. There were 252 appointed senators, obviously dominated by the military, and 301 House of Representatives members of parliament (MPs). General Prem was nominated by parliament and accepted the premiership. He was never directly elected.

The fact that the prime minister was not elected — and in addition came from the military — became a sticking point, and the main drawback of this constitution. Parliament debated an amendment that would have prevented appointees becoming ministers or prime minister four years after 1979, but General Prem dissolved parliament in February 1983 and staged an election to maintain the *status quo*. That continued throughout the 1980s until 1988 when the July election elevated to power an elected prime minister for the first time in fourteen years. General Prem at that time was asked by the winning parties to continue, but declined. General (Retired) Chatichai Choonhavan became a civilian prime minister, but his government lasted only until the military staged a coup on 23 February 1991. The reasons for the coup, the justifications, were similar to those heard recently — corruption, tampering with military promotions, parliamentary dictatorship, and a threat to the throne. There had been an investigation into an attempt on the queen's life that was not properly investigated — that became one of the justifications for the coup.

The military junta then called itself the National Peace-Keeping Council (NPKC) — today it is the Council for Democratic Reform (CDR, which later became the Council for National Security or CNS). They had their own constitution, an interim constitution that allowed dominance by the Senate, and made it possible for an unelected person to be prime minister. This led, of course, to the March 1992 general election, in which the military instituted and supported a conglomeration of existing MPs under the Samakkitham Party. Samakkitham won the most seats, formed a coalition government, and then appointed General Suchinda Kraprayoon, the NPKC chief, as prime minister — against his previous pledge not to accept the premiership. This in turn led to protests in the streets of Bangkok, and eventually in May 1992 to the confrontation between Suchinda and Chamlong Srimuang. That confrontation then led to bloodshed from 17–19 May, and finally the king's intervention on 20 May. General Suchinda left his post and then came a new period of reform — the post-1992 reform movement — which came to an end with the coup last week.

The post-May 1992 reform movement had a number of issues to solve. Among them were amendments to the constitution that would make the prime minister elected, and the House speaker president of parliament (previously the speaker of the military-dominated Senate was parliamentary president). Other reform targets were vote-buying, electoral fraud, and money politics. The driving logic of these efforts was to try and escape from the so-called vicious cycle of Thai politics. This concept is well known — after a new constitution an election is held, producing a corrupt government, leading to political crisis, engendering a coup, and then going back to the constitution again. Ajarn Chai-anan Samudavanija was the first to codify this vicious cycle in a diagram that appeared in his 1982 book, *The Thai Young Turks*.[2]

The reform movement tried to address this vicious cycle by getting rid of money politics, vote-buying, and fraud. Vote-buying relied on patronage networks with provincial bosses who came to power in Bangkok concurrently undertaking graft to recoup their investments. Shady scams and corruption scandals then led to the erosion and eventual crisis of legitimacy which laid the necessary conditions for military takeover. To eliminate this rampant money politics, reformers wanted to prevent corruption and promote more accountability of the executive branch and the legislature. They sought also to promote government stability, by getting rid of unwieldy and unworkable coalition governments.

This reform movement took off from 1993. It took shape first in the form of the Constitution Reform Committee, succeeded in 1995 by the Committee for Developing Democracy (CDD — sometimes also called the Committee for Democratic Development). The CDD went around the country organizing public hearings to see what people wanted out of the constitution. From May 1996 the CDD changed to the Constitutional Drafting Assembly (CDA) which took more concrete steps to codify concepts, ideas, people's grievances, demands and wishes into a charter, a document. The CDA was led by three main individuals from different backgrounds — Dr Prawet Wasi, a social activist and social critic; Khun Uthai Pimchaichon, a seasoned politician going back to the days of the Thanom Kittikachorn dictatorship (1963–73); and Khun

Anand Panyarachun, who was twice-appointed prime minister during the turmoil in 1991–92.

The CDA's final draft was finished on 15 August 1997. At that time a lot of people did not agree with it. Most politicians were opposed, and the battle for ratification was drawn out and contentious. In Bangkok there were also movements to pressure the politicians to ratify the constitution. In the end it was ratified and promulgated in October.

THE 1997 CONSTITUTION — KEY PROVISIONS[3]

What did the constitution address? What did it do? It sought to promote the stability and effectiveness of government, along with transparency and accountability. There were measures against vote-buying. Compulsory voting was introduced for the first time — you lost political rights if you did not vote. Democracy was seen as entailing responsibilities on the part of the electorate — citizens not only had rights but they had responsibilities, particularly the obligation to vote.

The constitution included a party-list system for 100 of the 500 members of the House of Representatives. The idea of this was that if some experts or able individuals wanted to join politics, they did not have to dirty themselves by engaging in the cut and thrust of electoral politics. They could join the party list. This system meant that if members of the party list became cabinet members, other list members from their party would move up without the necessity for by-elections.

Single-member constituencies, on the other hand, were designed to put MPs in closer touch with their constituents. Previously there were multiple-member constituencies with two or three members, blurring the lines of responsibility to the electorate. Now with single-member constituencies — roughly 150,000 people per constituency — MPs would be forced to be close to his/her constituents, thus promoting a more effective democratic system.

The constitution also contained measures to combat corruption. It set up the National Counter Corruption Commission (NCCC), which after a period of suspension is now back at work. Cabinet ministers were also required to declare their assets before and after taking office. This was intended to make assets more transparent — if these increased substantially during office tenure, this might imply that the office had been used to gain more wealth. An Anti-money Laundering Office was also established. And there were also quirky provisions, such as requiring all candidates to have a university Bachelor's degree. This was directed at people like former Prime Minister Banharn Silapa-archa. They hoped this measure would exclude provincial "mafia" figures from influence-peddling in the political process.

Several other independent institutions were established to protect the public from a powerful executive. A Constitutional Court was mandated to deal with issues related to the constitution. An Administrative Court was established to deal with conflicts between lay citizens and bureaucrats/officials, because in the past there had been a lot of abusive and corrupt bureaucrats who were not accountable to the people. A National Human Rights Commission (NHRC) and Ombudsman were created to allow people access to government, to the constitution, and to the machinery of government — if you did not like something you could petition the Ombudsman to look into it.

The constitution also promoted a strong executive. It had a ninety-day rule, which meant that while the prime minister had authority to dissolve the house with an election to take place within sixty days, MPs must belong to political parties for ninety days before they could contest the election as a member of that political party. This strengthened the executive, especially, the prime minister, because MPs would have less incentive to defect or jump ship as they did in the past. To censure the prime minister you needed 200 MPs, an innovation that made it very difficult to mount a censure motion. Besides that, the censure motion would have to include the name of an alternative prime minister in case the no-confidence motion succeeded.

The constitution also provided for a separation of powers. The prime minister had initially to be elected as an MP, but Cabinet members could not concurrently serve as MPs. This was to address a problem experienced in the past where MPs became Cabinet members and used this for patronage purposes. With the party-list system this could be managed easily, without the need for a by-election after MPs were promoted to Cabinet.

EARLY CONSTITUTIONAL ACHIEVEMENTS

The fate of the 1997 constitution is tragic because it worked — at least it did for a while. It worked well too, and people wanted it. There was initial euphoria, and a celebration after its promulgation. Newspaper headlines said this was a new era. With a people's charter, Thai politics was entering more promising territory where it would get out of this vicious cycle of election, crisis, coup, and constitution. Thais evidently have a very short memory. Looking back at some of the headlines and images from that period, there is no question that the constitution was widely accepted.

The first set of independent institutions set up under the new constitution — including the Election Commission headed by Ajarn Gothom, and the NCCC — also performed credibly. The Senate elections in March 2000 went off well. The Election Commission worked exceedingly hard. It was exhausting work because a large number of red cards and yellow cards were issued to candidates. (Red cards meant a clear violation of election law had occurred, and the candidate was immediately disqualified; yellow cards were issued when a violation was less clear cut, and required another election.) There were three or four sets of by-elections, but in the end a more credible Senate emerged from these.

The NCCC caught out Deputy Prime Minister Sanan Kachornprasart, on the assets disclosure rule, for 45 million baht that he had not accounted for. He was indicted, and to his credit he resigned. He resigned from the Democrat Party, and took a five-year ban from politics even before his case went to the Constitutional Court. He was also the first to say, after Thaksin's defiance in the face of a similar NCCC indictment, that Thaksin would have "no land to live on" [*mai mee paendin yoo*].

The NCCC, in those days comprising one woman and eight men, did a lot of bold things. Their main achievement and the achievement that eventually paved the way for the erosion of its power, was the indictment of Thaksin. This also had much broader implications, paving the way for Thaksin's subsequent undermining of constitutional rule.

THAKSIN'S ASSET CONCEALMENT CASE

The constitution was working well until Thaksin came to power and until the NCCC indicted Thaksin for asset concealment. It was unfortunate that the constitution faced this test so early in its existence. The case itself was clear-cut. The NCCC had voted 8:1 in favour of indicting Thaksin in December 2000. Thaksin had hidden hundreds of million of baht under the names of his driver and maid. Is it possible that he did not know about this? And that his wife also did not know about it? It is not possible. But the case was not tried on its merits.

Thaksin came to power in January 2001 when his Thai Rak Thai (TRT) Party won 248 seats out of the 500. It promptly absorbed smaller parties, starting with Seritham, followed by the New Aspiration Party, and eventually Chart Patthana. So TRT started out with just short of a majority, and after the quick absorption of Seritham gained a simple majority.

Thaksin campaigned on a popular platform, and achieved a coalition of forces that secured his 2001 election triumph. This put great pressure on the Constitutional Court before its August decision. If it decided Thaksin was guilty of knowingly concealing his assets, he would be banned from holding political office for five years.

The Thaksin coalition helped pressure the Constitutional Court to decide in favour of Thaksin. They argued that Thaksin deserved a chance because he was going to get Thailand out of the lingering economic malaise remaining from the 1997 crisis. Thaksin had a populist platform, which was an innovation, and wide-ranging support from many segments of society, including people that subsequently protested against him — like Sondhi Limthongkul, who supported Thaksin at the Constitutional Court on decision day.

Had the Constitutional Court decided against Thaksin, there would have been pandemonium in front of the court. The crowd for Thaksin hugely outnumbered those supporting the NCCC. Chamlong Srimuang was sitting on Thaksin's side at the Constitutional Court. Sondhi was outside and his *Phujatkan* media group played up the case as the end of Thailand if Thaksin were convicted. And if the Bangkok grapevine is to be believed, even former Prime Minister General Prem, the head of the king's Privy Council, wanted to see Thaksin acquitted and was involved in behind-the-scenes manoeuvrings. Heavy lobbying was conducted by other senior figures, including a former chief of the Supreme Court and senior commercial bankers, who wanted to give Thaksin a chance. The pressure for acquittal was so immense that the Constitutional Court would have had a very difficult time fending off recriminations and retributions had it convicted Thaksin in August 2001.

Unsurprisingly but controversially the Court ruled 8:7 in favour of acquittal. Thaksin was off the hook. He shed a few tears of relief. I have always maintained that this was the wrong decision, and became an early Thaksin critic because the price paid for this ruling was not worth it. This violation of the rule of law dealt a major setback to the fledgling constitution just to allow this one person to rule and to ostensibly rescue Thailand. Moreover some of us even back then did not believe Thaksin was intent on rescuing the Thai economy.

The decision to acquit Thaksin sounded rather contrived. Seven judges said Thaksin was guilty. The other eight who issued a not guilty verdict included four who said the court did not have jurisdiction and another four who said Thaksin did not know about his asset concealment. No one then seemed to care much about the reasoning. Yet if the same trial were held now in September 2006 the decision would be a 15:0 guilty. This point is raised because the judiciary's role has been compromised. The judiciary was politicized and manipulated, and there is a danger that this has set a precedent for years to come.

THAKSIN'S RISE AND DECLINE

Thaksin was an attractive person to become prime minister because he had a new party platform — a populist focus on the rural-urban divide — and he was able to overcome the factions for the first time. In Thai politics, factions normally have more leverage than parties. Thaksin was able to overcome this by connecting directly with voters. This is not something unique to Thailand — Japan's Prime Minister Koizumi had done the same, and also Chavez in Venezuela. You connect with the voters, use that popularity to overcome the party factions, and rule the country directly.

Thaksin's popularity was not just a result of vote-buying or money politics. More important was the fact that he delivered on policy promises. He promised the 30 baht healthcare scheme, the village fund and debt suspension, and he delivered. He also combined populism with nationalism promoting Thailand to become a developed country and member of the Organization for Economic Cooperation and Development (OECD). He was wildly popular from 2001 through to 2004.

It is very difficult to pinpoint which episode or period marked Thaksin's descent and slippage. There was a confluence of factors that led to his downfall, certainly from 2004. The south was the first crisis that he could not solve — it made him look bad and it made him look worse the more he tried to handle it.

Still Thaksin's acquittal in August 2001 was critical to subsequent developments, because it led to the decline of the 1997 constitution. It violated the spirit of reform — neither the letter of the constitution nor substantive provisions *per se*, but the spirit of the constitution. It paved the way for the politicization and penetration of the constitution by Thaksin's lawyers and by vested interests under him. Eventually this allowed Thaksin to capture the independent institutions under the constitution — putting their lawyers and allies in the Election Commission, the NCCC, the Constitutional Court, even the Anti-Money Laundering Office. The other institutions such as the National Economic and Social Advisory Commission (NESAC) and the NHRC were marginalized or disregarded. So the constitution became compromised after August 2001. It went into crisis later because it had been taken hostage by Thaksin, monopolized by him. Democracy under Thaksin was not healthy or robust. It does not justify the coup, but at the same time we need a rounded perspective of the Thai constitution and of democracy under Thaksin.

Thaksin was able to dominate the constitution because of a combination of attributes. That he had ideas is indisputable. He had financial muscle and organizational and management skills too. His CEO leadership was very controversial, but he got a lot of things done.

WHITHER CONSTITUTIONAL CHANGE?

The 1997 constitution succeeded in doing many of the things that it set out to do — promote transparency and accountability of the political system and stability and effectiveness of government. Thailand has just a few big parties now. The days of unwieldy, unworkable coalition governments were numbered. But the correction went too far. Thailand ended with one-party rule, and with few effective checks on this party. The opposition was too weak. The Democrats themselves were partly to blame for this. They were unable to muster the wherewithal to come up with an alternative. They could not match Thaksin's innovations, policy schemes, stature, and prominence.

Indeed, the 1997 constitution is dead and abolished. We do not yet know what will replace it. There are two major approaches to constitution drafting — one is to amend the existing constitution; another approach would be to write something completely new. Thailand has sixteen constitutions to draw from, but the effort required to write a new constitution would be a drawn-out process. The last time it took five years, including a very intensive nine-month period towards the end of this. So amendments and alterations rather than wholesale rewriting would be the preferred approach. However the major concern is that the pendulum not swing back too far away from the objectives of the 1997 constitution.

A number of constitutional changes are currently being talked about to weaken executive control, including getting rid of the ninety-day rule, promoting more checks and balances by reducing the number of members needed to censure the prime minister from 200 down to 125 or 100, and to censure Cabinet ministers, from 125 down to maybe 100. But you have to be careful in trying to find this new equilibrium because if you go back too far the other way you end up with the past. Leverage now is shifting back to factions and smaller parties. Hopefully it will not mean a return to the old days of fractious politics, and fractious, unwieldy and unworkable coalition governments.[4]

PROSPECTS

I blame the demise of the 1997 constitution on a lot of people — on the Thaksin people certainly, for being so brilliant and shrewd in undermining, politicizing and capturing the constitution. I also blame many others who are against Thaksin today, for violating the spirit of the constitution in Thaksin's 2001 court case, and allowing Thaksin to get away with other violations for several years. Now they do not like Thaksin and are pleased that he has gone. But the situation is extremely messy — an even bigger mess than before.

The current situation is very precarious for the military. It is uncertain that it knows what it is doing; it seems to be making things up as it goes along. Initially it felt it had to act, and was pleased that the coup had solved the crisis in the short term. But the major problems have not gone away. Polarization still exists and corruption charges against Thaksin are yet to be proven. The military is very slow in prosecuting and in proving these. It needs to justify the coup by proving these corruption allegations very quickly, and to publicize and disseminate this information. It is not media savvy. It controls television but does not use it — it only blocks certain television and news programmes instead of using them to convey its own messages. Progress on the corruption front is also necessary to prevent Thaksin and his cronies from making a comeback. The charges need to be made so convincingly that Thaksin will not want to return.

Finally, to move forward along this murky path in the coming weeks, the military and the interim government have to address and incorporate Thaksin's positive legacies. No doubt it is very hard to do — there is an obvious temptation to reject everything Thaksin stood for. The People's Alliance for Democracy (PAD), the anti-Thaksin coalition, feel emboldened and vindicated. The *Phujatkan* website is conducting a vendetta now, going after the entire so-called Thaksin regime. The problem is where to stop. There were hundreds of people under Thaksin within his government machinery. You cannot just put them in jail without some sort of legitimate trial. Nor, however, can they just be let loose, because they will go out and agitate.

There are other benefits in incorporating some of Thaksin's legacies. His focus on the grass-roots was unprecedented — even though it was paternalistic, patronizing, and at times he just threw cash around. It may be true, as Peter Warr argues in this volume, that abject poverty actually did not improve under Thaksin, and that Thaksinomics may not really have been that great for the Thai economy. But people liked it nonetheless. They may not know that it has not made a difference, or that they are actually more indebted. But Thaksin struck a chord and connected with the grass-roots majority of the electorate; he won hearts and minds in a very short time. This is something that must be neutralized and incorporated into the new constitution. The military has to address this question quickly. I have never heard the PAD talk about the rural poor; they just wanted to overthrow Thaksin. In fact, some Bangkokians even think that money should not be going to the poor, to the countryside. They argue that because most of the money is made in Bangkok it should be going to the underground rail system, to build more crossovers, roads and so on.

It is too early to count Thaksin out. All the evidence shows that he is a man who does not like to lose, and who will not be happy out of power. He was never happy being number two in Thailand. That in essence was the reason for this crisis.

I hope the coup leaders will go for amendments and stick to the main parts of the 1997 constitution, rather than drafting a new one. It was a good constitution, which certain people allowed to be abused. But constitutional change is unlikely to be a panacea. And it will do little to alleviate Thailand's critical problems if it does not address the division between urban affluence and rural poverty.

NOTES

1. This chapter is based on an oral keynote address to the National Thai Studies Centre's September 2006 Update.
2. Chai-anan Samudavanija, *The Thai Young Turks* (Singapore: Institute of Southeast Asian Studies, 1982).
3. For an English language version of the 1997 constitution, see Foreign Law Division, Office of the Council of State, *Constitution of the Kingdom of Thailand, B.E. 2540 (1997)* (Bangkok: Office of the Council of State, 1997).
4. As other contributions in this volume reveal, coup leaders opted for a wholesale re-writing of the constitution, producing a charter that placed major restrictions on a strong executive and strong political parties.

3

The NESAC, Civil Society, Good Governance and the Coup

Gothom Arya

Thailand's NESAC, or National Economic and Social Advisory Council, took its model from France, more or less. In French, they call it *Conseil Economique et Social*. According to this model, the council is an institutional representation of civil society. The council comprises many groups: employers, trade unions, farmers, consumers, professional associations, social associations and so on, which interact with the government. This is the concept. To do what? To bring the concerns of various sectors to the attention of the decision-makers; to provide a platform for dialogue among the diverse sectors of civil society; to minimize conflict; and to promote a culture of sharing and caring as well. So there are two or three big roles. I do not know whether the people in NESAC understand all this or not, but this was the original idea.

Actually more than fifty countries around the world have established advisory councils. However in East and Southeast Asia there are only three — in Thailand, China and South Korea. There are also councils at the regional level for the European Union — the European Economic and Social Committee — and in Latin America.

That, broadly, is the concept. Now, to NESAC itself. NESAC is mandated by Section 89 of the abolished 1997 constitution. Fortunately, there is a piece of legislation (see Appendix). According to the act, NESAC is an organization that echoes or mirrors economic or social concerns to the government, with no personal interest allowed or involved (ideally). It comprises the council and the office. The office, strangely, is a governmental department reporting directly to the prime minister but supervised by the NESAC chairman. The council has ninety-nine members, self-selected from a broad range of interest groups, who serve three-year terms. The make-up of the council is as follows: 50 members from the economic sector, industrial, agricultural and services; 19 from social organizations like women's groups, handicapped groups and the education and health sectors and so on; 16 members from the resource-based sector; and 14 "highly-knowledgeable persons" (see Appendix).

NESAC's role — and this is very formal — is to advise the government or the cabinet and to comment on government development plans. It can receive a request from the government, although so far this has happened only twice, or it can initiate advice. This has happened 110 times since the first council chaired by former Prime Minister Khun Anand Panyarachun (chair from August 2001 to August 2005). There have only been about ten recommendations since I took over the second council in August 2005. The council is also to conduct studies on issues under report on the economic and social state of the country. Other details give rather extensive powers to the chairman, aided by two vice-chairmen, to oversee the activities of the council and the office.

Recommendations to the cabinet by the second council have included one on free trade agreements (FTAs), one on ways to improve Buddhist institutions, one on educational reform, and one on the mass transit trains in Bangkok. It has also just finished comments on the Tenth Five-Year Economic and Social Development Plan — NESAC is mandated to do this for every National Economic and Social Development Plan, which is what it has done.

INSTITUTIONS FOR GOOD GOVERNANCE

The NESAC is one of a number of institutions set up under the 1997 constitution to try and ensure good governance. Where does NESAC fit into these arrangements?

One group of good governance institutions is judicial. Within the Courts of Justice mention was made in the 1997 constitution of a division — a criminal division — to handle offences by political office-holders

(Article 272). So for political office-holders there is a division under the Supreme Court. The constitution also provides for Administrative Courts to rule on disputes that involve the public service, and a Constitutional Court to adjudicate on all matters touching on the constitution itself.

In addition there is what may be called political good governance bodies. NESAC is one of these. Strictly speaking, they are not political, nor are they judicial. They include the Electoral Commission, the National Human Rights Commission (NHRC), the National Counter Corruption Commission (NCCC), the State Audit Commission and the Ombudsman. Why is there an Ombudsman in addition to these other bodies? One reason is that it only deals with problems created by state officials, but an extra power it has is to report cases to the Constitutional Court. Normally, it is very difficult to take cases directly to the Constitutional Court, but often people petition the Ombudsman so that the case will be sent there.

How are these independent organizations established? Normally, there is a select committee which nominates twice the number of candidates as there are placements to the Senate. For instance, in the case of the NCCC, eighteen are nominated and the Senate selects nine for royal appointment — though changes to this are likely following the abolition of the 1997 constitution.

INSTITUTIONAL CHANGES AFTER THE COUP

The fate of these independent institutions was profoundly affected by announcements and actions of the coup group, calling itself the Council for Democratic Reform (CDR). One of their first orders was to abolish the constitution and political bodies like the Senate, the House of Representatives and the Council of Ministers, plus one judicial body — the Constitutional Court. Coup leader General Sonthi Boonyaratglin, in one of his first interviews, maybe the first one, said that all the other bodies would be abolished with the constitution. But subsequently he retracted this statement to a certain extent. So, among those bodies mentioned, the political bodies are gone — The House of Representatives, the Senate and the Council of Ministers. A new Council of Ministers will be established after coup leaders select a prime minister.

Then, the CDR also changed two other institutions, rather than abolishing them. It changed the Constitutional Court judges, with the old group being replaced by new appointees and renamed the court the Constitutional Tribunal. Former members of the State Audit Commission were also banished, but the state audit governor was assigned two roles

— as the governor and as the commissioner at the same time, which is very strange. Here the power was concentrated in one person, namely Khunying Jaruwan Maintaka. Also, the CDR appointed, without going through the process of selection by the Senate (since it had been abolished), nine people to the NCCC while five newly selected and appointed Election Commissioners were confirmed. What do these decrees mean? They mean that only the political bodies are gone. The judicial bodies remain with some changes at the level of the Constitutional Tribunal. And all other good governance bodies remain.

How did the coup affect laws? The CDR initially said that all organic laws (those mandated in the 1997 constitution) were abolished, except where the CDR decided to the contrary. Among the eight, some have been modified slightly and continue to be enforced. However, two obviously related to the political process have been annulled. One is about the election of members to the House of Representatives and the Senate. The other is the organic law on referendums. If the CDR thinks ahead it may have to resurrect the organic law on referendums — because they plan to have a referendum after the drafting of the new constitution.

How about the secretariats? The CDR abolished the House of Representatives and Senate altogether, but clarified that the secretariats were to continue. So now the civil servants are very happy — they have salaries without having to work!

What happened to NESAC then? NESAC was established by an ordinary law, not an organic law, in the same manner as the National Human Rights Commission (NHRC). Therefore both stayed in place. However, in order to show that it received some favours from the coup group, on 25 September the CDR met and discussed the NESAC. The CDR said something like this: "People are concerned about big issues like Free Trade Agreements and privatization. So we need to provide the people with channels through which they can make sensible petitions." Thus, the CDR asked its secretariat to set up a unit to receive suggestions from the public, to screen those suggestions and to send them to NESAC. The NESAC would in turn analyse and synthesize those suggestions in order to make recommendations either to the CDR or the future Cabinet. This is what was contained in the minutes of the meeting. So now maybe the NESAC has to do more work!

Around the same time the CDR announced a clarification of its structure. It followed a strict hierarchy. The supreme commander was chief adviser. General Sonthi, from the army, of course remained the leader. The first deputy leader was from the navy, followed by second and third deputies from the

air force and the police, respectively. The secretary-general of the National
Security Council was appointed CDR secretary. The CDR subsequently
also announced they would be assisted by advisory groups. Among those
there is one which is particularly interesting: its name is Advisory Group
on Reconciliation and Social Justice. I mention this because three NESAC
members are among these twenty-six advisers, and seven former members
of the National Reconciliation Commission (NRC) are also included. So
hopefully this is a good sign that there is some recognition of the ideas
of the NRC.

COUP JUSTIFICATIONS AND ITS IMPACT
ON CIVIL SOCIETY

Now to the coup. The CDR on the first day, 20 September, had already
asked about forty diplomats to join a press conference. That was not
enough, so on 25 September it invited the diplomats for a second briefing.
The explanations which were given as to why the CDR took power were:
firstly, that the Thai people were divided and they (the coup makers) were
apprehensive of violent confrontation. There were apparently some rumours
that on the 20th, the People's Alliance for Democracy (PAD) planned to
organize a rally and that Thaksin wanted to arrest the leaders and announce
a national emergency in order to control the situation. So, in order to
prevent Thaksin from doing that, it was necessary to launch pre-emptive
action. This is very hypothetical. Mention was also made regarding the
problems in the south, in the message to the diplomats.

There was mention of the king — but initially this was only indirect.
An early announcement of the coup said that some actions of the previous
government were "verging on *lèse-majesté*". But that was dropped in
the announcement on the royal appointment of General Sonthi, which
however affirmed that "His Majesty the King has graciously granted a
Royal Command appointing General Sonthi Boonyaratglin as Leader of
the Council for Democratic Reform."

The previous regime was also accused of rampant corruption and
malfeasance, and corrupting and undermining independent agencies, the
electoral process and the entire civil service. For all these reasons, it was
argued, there was no choice but to stage a coup.

Here I would like to reflect a little on what has been going on in civil
society in Thailand. During the earlier Thaksin period civil society was
divided between pro- and anti-Thaksin groups, but as his rule developed
most moved to the anti-Thaksin group. However, there were still some who

saw Thaksin as having positive sides. But when the coup came, the divide changed. Now the divide may be half and half, although this is not clear. The divide is now between those who would like to accommodate the coup and those who strongly oppose the coup. Those willing to accommodate — I would not say they are apologists, but rather that they are willing to accommodate — accept all the reasons given above. These I would call Group A, the "no choice" group.

And as for Group B, I would refer to a letter by former Senator Jon Ungphakorn, which was circulated among civil society people. I would describe Group B as the "have choice" group. They would like to oppose the coup not only as a matter of principle but, more importantly, because they believed the political crisis could have been resolved within the constitutional framework — such as through the courts, elections, or even direct action like civil disobedience and so on. They are apprehensive of military power because it is an absolute power and we cannot really trust absolute power. Also, there was uncertainty as to whether the old power of the elite groups among the bureaucrats or the academics might take this opportunity to stage a comeback and occupy a greater space than the people in the political arena. After the announcement of the outline of the interim constitution, those in Group B felt even more certain that their apprehensions were justified.

To these may be added a third category, a "no choice but" group. The first group, Group A sees no choice — we had to have a coup. Group C, the "no choice but" group, used to belong to Group A but are starting to have doubts and convert somewhat to Group B. They argue something like this: "Why did the CDR have to abolish the entire constitution instead of choosing to stop the enforcement of only certain sections or certain chapters whilst keeping the good sections in place?" For instance, general principles, human rights and so on, are not concerned with the political struggle. Why should the CDR muscle in on the media, and not allow freedom of expression and freedom of assembly when this is carried out in good faith? Why do they not talk about people's participation in political reform? And why does the interim constitution envisage the CDR becoming the Council for National Security (CNS)? The CNS is mentioned in the interim constitution and will retain a lot of power.

WHAT SHOULD CIVIL SOCIETY DO?

Let me approach this final issue by first making a small criticism of civil society. Thailand needs a strong leader, but it also need someone who is humble. That is precisely a quality which Thaksin lacked. Does Thaksin deserve, or merit, being criticized? Yes, but does he merit being "bashed"? That is not obvious because "bashing" someone can lead to hatred and fear. The PAD is not a monolithic group, but part of it used what might be called a tactic that would create hatred. They used nationalism against "selling out the country". They called for the restoration of the nation, a *kuu chat* movement. The implication here was that Thaksin did not love the country, and that somebody who did not love the country should be hated. He was presented as all bad, and someone who sold out the country. They also invoked the monarchy, arguing that Thaksin was not loyal to the king.

To me, this was not very fair. Those who feared Thaksin correctly pointed out that his populist policies seemed to be unbeatable among the electorate, and his cronyism was eating up the fabric of Thailand's political system. Thailand has to fight both populist democracy and cronyism with all its force. But it should not fear these things so much as to cause it to throw away the basic principles of democracy.

The divide between those who would like to collaborate and those who refuse to collaborate with the CDR has been mentioned. So what should we do? I would like to appeal to academics and civil society to transcend that divide through dialogue and solidarity, and propose the following as common ground.

We have to insist on the principle of the sovereignty of the people, whilst still thinking of safeguards against populism and money politics. We have to insist on the ideology of nationalism whilst at the same time also insisting upon the respect of everyone's human dignity and for all cultural and ethnic diversity. We have to preserve the constitutional monarchy by building safeguards against politicizing the monarchy itself. We may agree that in the absence of representative democracy during the coming year, we have to advocate both participatory and deliberative democracy. But we have to get organized, we have to mobilize, and we have to start now the participation and the dialogue on political reform. There is a lot of work to be done and there is a lot of danger ahead. But we should look forward and make a better constitution within a year.

Appendix: Extracts from The National Economic and Social Advisory Council Act B.E. 2543 [A.D. 2000]

Article 4.   The Prime Minister shall have charge and control of the execution of this Act.

Chapter 1 Member of the National Economic and Social Advisory Council

Article 5.   Let there be a National Economic and Social Advisory Council, the membership of which is made up of ninety-nine people who are elected to represent organized groups in the economic and social sectors, with the latter being drawn from various resource bases and the highly-knowledgeable persons. The aforementioned groups, the number of each is shown in the attachment of this Act, are defined in accordance with the state's fundamental policies set forth in the constitution.

Article 6.   Membership pursuant to Article 5 shall be derived from the following procedures:

(1) When there is a need to elect members, a Selection Committee for members of the National Economic and Social Advisory Council shall be set up with 21 committee members comprising:

[a] Chairman of the National Economic and Social Development Board, as ex-officio committee chairman;

[b] Permanent-secretaries of all ministries, elected through self-selection down to four;

[c] Presidents of all the tertiary educational institutes, which are incorporated as juridical persons, elected through self-selection down to three;

[d] A representative of presidents of all the Rajabhat Institutes and Rajamangala Institutes of Technology, elected through self-selection;

[e] Four representatives of the institutions in the production sector, i.e., one each from the Board of Trade of Thailand, the Federation of Thai Industries, the Thai Bankers' Association, and the Agricultural Co-operative Federation of Thailand, Ltd.;

[f] A representative of all trade unions, elected through self-selection;

[g] Representatives of non-governmental organizations that operate without seeking profits, nor sharing the proceeds, elected through self-selection down to four, i.e., one each from those whose main objectives are as follows:

(i) Rural community development, urban community development, natural resources management, environmental management, alternative agriculture management, or management of appropriate technology;

(ii) Livelihood development for children, youth, women, the elderly, the disabled, the AIDS-affected people, or patients;

(iii) Advocacy for civil rights and liberty, consumer rights, democracy promotion, or labour development;

(iv) Public health, education, or arts and culture.

[h] Three representatives, one each from the print, radio, and television media, elected through self-selection.

The secretary-general of the National Economic and Social Advisory Council shall be the secretary of the Selection Committee.

Article 7. Qualifications and prohibited attributes of members are as follows:

(11) Not being a member of the House of Representatives or the Senate, a political office holder, a member of a local council, an administrator of a local administration, or an office holder in a political party.

Article 8. Members shall be in office for a term of three years from the date a list of members is published in the Government Gazette. A member may be re-elected, but cannot stay in office for more than two consecutive terms.

Chapter 2 Authority

Article 10. The National Economic and Social Advisory Council is an organization that reflects economic and social problems, and not to be misused as a bargaining tool to benefit any person or group of persons. Its authority is as follows:

(1) To provide advices and suggestions to the Council of Ministers with regards to economic and social problems

for the benefit of implementing the Directive Principles of Fundamental State Policies as prescribed in Chapter 5 of the Constitution of the Kingdom of Thailand.

(2) To provide comments on the National Economic and Social Development Plans, other plans according to Article 14, as well as any plans prescribed by law to be previewed by the National Economic and Social Advisory Council prior to their official implementation.

Chapter 3 Operations

Article 18. There shall be a Chairman of the National Economic and Social Advisory Council and two Vice-Chairmen. At the inaugural meeting of the National Economic and Social Advisory Council, members shall elect one of their fellow members as Chairman of the Council, and two as vice-chairmen. The two are to perform their duties as First Vice-Chairman and Second Vice-Chairman.

Article 19. The Council Chairman shall hold the following authorities:

(1) To conduct meetings, and is empowered to issue any instruction as deemed necessary to keep the meetings in order;

(2) To control and operate the council's affairs in accordance with the by-laws and resolutions of the council;

(3) To represent the council in the affairs that involve outsiders;

(4) Any other authorities as provided by laws.

List of Groups

1. Groups in the Economic Sector   Total: 50 members

(1) Agricultural production, e.g., rice farming, crop growing, fruit orchard and gardening, livestock farming, genetic improvement of plants and animals, fishery, processing of farm produce or other agricultural products.   *16 members*

(2) Industrial production, e.g., mining, including rock excavation or quarrying, production of food and beverage, textile, apparel, leather, wood products, furniture, paper, chemicals, medicine, petroleum products, natural rubber, glass, cement, ceramics, construction materials, jewelry, ornament, metal, machinery, motoring equipment and spare parts, electrical and electronic appliances and tools, or other industrial manufacturing.   *17 members*

(3) Service provision, e.g., logistics, transportation, communication, telecommunication and information technology, import-export, domestic agricultural and industrial trading, tourism, legal services, accounting services, architectural services, engineering services, construction, sporting and recreation, artists and writers, government officials, restaurant business, mass media or other services. *17 members*

2. Groups in the Social Sector, Resource-Based Sector, and the Highly-Knowledgeable Persons   Total: 49 members

Groups in the Social Sector   *19 members*
(1) Community Development   *2*
(2) Public Health   *2*
(3) Education, Arts and Culture, Religion   *4*
(4) Development and Care for the Disabled   *2*
(5) Development of Children, Youth, Women, and the Elderly   *4*
(6) Labour Development   *4*
(7) Consumer Protection   *1*

Groups in the Resource-Based Sector   *16 members*
(8) Resource bases, e.g., land, forest, water supply, water basin, sea, air, or biodiversity   *10*
(9) Agricultural System Development   *4*
(10) Industrial System Development   *1*
(11) Service System Development   *1*
Group of the Highly-Knowledgeable Persons   *14 members*

Source: <http://www2.nesac.go.th/english/law/pdf/The_National_Economic_and_Social_Advisory_Council_Act2543.pdf\ t2543.pdf\>.

4
Military Coup and Democracy in Thailand

Chairat Charoensin-o-larn

OVERVIEW

Thailand's military coup on the night of 19 September 2006 came as a surprise, and was greeted with resentment by some and with joy, relief, and hope by others. The former were afraid that the coup was just the beginning of yet another military intervention in Thai politics, a tradition that represents a bitter revival of events fifteen years before in the 1991 coup and bloody incident of May 1992. Representatives of this group ranged from a number of students and university lecturers who called themselves the "19 September Network against the Coup",[1] to a taxi driver who ran his car head-on into an army tank stationed at the Royal Plaza to show his discontent with the coup for destroying Thailand's democracy.[2]

For educated people within this group, using the military coup as a means to restore democracy was simply indefensible. Low-income people (including taxi drivers), on the other hand, were benefiting greatly from a number of generous financial schemes emanating from the populist policies designed and implemented by Prime Minister Thaksin after he came to office in 2001. These schemes included universal healthcare, village investment funds, the People's Bank, and cheap loans.[3] The departure of Thaksin from power has meant the loss of many of these benefits.

However, in mentioning this, I do not mean to argue that these low-income groups, particularly the rural masses, are the "victims" of Thaksin's populist policies, as most middle-class and urban intellectuals have been fond of pointing out.[4] On the contrary, the victim thesis overlooks the significant fact that the rural poor have persistently struggled throughout Thai history to bring political pressure to bear on various governments. The populist policies of Thaksin are in part the result of this long and arduous struggle.

Against the background of military intervention in Thai politics, the recent coup is thus seen by this group as redemption for the army, which is now in a position to reclaim its former prominent role in Thai politics after a long hiatus. The picture will become clearer after 30 September 2007 when General Sonthi Boonyaratglin, chairman of the Council for National Security (CNS) and leader of both the coup and the former Council of Democratic Reform (CDR), retires from his army post. Meanwhile, General Sonthi has kept the Thai public guessing whether or not he will enter politics, and if so by what means. Nonetheless, within the context of Thai politics, such reluctance on the part of General Sonthi to deny or acknowledge reports of his future role in politics is simply taken as a confirmation of the reports.[5] Sonthi's succession is also a delicate matter and has potential to cause political turmoil if it is not handled with care. For example, a rift among the three top contenders for the post of army chief could pose a threat to political stability.

To those for whom the coup brought joy, relief, and hope it is believed that the coup will bring back normalcy and stability to Thai society after a prolonged and profound conflict between the supporters and opponents of the deposed Prime Minister Thaksin Shinawatra, who is now living in self-imposed exile in England in the aftermath of the coup.[6] This second group, which is composed mainly of the neo-royalists, the old elite, the armed forces, the middle class, and a substantial portion of urban intellectuals, regards the coup as legitimate because it is the "last resort" to solve political conflicts after all other measures have failed. One advocate of this formidable coalition argues that the September military putsch was not really a *coup d'état* but rather a *coup de grâce*.[7] This is because the coup was launched without bloodshed, and it effectively ended a lengthy period of political turmoil. According to this group, the coup was carried out not for anyone's personal gain but for the sake of the Thai people and the Thai nation as a whole.

The coup was quickly endorsed by the king, soldiers and tanks involved in the coup displayed yellow ribbons — yellow is the king's colour — to symbolize their loyalty to the king, and the coup leaders, immediately after successfully seizing power from the elected government, initially referred to themselves as the Council for Democratic Reform Under the Constitutional Monarchy (CDR). One academic called the event "a royalist coup".[8] In addition, during the night of the coup, all radio stations and television channels played songs composed by the king, interspersed with pictures of the king's activities in development projects initiated by the royal family. This display has led another academic shrewdly to call it the "unread announcements" of the coup leaders.[9]

In the opinion of this group of academics, the September coup was the culmination of months of shadow-boxing between the "network monarchy" and the network of ousted Prime Minister Thaksin.[10] In an exclusive interview with *The Nation* newspaper shortly after the coup, General Sonthi recited his military-cum-royalist script concerning the coup:

> I like to say two things about the military coup. First, I received calls for the coup from many people. Second, soldiers are obliged to protect national security, safeguard the nation and uphold loyalty to the monarchy. The military cannot tolerate any leaders who lack or have limited loyalty to the King.[11]

During his annual birthday speech on 4 December 2006, the king explicitly made known his support for the Cabinet headed by General (Ret) Surayud Chulanont, stating that "the elderly are not greedy and don't want to accumulate power for themselves".[12] The new cabinet, dubbed by the media as "old ginger", was composed of a host of elderly, retired civil servants. Of Prime Minister Surayud in particular, the king said that he was a man of principle and had sacrificed himself to work for the good of the country. Thus, the king had openly endorsed and supported the junta-installed cabinet. This prompted one academic to comment that the "direct boost to the Surayud Cabinet is an indirect approval of the military's putsch and its post-coup efforts".[13]

The junta accused the elected government of ousted Prime Minister Thaksin of causing an unprecedented rift in society, accompanied by corruption, nepotism, human rights violations, interference in the independent agencies set up by the now-abolished 1997 constitution, meddling with the army, and insults to the king. Therefore, the junta deemed it as its duty to unite the nation through a brief intervention in order to restore peace, order, justice, and the prestige of the monarchy.

However, almost a year after the coup, there is still no light at the end of the tunnel. Violence in the south broke out in January 2004 and has since escalated despite various attempts by the state to deal with it. When Prime Minister Surayud, a privy councillor and former army chief, assumed power, an early act was to apologize publicly to the Muslim population in the south for the violence and the mishandling of their situation by the previous government. He then announced a policy of reconciliation toward the south.

Political conflicts and power struggles between the coup leaders and their network and the network of former Prime Minister Thaksin seem to have intensified rather than subsided, especially from late May after the Constitutional Tribunal dissolved Thaksin's once powerful Thai Rak Thai (TRT) Party and the Assets Scrutiny Committee (ASC) decided to freeze his family's financial assets and to indict Thaksin in connection with several corruption cases. The junta-appointed ASC, and its sister organization, the National Counter Corruption Commission (NCCC), are comprised mainly of opponents of Thaksin. This meant that the September coup has had the effect of deepening the existing "partition of the perceptible"[14] in Thai society, and has diminished hopes for a quick return to the normalcy and stability that had initially been promised by the coup.

The junta also had the leading role in selecting a National Legislative Assembly. This comprised largely active-duty and retired military personnel, government officials, and members of anti-Thaksin groups such as the People's Alliance for Democracy (PAD), whose tenacious protests and demonstrations not only led to the downfall of the Thaksin regime but were also an invitation to the army to stage the coup.[15] Such a selection process does not truly represent either the spirit of democracy or the kind of citizen participation promised by the coup leaders under the banner of "political reform". Therefore, the deep division between the urban middle class and the rural population continues.

Indeed, it was the hope for a return to normalcy that helped make the coup, in its first few days, appear like an exhibition of artillery hardware in the capital city of Bangkok. Coup supporters and the general public had their pictures taken with soldiers on duty with their tanks. Flowers, food, and drink were offered to soldiers to show the public's appreciation. All of this led the coup leaders and their supporters to conclude that this was a "special" coup, that is, a coup with a human face.

More significantly, the promise by the coup leaders for a quick return of power to the people and to normalcy tends to obscure the historical dimension of the military *coup d'état* in Thai society. The announcement of such a coup made it appear like an unavoidable and necessary measure to solve a political crisis or break a political impasse. The *coup d'état* as a crucial form of power struggle in the history of Thai politics has been used, with some sophistication, as a legitimate technique for solving national problems under such political slogans as "a quick return to normalcy" and "a restoration of democracy".

Finally, there is no better demonstration of this sharp "partition of the perceptible" in post-coup Thailand than the intense campaigns surrounding the referendum on the junta-sponsored draft constitution, which was held exactly eleven months after the coup, on 19 August 2007. Tension mounted between the interim government, the CNS, the former opposition parties, and the coup supporters, who sided with the draft charter, symbolized by the colour green, and the supporters of Thaksin and the various networks of those who opposed the coup, who united together under the umbrella of the United Front of Democracy against Dictatorship (UDD), which campaigned against the charter under the symbol of the colour red. The conflict between these two groups has dominated the political space since 6 July, when the Constitution Drafting Assembly endorsed the draft charter and offered it for referendum. The referendum thus turned into a political contest between the supporters and the opponents of the coup, reminiscent of the former polarization between the supporters and the opponents of Thaksin prior to the coup.

Perhaps the root cause of the political conflict in contemporary Thai society that has led to all this turmoil lies neither in the abrogated 1997 constitution nor in the 2007 draft charter. Rather, it is an inherently weak Thai society and culture that does not believe in people's power and always looks for a white knight to solve political crises.[16] Consequently, to restore democracy, Thailand needs neither a military coup nor an authoritarian leader but a wise and active citizenry who are capable of transforming what Chantal Mouffe has called "antagonism" into "agonism".[17] This is an ability to perceive the other not as an enemy to be defeated but as an adversary "whose ideas we combat but whose right to defend those ideas we do not put into question".[18] If antagonism treats opponents as enemies to be obliterated, then agonism considers them as legitimate opponents. This represents democratic tolerance and the utilization of a democratic means for handling conflict that Thailand needs to learn and to build on.

With the passage of time, the coup has proven not to be a workable solution to the increasing complexity of Thai society. Thailand's globalized economy and society are incompatible with the rigid rule of a military junta. Investment has dropped due mainly to an 18 December announcement that investors must set aside 30 per cent of their money before being allowed to invest. If they withdrew funds before the end of a year the investment would be subject to a 10 per cent withholding tax. This requirement had severe negative repercussions for the stock market. The SET index dropped 15 per cent within a day, resulting in a loss of 820 billion bath (US$22.9 billion). Just one day after the measure was introduced, the Bank of Thailand removed capital controls on equity investments, leaving intact only capital controls on the money market.[19] Before the reserve measure, foreign funds had been pouring into Thailand, particularly for the purpose of speculating on the baht. This means that foreign investors did not care much about either the coup or the new constitution. However, they did care about capital controls. Though the stock market quickly regained much of its lost ground, these policy changes damaged Thailand's financial credibility in the early months of the interim government.

Furthermore, the export sector has declined due to the strong baht. The baht has appreciated to the extent that several textile and footwear companies have been forced to close down. In August 2007 the country's fourth largest rice exporter in Phichit Province, President Agri Trading Co., was shut down due to an accumulated debt of one billion baht.[20]

From January to July 2007, it was reported that the baht had gained 7.1 per cent against the U.S. dollar and that the Bank of Thailand had spent more than 1.7 trillion baht to defend the baht from speculators. The 30 per cent reserve on capital control mentioned above was part of the package to stabilize the baht. The stronger baht, the United States economic slowdown, and fallout from the sub-prime mortgage crisis have combined to dampen Thailand's export performance in July, giving it the lowest figures in twenty-nine months.[21] The level of household debt in August also hit a historic high mainly because the economy has slowed down and forced people to borrow more to survive.[22] However, many economists have argued that greater availability of credit, particularly from Thaksin's populist programmes, have contributed to the increase in household debt.

Meanwhile, the labour union of the Telephone Organization of Thailand (TOT) has called for the entire board, including its chairman, General Saprang Kalayanamitr, one of the coup leaders, to resign.[23] They argued that the board's lack of business experience and its internal conflicts are hurting the company's overall performance.[24] The minister of information and communication technology admitted that the trouble-plagued TOT was on the verge of collapse and needed to find quick solutions.[25]

The prices of agricultural produce, notably longan, rambutan, mangosteen, and longan, have plunged.[26] It was reported that former MPs had to buy tons of these fruits from local growers and give them away free in a bid to help shore up prices.[27] The interim government also assigned the Royal Thai Air Force to provide C-130 carriers to transport longan fruit from airports in the southern provinces for sale at the China International Halal Food and Muslim Commodities Festival held in China's Ningxia province.[28]

Tourism has also slowed down compared to the same period of the previous year. Factors from all sides have contributed to such a slow down. In addition to the coup and violence in the south, which has seen daily bombings and indiscriminate killings, other factors include the stronger baht which makes travelling to Thailand more expensive, and the domestic political situation which has been marked by bombings in the city, school torching in the provinces, and demonstration against the junta.[29]

Economic hardship has also been felt. One college student in Nakorn Srithammarat was reported to have committed suicide in late July because she could not endure hardship while waiting for government student loans.[30] The interim government had run out of funds for the student-loan project.

Civil liberties are restricted and thirty-five provinces are still under martial law — under the watchful eyes of soldiers, the police, and local administrators. Meanwhile, a referendum for the new draft charter on 19 August was held amidst a decidedly undemocratic atmosphere.

The neo-royalist network's coup has not provided a democratic alternative to Thaksin's authoritarianism. Although a general election was scheduled for the end of 2007, and the draft charter passed the 19 August referendum by a narrow margin, there are certain signs pointing to an increasing role by the military in the future of Thai politics. Suffice it to say that a new constitution and a general election will not be able to keep the armed forces out of politics. Rather, these two facilitators of democratic governance will be used as avenues for the armed forces to enter politics and to hold on to their power.

POLITICAL CLEAN-UP: PHASE I

Power Consolidation

The political situation in Thailand since the September coup can be divided into two major periods. The first phase was from 19 September 2006 to April 2007. The second phase began from May 2007, and continued throughout the year. The first phase of post-coup politics was marked by a sense of hesitation and uncertainty regarding how to deal with the deposed Prime Minister Thaksin and his network.[31] Unlike previous coups, which were able to maintain law and order, this coup and its interim government have been struggling to contain Thaksin, his supporters, and insurgents in the south.[32]

Instead of using the existing Anti-Money Laundering Office to freeze the assets of politicians suspected of corruption — as the anti-Thaksin group called for — the junta and the interim government opted for establishing special panels to deal with this problem. This then allowed the suspected politicians time to transfer their assets at their own discretion. Such hesitancy and uncertainty caused a rift within the CNS and between the CNS and the interim government of General Surayud. In January 2007, at the height of these concerns, a rumour was spread that another coup would take place in which an attempt would be made to seize power from the interim government. The coup rumour forced the junta to make a televised announcement on the army-run TV5 to deny it.[33] Prime Minister General Surayud himself warned the public to be alert and prepare for the "new threat" to their lives.

The Assets Scrutiny Committee (ASC) was the main institution established by the junta to tackle the remnants of the "old power" and the "undercurrents" — the CNS's terms referring to an alleged pro-Thaksin movement. It also reconstituted the Constitutional Court as the Constitutional Tribunal, and appointed a new National Counter Corruption Commission after this had been in abeyance for two years. Meanwhile, the majority of the bureaucracy had decided to assume a "neutral" stance by feigning indifference and being uncooperative to the new power holders, partly because they were afraid that the "old power" might strike back, and partly because they were part of the Thaksin network. The situation was serious enough that the ASC had to present to Prime Minister Surayud lists of individuals and agencies that failed to cooperate with the committee in an investigation into alleged corruption cases.[34]

During this first phase of the political clean-up, the coup leaders and the coup-installed Prime Minister Surayud saw Thaksin as a threat to national security and kept repeating that Thaksin should stay abroad until after the new election was completed and the new government formed. They anticipated that Thaksin's return would set off conflict and violence, a scenario that most Thai people were familiar with before the coup took place. One of Thaksin's hired lawyers at the U.S. law firm Baker Botts told the *Associated Press* that the coup leaders had explicitly told the ousted premier to stay away from the kingdom.[35]

Just a week after the putsch, an editorial in *The Nation* commented on the slow move of the coup leaders as "a disappointing start" because they had failed to freeze the assets of politicians suspected of gaining their wealth through unusual means.[36] This failure is significant because one of the reasons the coup leaders used to justify their action was alleged widespread corruption in Thaksin government.

Another justification used by the coup leaders was that they needed to resolve a protracted political crisis and to restore harmony among the people. However, this objective could not be realized either — several bombs exploded in many areas of the capital during New Year's Eve, killing three and injuring forty-two, and schools in the northeast and the south were being set on fire almost daily. This is not to mention the daily violent outbreaks in the deep south. In both the bombing and school torching cases, the only explanation the authorities could come up with was that they were the work of the old power. The authorities failed to find the culprits and these cases are still unresolved. Thus, it is quite clear that the CDR and CNS did not have a clear strategy to deal with the old power at the beginning of their rule.

During this first phase of political clean-up, many police officers, civil servants, and provincial governors loyal to, or appointed by, the Thaksin government, and his former Class 10 classmates at the Armed Forces Academies Preparatory School, were removed or transferred to inactive posts and replaced with officers trusted by the new regime. The junta reasoned that these people could pose a threat to national security if they were to remain in their positions. This removal was effected for the stated purpose of achieving "national reconciliation".

Meanwhile, the junta leaders appointed themselves and their associates to the boards of directors of several key state enterprises such as the Airport of Thailand, Thai Airways International, the Port Authority of Thailand, and the Telephone Organization of Thailand — a practice that has a long history in the tradition of the military junta in Thai politics. Faced with criticism, interim Prime Minister Surayud came out defending the practice by insisting that such appointments were based on ability and expertise and were not the result of nepotism, as had been the case with political parties in power in the past.[37] General Sonthi too supported the practice, saying that high-ranking military personnel were put in positions of authority on the boards to prevent corruption and to ensure national security. General Chavalit Yongchaiyud, a former army chief and prime minister, made a surprise criticism, reportedly because his men failed to get appointed to any of the boards.

Furthermore, the Surayud Cabinet approved substantial salary increases for the coup leaders and their appointed bodies. For example, General

Sonthi, chairman of the CNS and coup leader, received a monthly salary of 119,200 baht — doubling his regular salary as army chief. The salary for National Legislative Assembly chairman was 115,920 baht, and the ASC chairman received 108,500 baht. These figures were astonishingly high when compared to the amount received by members of the National Peace-Keeping Council after the 1991 coup, which was 20,000 baht per month.[38]

By April 2007, with the completion of the mid-year military reshuffle, the junta had begun to consolidate its power. All mechanisms set forth by the junta to handle Thaksin and his associates had begun to produce concrete results. This marked the beginning of the second phase of the post-coup political clean-up in Thailand.

POLITICAL CLEAN-UP: PHASE II

Party Dissolution

On 30 May 2007, dubbed "Judgement Day" by the media, the whole nation was glued to their television sets, watching with anticipation as the junta-appointed Constitutional Tribunal read its lengthy verdict on the dissolution of the TRT Party and the dismissal of all charges against the Democrat Party.[39] The TRT was charged with election fraud during the 2 April election because it had purportedly hired smaller parties to contest in the polls. The idea was to avoid the requirement of having to win 20 per cent of eligible votes where only a single candidate contested. The main opposition parties — the Democrats, Chart Thai, and Mahachon — boycotted the election by withdrawing their candidates from the contest. In the same verdict, the tribunal also imposed a five-year ban on 111 TRT Party executives from participating in politics. In other words, these executives were stripped of their rights to hold office in a political party, to vote and to run in an election.

The verdict was controversial not only because it acquitted the Democrat Party of all charges while finding the TRT guilty, but also because there appeared to be a conflict in interpretation and an attempt at manipulation. A week before the scheduled verdict, King Bhumibol gave a rare speech to the Supreme Administrative Court judges. The thrust of the speech emphasized the king's grave concern over the upcoming Constitutional Tribunal verdict on the future of the two major political parties of the country. In his speech, the king asked the country's top judges to do their best for the country and yet brace themselves for heavy criticism. "You have the responsibility to prevent the country from collapsing", he warned them in the speech, which was televised on all national television channels simultaneously on the evening of 24 May 2007.

The king further asked the visiting judges, led by Supreme Administrative Court President Ackaratorn Chularat, who was concurrently vice-president of the Constitutional Tribunal, to "rightly interpret" what he was trying to say:

> Whatever court you belong to, judges need to make the right interpretation, otherwise the country will be doomed. … You have the responsibility to judge, but not with the hammer. You can only decide within your heart whether the Constitution Tribunal makes the right ruling. Your responsibility and duty are to criticize the ruling. I have no right whatsoever to say if they are right or wrong, but in my heart I have to know whether they have done right or wrong. If they are wrong, there will be trouble whether or not political parties remain. I have the answer in my heart but I have no right to say it. Neither do you. … [We] can't issue any ruling because we are not the Constitution Tribunal. … But if you [have] listen[ed] to [the] radio over the past two days, there has been heavy criticism [of] the courts. …[40]

The exact meaning of this advice from the king was not clear, and interpretations varied. Some observers saw it as a suggestion to the judges not to make a compromise ruling; others saw it as a warning against dissolving the two parties. The king was careful not to say where he stood on the merits of the case. The parties concerned had to read his mind.

Meanwhile, it had been reported that General Sonthi, the coup leader, had met with Judge Ackaratorn on 29 May, one day before the verdict. However, General Sonthi denied that he was lobbying the judge on the dissolution case. He said that it was simply a casual get-together of two Muslims for a round of merit-making.[41]

Finally, shortly after the verdict, there was a report of an attempt to bribe some of the Constitutional Tribunal judges to deliver a favourable ruling for the TRT. This led Supreme Court President Panya Thanomrod, who was also president of the Constitutional Tribunal, to appoint a disciplinary committee to conduct a formal inquiry on the report. By mid-August, the committee found that a certain high-ranking officer of the Justice Ministry and a retired police colonel had lobbied certain Constitutional Tribunal judges for a favourable ruling.[42] An arrest was made and the case is now under judicial process.[43] It is uncertain whether the king had known about this bribery allegation and thus came out to warn the judges in his speech mentioned above.

The controversy over the verdict had less to do with banning the TRT than with the tribunal's sweeping imposition of the five-year ban on political participation by all TRT executives. The decision, reached by a 6-3 judicial majority, was based on CDR Announcement No. 27, issued shortly after the coup. The announcement amended the Political Parties Act by stipulating that executives of the dissolved party will be stripped of their voting rights for five years for violating election law, making them ineligible to stand for office. In effect, Announcement No. 27 forced TRT executives and MPs to resign en masse from the party in a desperate attempt to keep their political careers alive in case the court ordered the party to be dissolved. Thaksin himself also resigned as the leader of the party by faxing his handwritten letter of resignation from London.

Since the CDR Announcement No. 27 came after the alleged offence, it is questionable whether it is acceptable for the Constitutional Tribunal to base their decision on it. To do so is tantamount to making the punishment retroactive. Legally speaking, punishment must be in line with the law in effect when an offence occurs. Furthermore, retroactive application of a law is acceptable only when it benefits the accused. A retroactive effect that harms or intensifies the punishment is against the international principles of justice.

More significantly, by invoking the power conferred by the coup leaders in Announcement No. 27, the Constitutional Tribunal has actually validated and endorsed the military coup. In other words, the ruling was seen by some critics as the coup leaders using the court to carry out their order. The grave concern of the critics was that the verdict would set "a dangerous precedent" for the future of democracy in Thailand: "The court severely punished Thai Rak Thai for breaking a law under the 1997 constitution while upholding the military's right to rip that constitution to shreds", wrote one critic.[44] Article 63 of the abolished 1997 constitution, which had its roots in the bloody incident of May 1992, explicitly forbade anyone to "overthrow the democratic regime of government with the King as Head of the State" by force. Therefore, the tribunal verdict ended up legitimizing both the present and future coups.

More striking and more revealing with regard to the TRT dissolution case is the "strange" manoeuvre of General Sonthi, the coup leader. Just two days after the verdict, he came out publicly with the idea of offering amnesty to the TRT executive party members concerning their five-year ban from politics. The idea caused a public uproar and was rejected immediately.[45] General Sonthi publicly apologized to the judges for his hasty thinking. However, the event was quite revealing concerning its ramifications for the future of Thai politics and Thai democracy.

It seems that General Sonthi has enjoyed his sovereign power since the coup — so much so that he may think that every one of his utterances could become the law of the land. In his capacity as a coup leader, he was indeed a sovereign in the sense of being able to declare a state of exception from any existing laws, notably the constitution.[46] Thus, instead of letting justice take its course according to the original verdict, he has decided to intervene on the platform of a reconciliatory mission: "I do believe that the idea [of amnesty] will be part of a process to restore peace and order and reconciliation."[47] Should he be allowed to have his way, months of hard work by the tribunal judges and their ten hours of verdict reading would amount to a total waste of time. It is thus not difficult to imagine how a strategic man like General Sonthi can come out with such an idea acting as a sovereign implementing a "state of exception" in an overt attempt to suspend the original verdict. In other words, his amnesty idea would overrule the tribunal's verdict.

However, some analysts have argued that General Sonthi and his CNS might have analysed the situation incorrectly, in part by misinterpreting the king's speech. This would then have led to the conclusion that the tribunal should only punish individual executives linked to election fraud but spare the parties from dissolution.[48] In addition, the amnesty idea would clear the path for some banned executives close to the junta to undertake political activities on behalf of the junta, after Sonthi reaches mandatory retirement age in September.[49]

Assets Freeze

Less than two weeks after the dissolution of the TRT Party, on the evening of 11 June 2007, the junta-installed ASC televised their announcement to freeze more than 52 billion baht possessed by deposed Prime Minister Thaksin, his wife, two adult children, and two other relatives. These frozen monies were in twenty-one accounts and some were related to the controversial sale of shares in Shin Corp to the Singaporean investment arm, Temasek Holdings, in early 2006 — worth a total of 72 billion baht. Later an additional 20 billion was frozen. The sale of these shares was alleged, among other things, to constitute tax evasion, with resultant damage to the state worth around 33.108 billion baht, according to the ASC's estimates.[50]

The ASC order was based on alleged acts of dishonesty and abuse of power to accumulate unusual wealth. The ASC derived its authority from CDR Announcement No. 30, issued shortly after the coup. The announcement authorizes the ASC to freeze or confiscate assets of state officials suspected of malfeasance or corruption, where these may cause damage to the state. Any bank which allows transactions in these frozen assets could face legal action. The assets will be unfrozen if the accused can verify within sixty days that they earned these assets through legal means. On 27 July the team of lawyers for Thaksin filed a court case demanding that the ASC unfreeze his assets.

In addition to alleged malfeasance in the sale of Shin Corp shares, the ASC found enough evidence to charge Thaksin and his wife in five other malfeasance cases and six cases of abuse of power, in both instances for the purpose of obtaining unusual wealth.[51] The five malfeasance cases consisted of the purchase of land worth 772 million baht from the Bank of Thailand's Financial Institutions Development Fund; the purchase of rubber saplings worth 1.44 billion baht by the Department of Agriculture, Ministry of Agriculture and Co-operatives; the purchase of luggage conveyor belts and CTX 9000 bomb scanners; the issuance of two- and three-digit lottery tickets by the Government Lottery Bureau; and loans by Krung Thai Bank executives.[52]

The six cases of abuse of power included altering an agreement on revenue sharing for prepaid mobile phone services to benefit Thaksin's company, the Advanced Info Service (AIS); altering an agreement on the rate of revenue sharing between the Telephone Organization of Thailand (TOT) and AIS; the issuing of an executive decree on telecommunications excise taxes and a cabinet resolution turning concession fees into excise taxes; instructing TOT to rent and invest unnecessarily in the satellite frequency held by Shin Satellite; ordering Exim Bank to allow the Burmese government to draw loans amounting to 1 billion baht in order to buy products and services from Shin Satellite; and, finally, using international trade negotiations to trade national interests for those of the satellite businesses of Shin Corp, adding considerable business value to Shin Satellite.

Among the five malfeasance cases above, the case involving the purchase of the Ratchadaphisek land, worth 772 million baht in 2003, had already been forwarded to the public prosecutors and indictments had been issued. As prime minister, Thaksin gave consent to the land purchase while he was in charge of overseeing the Financial Institutions Development Fund, which owned the land. The purchase was thus considered to be a case of conflict of interest.

The Ratchadaphisek land deal case was then sent to the Supreme Court's Criminal Division for Political Office Holders for trial. The first hearing was set on 14 August but Thaksin and wife did not show up, citing a concern for their safety should they return to stand trial in Thailand. The summons was posted in front of Thaksin's residence in Bangkok with much media fanfare. The court postponed the hearing to 25 September and issued the couple arrest warrants for their evasion of judicial proceedings. If Thaksin and his wife failed to turn up for the second hearing, the prosecutors would start extradition proceedings with the British government.[53]

Veteran politician, Samak Sundaravej, a former Bangkok governor and a former leader of the Prachakorn Thai Party, had argued that what the CNS, the interim government, and its bureaucracy had tried to do in the land deal case was to discredit Thaksin. The issue of an arrest warrant was just a standard procedure of the judicial process when a defendant failed to appear in court. Besides, the Ratchadaphisek land deal was not a corruption case because the former NCCC had already ruled that the purchase was not in violation of Article 100 of the NCCC bill. Although Thaksin supervised the Bank of Thailand (BoT) in his capacity as prime minister, he did not actually administer the bank. Furthermore, the Financial Institutions Development Fund did not feel that the purchase had caused them any damages. Nonetheless, the junta-installed ASC forced them to file a complaint so that the case could be processed.[54]

Immediately, and perhaps coincidently, after Samak's remark, the Office of the Auditor-General (OAG) recommended criminal proceeding against Samak by sending an urgent letter to the police chief to investigate the charge of abuse of power while Samak served as Bangkok governor. The OAG asked the police to send the investigation report back within ninety days. Samak was then charged with hiring private companies to undertake waste management in 2003 by choosing bidders who had offered a higher service fee but had provided low-quality work, causing damages to the state worth 558 million baht. Samak responded publicly that he had anticipated that this kind of allegation would emerge after he agreed to lead the TRT's new shelter, the People Power Party (PPP). In other words, Samak saw it as a politically motivated charge.[55]

It is interesting to note that the return of Samak and other members of the old guard to the political limelight seemed to display a dearth of leaders among Thai politicians once the former 111 TRT executives were barred from political activity. This is one of the side effects the junta had failed to foresee when launching its political reform project. If the interim government was dubbed "old ginger", then the upcoming electoral politics in

Thailand could be described as a return of the "old skeletons".[56] Old ginger and old skeletons will definitely play a crucial role in the coming elections, and the future prospect for democracy in Thailand looks very bleak.

Meanwhile, Thaksin's lawyer said that his clients were determined to clear their names but would do so after the junta relinquishes its power. Speaking from London, Thaksin was quoted as saying: "I will defend myself against all charges when I am confident I can do so in a fair and just process. This is not possible while the military control what should be a proud democracy."[57]

Former Prime Minister Thaksin will have to face several other charges and will receive several other arrest warrants in the near future for his alleged wrongdoings. The junta hopes that all these cases, together with the dissolution of the TRT Party and the implementation of the new constitution, which will be discussed below, will once and for all put the last nail in Thaksin's political coffin.

If the first phase of the political clean-up saw the coup leaders and the interim government worried about Thaksin's return for fear it might encourage violence, then the second phase of the clean-up has been marked by a growing eagerness to persuade Thaksin to return to face trial for all of the charges against him. The coup leaders, the prime minister, the cabinet members of the interim government, and the national police chief have all repeated the same line by calling upon Thaksin to come home to fight these charges. They would guarantee his safety. The political situation has obviously changed to the benefit of the coup leaders during the second phase of the political clean-up.

Referendum and New Constitution

The 2007 draft charter passed the referendum on 19 August with 14 million votes, while 10 million voted to reject the draft, and half a million ballots were voided. There were 45 million eligible voters nation-wide. Thailand now has its eighteenth constitution. Though the results of the poll were not very impressive, the approval of the junta-supported constitution at least brought an end to the last leg of the second phase of the political clean-up. With the new constitution in place, the whole political process was now able to proceed in a clear direction.

Interpretations of the referendum voting patterns have varied. Above all else, voting patterns on the draft charter show that a sharp political division in Thai society still existed eleven months after a military coup whose primary proclaimed objectives included the healing of a national rift and restoration of national harmony through an emphasis on "national reconciliatory" policies. The votes against the draft charter came mainly from the northeast and the upper north, which were the strongholds of the former TRT. Nonetheless, it would be quite unrealistic to come to the conclusion that the 10 million negative votes were from Thaksin's supporters alone. Many people voted "no" to the draft because they did not like the military coup and did not want the military to intervene in politics. This includes the pro-democracy groups, who were against the coup from the beginning.

Meanwhile, the 14 million voters who supported the draft did not necessarily signify that they entirely supported the coup, either. Most of these voters are pragmatists and simply wanted to see political certainty and the return of normalcy to the country. By voting "yes" to the draft charter, they believed the democratic process would get back underway, leading to the end of military rule. In other words, in part, the "yes" votes on the referendum constitute a national vote for political stability and for a return to democracy, and were not a signal of approval of the coup. Given the fact that the content of the draft charter played an insignificant role in determining the outcome of the voting, it was indeed a vote for normalcy.

Furthermore, as the Democratic Party leader has argued, it is quite simplistic to say that the voting patterns in the referendum showed Thaksin's popularity to be in decline. Such a statement does not bring into consideration the atmosphere in which the referendum took place. Those who voted against the draft had to face all manner of threats and pressures from the state. Several anti-junta campaigns were blocked.[58] Many activists who campaigned against the charter were arrested.[59] Stickers attached to the rear windows of taxis in Bangkok saying "Take passengers but don't take the draft charter" had to be removed within a few days as they were ruled to be against the traffic law.[60] A team of soldiers and police confiscated anti-charter campaign materials from the house of a former TRT MP in Kamphaeng Phet and from the house of Prateep Ungsongtham-Hata, the rights activist and a former senator, in Bangkok's Klong Toei slum.[61]

Thai voters were faced with threats of all kinds of negative consequences; the junta and its functionaries made it known that if the draft charter were rejected, the people would face something worse than the present situation. No alternative version of the constitution was offered and there was no requirement for a minimum turnout of voters necessary for the referendum to be valid. In short, Thai voters were being railroaded, via the ritual of referendum, into accepting what was being offered.

Ironically, while the coup leaders had deposed an elected government on the ground that voting alone was not the only legitimate source of power, they committed the same sin by trying to galvanize votes without laying the groundwork for a fair and just referendum. The interim government set aside a budget of 576 million baht to "educate" the public about the draft charter, and the whole referendum process cost more than 1.5 billion baht. General Sonthi was reported to have instructed 400,000 members of the armed forces and the police to support the constitution.[62]

The CNS campaigned strenuously for the draft charter as its approval would be used to justify their removal of the elected government. All kinds of state functionaries close to the people were mobilized in the campaigns to support the charter: the traditional *kamnan* and village headmen, village health volunteers, teacher leaders, army regional headquarters throughout the country, and the Internal Security Operations Command (ISOC). "Mother hens" [*Vitayakorn mae kai*] were sent out to knock on people's doors and lecture them on the coup-sponsored constitution, the 19 August referendum, and the planned general election. These were Interior Ministry volunteers whose job was to usher in the new constitution and to promote democracy to their "chickens" — the community leaders. The initiative was part of the government's Democracy Development Volunteer project. This promotional style was derived from a successful commercial direct-sales technique. Prime Minister Surayud himself volunteered for the job and was made an "honourary mother hen". After the referendum, these "mother hen" volunteers would shift to campaign for a clean and fair election.[63]

Since the CNS and its installed government controlled all access to the mass media in an attempt to influence the opinion of local leaders, from the major cities to the small communities, the narrow margin in the referendum therefore came as a disappointing surprise to both the coup leaders and their supporters. Despite many unprecedented arrangements to ensure that people voted, including free transportation to the polling stations and an extra public holiday on Monday 20 August, the day after the referendum, the junta could not gain the 70 per cent approval that they had expected. Even with all the forms of control at their disposal, and despite the one-sided public information campaigns, the junta failed to achieve a convincing victory. Without the vigorous campaign against those who opposed the draft charter, the number of people turning out to vote "no" would have been far greater.

The referendum was the first crucial test of public sentiment since the September coup. It served more or less as a barometer to gauge public opinion toward both the coup and the future direction of Thai politics. The overwhelming "no" votes in the northeast provinces prompted Lieutenant-General Sujit Sitthitprapa, the Second Army Region chief who is responsible for that area, to conclude that it was a setback for the army.[64] Many provinces in the north and northeast that voted "no" to the draft charter are now under martial law.

The 19 August referendum thus represented another example of how major portions of the population were compelled to take sides. Because of this sharp divide, it is difficult to tell exactly how many votes were cast without any influence either from the junta and its government or from the anti-charter groups. Therefore, it was both amusing and astonishing to hear General Sonthi say on television that the 14 million votes for the charter were all "innocent" votes, as they were not manipulated by the junta and its installed government.

Although the contents of the draft charter played a secondary role in determining how people voted in the referendum, to discern the future prospects for Thai politics at this crossroads, it is appropriate to have some knowledge about these contents. Overall the new charter has been criticized as being undemocratic because it limits the power of politicians and gives immense power to the courts to rectify weaknesses in the suspended 1997 constitution — particularly relating to the monopoly and abuse of power by the executive branch and by the military under the name of national security.

The 2007 constitution deliberately sets out to weaken the prime minister and political parties. It is written mainly to prevent Thaksin or Thaksin-like politicians from returning to power. For example, only one-fifth of the MPs are required to submit a no-confidence motion against the prime minister, while under the abrogated 1997 constitution, two-fifths were required. Therefore, if the emphasis of the abolished 1997 constitution was on building a strong government with an eye to political stability by bypassing the system of strict checks and balances, then the aim of the new constitution is to reduce the government's and people's power by increasing the power of the judiciary. The content of the new charter reveals a deep mistrust of politicians and of the voter's ability to make informed decisions. However, the writers of the new constitution claim that it gives more power to the people than the abrogated 1997 constitution. For example, Article 291 stipulates that 50,000 eligible voters can petition to have the constitution corrected and Article 212 allows eligible voters to file cases at the Constitutional Court.

Nonetheless, critics argue that the rights and liberty of the people cannot be guaranteed when there are several other articles in the charter that tend to undermine democratic institutions and principles. For example, half of the senators in the new charter would be appointed by a special panel composed of judges and chiefs of independent organizations such as the Election Commission, the National Counter-Corruption Commission and the auditor-general.

Furthermore, there are many provisions that run counter to civil and human rights concerning the eligibility of applicants for the Senate. For instance the following persons are barred from running for Senate: parents, spouses, and children of an MP or holder of a political position; members or holders of positions in a political party (also the case under the 1997 constitution); and those who have resigned from political positions less than five years before the application date. Yet at the same time as blocking some political participants, the new constitution does not bar the coup leaders from entering politics.

The good side of the new charter is the injection of integrity and ethics into politics and the installation of a better system of checks and balances. As mentioned earlier, the new constitution is clearly drafted as a reaction to the misdeeds of the previous government, some of whose members are embroiled in real or perceived conflicts of interest, abuse of power, and interference with independent organizations. Representatives of political parties are excluded from sitting on committees that select members of independent organizations under the new constitution such as the NCCC, and the Constitutional Court. Most members of the selection committee are drawn from among judges.

Clearly, the writers of the new constitution do not trust the judgement of the people and have faith only in judges or those in the judicial branch. However, this is quite worrisome because the stated role of members of the judiciary is to be impartial as they determine the fate of other people. Involving the judiciary in politics would cost them their impartiality.

Thus, instead of using foresight to design a political system that is capable of dealing with the complex changes taking place in a globalized world environment, and to design institutionalized mechanisms to handle political conflict in a complex society, the writers simply reduced their task to curtailing the power of the executive branch. Political reform is narrowly defined as techniques of controlling the government. In this regard, the whole process of political reform from the implementation of the abrogated 1997 constitution to the 2007 new constitution has been labelled by one academic as another "wasted decade" for Thailand.[65]

MILITARY DOMINANCE LINGERS ON

At least three obvious issues have emerged out of the political situation in Thailand after the 19 September coup. First, based upon the result of the referendum on the junta-sponsored constitution, in which the number of voters opposed to the charter was incredibly large, it is certain that the junta has failed to contain the power and the popularity of former Prime Minister Thaksin. This could prove worrisome to the coup leaders and their supporters in the December 2007 election.

Second, the deep division within Thai society that the junta was supposed to heal has not healed. The sharp divide between the supporters and the opponents of the draft charter — supported by only 57.81 per cent of those who voted — should remind us of this deep divide. After almost a year of hard work and harsh measures on the part of the junta, the political divide in Thailand runs even deeper.

And finally, the main objectives of the junta, which provided the justification for the coup, remain unfulfilled. The tough measures that have been taken against Thaksin and his network, such as the dissolution of the TRT, the freezing of assets, and the weakening of politicians and elected members of government, as stipulated in the new constitution, have so far failed to eradicate Thaksin from the Thai political map, not to mention from the consciousness of the rural masses.

Therefore, there is no doubt that the armed forces will stay on in politics to accomplish their remaining proclaimed tasks, but they will stay on in a more civilized/civilianized form. Following the December 2007 election we will see more clearly the pattern of military domination in Thai politics. However, political participation by the army in the form of another military coup can never be ruled out. As one of the leaders of the September coup once said, in a script that reflects clearly the fundamental thinking of men in uniform as guardians and saviours of the nation: [A] military coup should never be ruled out. ... [A] coup will take place if there is a cause and that cause is justified. ... If the country plunges into crisis, a coup can always happen.[66]

Asked on the referendum day whether the new constitution would last if it passed the referendum, General Sonthi, the coup leader, said that the life of the constitution would depend largely on how the future administration behaves. If they are "honest and patriotic", then the constitution will last.[67] In other words, there is no guarantee from the military that the new constitution will not be shredded in the future.

General Sonthi's comment here is quite revealing regarding the future prospects for Thai democracy. Based on this comment, it is obvious that the military still thinks of itself as the guardian of democracy and the "white knight" that will come to rescue the nation whenever it deems necessary. Consequently, it would never understand, as one critic has pointed out, that the 19 August referendum was for and on the constitution, not on the CNS, the coup, or its administration for the past eleven months. Therefore, nobody has a mandate to change the rules once the people have endorsed them except the people themselves.

The dominance of the military in the future of Thai politics is guaranteed by the new charter. The controversial Article 309, which is the very last article in the new constitution, grants *de facto* amnesty not only for the junta's past deeds but also for their future actions. The article stipulates that anything compliant with the 2006 interim charter, issued shortly after the coup, should be deemed legal afterwards. Having such an article in the constitution simply undermines the entire principle of the constitution being the supreme law of the nation. Article 309 is tantamount to allowing the military to declare a "state of exception" whenever it deems necessary and appropriate.

Moreover, the less noticed Article 77 of the new charter stipulates that it is the state's duty to provide the armed forces with "modern", "necessary", and "adequate" [*phieng phor*] (not *phor phieng*, or sufficient) personnel, weapons, and technologies to protect national independence, national sovereignty, national security, the monarchy, the national interest, and the democratic form of government with the king as the head of state. Critics have argued that these three adjectives, which did not appear in the abrogated 1997 constitution, would certainly lead to an increase in the military budget in the near future.[68]

Such an expectation is not exaggerated, judging from an unprecedented increase in the military budget and spending after the September coup. With an increase in military spending comes an increase in the role of the military in society and politics. Three months after the coup, it was reported in the newspapers that the junta had used 1.5 billion baht from its "secret funds" to stage the coup in September. General Sonthi, the coup leader, did not deny the report; he simple stated that the money was needed for food for troops and other necessary expenses.[69]

In addition to the expenses incurred by the coup, the military's budget has increased tremendously. For example, in late December 2006, the Surayud Cabinet approved 556 million baht for the formation of a 14,000 strong special operations force with a mandate to control anti-junta protests. The fund allocation came from a request by the CNS. This is a rapid deployment force, which began its operations before the approval of the budget. The practice runs counter to the directives of the Prime Minister's Office, so the appropriation was approved retroactively. The money would be drawn from the government reserve fund for emergency situations. General Saprang Kalayanamitr was appointed commander of the force to crack down on anti-junta protesters.[70]

Prior to the coup, the armed forces were working with a budget of 86 billion baht. However, in the proposed budget for fiscal year 2008, they have asked for 143 billion baht. The figure rose from 115 billion baht for fiscal year 2007. Thus, in less than two years, the military has increased spending by 66 per cent, raising the question of whatever happened to the idea of a self-sufficient economy, which the junta had strongly supported. The increase in the defence budget of 33.8 per cent in 2007 and 24.3 per cent in 2008 has raised concern about the return to political dominance of the armed forces.[71]

In May 2007 it was revealed that the First Army commander, General Prayuth Chan-ocha, had been placed in charge of a secret army unit with a budget of 319.1 million baht for mobilizing mass support for the junta.[72] The sending out of millions of SMS messages to mobile phone users throughout the country to discourage the people from attending the protest rallies against the party dissolution verdict mentioned above was part of this mass-mobilization project.

It has been alleged that the violent clash between anti-coup demonstrators and the police in front of Privy Council President General Prem Tinsulanonda's residence on the night of 22 July was part of the work of this unit.[73] It was estimated that 100 demonstrators and 200 police were injured in the clash. Nine key leaders of the protesters were later arrested.[74] The protesters demanded that Prem resign from his privy councillor post because he was the mastermind behind the 19 September 2006 coup.[75] Interim Prime Minister Surayud came out to condemn the protesters as being part of a conspiracy to undermine the monarchy.[76] Such a remark only served to widen the national divide and inflame already heated feelings.

Since the coup a large police and military presence has been maintained throughout the country. Military and police set up checkpoints and intercepted and deterred groups of people heading into Bangkok and other places for fear they were attending the protest rallies against the coup. This caused great inconvenience to a large number of people throughout the country. Furthermore, the armed forces had requested 17.6 billion baht to fund counter-insurgency efforts in the far south for the next four years, starting from 2007 to 2011, and 456 million baht for a "secret budget". Sixty per cent of the military budget for southern security operations in the past had been spent on salaries and welfare benefits.[77]

The CNS also proposed a controversial security bill, which was approved by the Surayud Cabinet and forwarded to the Council of State for review before being sent to the National Legislative Assembly (NLA) for final approval. The new draft national security bill would give sweeping powers to the Internal Security Operations Command (ISOC), headed by the army commander, to handle "new forms of threats" to the country such as acts of sabotage, transnational crime, and propaganda. If approved, the bill would provide an alternative to the Executive Decree on Public Administration in Emergency Situations issued during the Thaksin government.

Critics of the security draft bill see it as a means for the military to hold onto power. The proposed security bill would in effect set up a permanent military dictatorship. Even after the election, the armed forces would have the power to set curfews or ban political gatherings at any time without bothering to declare a state of emergency. Faced with criticism from civil groups, interim Prime Minister Surayud temporarily backed off, first by offering a change in the person responsible under the bill from the director of ISOC to the prime minister, and later adding that it is not an urgent matter. Therefore, the government would not submit the draft to the NLA until it is acceptable to all parties concerned.[78]

Finally, shortly after the referendum's defeat in the northeast and the north, the junta launched a populist project worth 10 billion baht to win the hearts and minds of the people in these two regions.[79] The Center for Poverty Eradication and Rural Development under the Philosophy of Self-Sufficiency Economy has been set up under the direct supervision of ISOC. The military firmly believes that if they can eradicate poverty and improve the people's lives in the regions, people would turn to support the army's cause. During his five-year rule, Thaksin had changed the contours of Thai politics and the aspirations of the Thai rural masses in such a way that simply dispatching more troops and injecting more monies into the village can hardly win their approval. Besides, this is not the proper role and duty of a professional military under a democratic form of government.

CONCLUSION

All evidence points to an increasing role for the military in Thai society and politics. The most recent military coup, which aimed at restoring democracy, would end up containing democracy under military control.

The past seventeen coups should be a reminder that military interventions, no matter how justifiable they may at first appear to be, are never a good solution to the problems of democratic politics. The use of force to move politics to the desired goal has proved futile. History has proved that soldiers, once they get a taste of power, tend to hold onto it.

Thaksin is out but he has not yet been defeated. Indeed, Thaksin has changed Thailand more than his opponents and enemies would care to admit. The new round of power struggles will be in evidence in the coming election. If General Sonthi were granted another six-month extension as commander-in-chief of the army, as one report had it,[80] then this will show that there have been conflicts within the army regarding the issue of succession. An extension would also serve as a clear sign from the army that it intends to further contain Thaksin and his former TRT group in the coming election.[81]

Politics will only become stable when the political system can accommodate all the important social forces within it. Reconciliatory politics and military coups work against each other. Coups represent the exclusion technique of governance rather than inclusion. The junta will definitely try to isolate the former TRT groups either by forging an alliance with the former opposition parties led by the Democrats or by arranging a realignment of political groups into a new party as an alternative to both the Democrat-led and the former TRT-led parties. The strategies of fragmentation and isolation at best will push the former TRT group into the opposition camp after the general election and at worst will intensify the great political divide in Thai society.

Despite the impact on the changing contours of the Thai political map, the historic verdict of the dissolution of the TRT and other measures taken by the junta to clean up "bad" politics have left open several spaces for future debates. The end of the TRT is in no way a guarantee of the Democrats' rise to power. Neither does it mean a better future for the country and for democracy. People's high expectations of the coup and the new election will be met with frustration. With the approval of the junta-supported constitution in the referendum on 19 August, we can expect a return of the military and the big bureaucrats to the Thai political scene.

The security state and the bureaucratic polity will re-emerge on the Thai political map in the forms of coalition government, appointed senators, committee members of independent organizations, and the controversial internal security bill. Elections will not solve the problems the nation faces; they will only serve to convince the world community that Thailand has, once again, a democratic form of government. Unless Thailand is able to design a system of institutionalized conflict management such as a strong and respected parliamentary system that is capable of converting "antagonism" into "agonism", then the future prospects for democracy in Thailand are still in doubt.

Amnesty as a means to solve political conflicts, which has been effective in the past, can hardly be used to solve the current conflicts. The conflicts among the elites this time are too deep and too complex, and too many parties are involved to allow amnesty alone to bring peace, stability, and normalcy to the country. These conflicts are structural rather than individual-based and need institutionalized rather than individualized mechanisms to solve them. For example, despite vigorous campaigning on the platform of reconciliatory politics, the military basically thinks in terms of antagonism and always looks to eradicate differing views perceived as threats to national security and the monarchy, and thus as enemies to be destroyed.

Ironically, before the September coup, educated and urbanized Thais showed their contempt for elections and elected politicians that depended greatly on a patronage system focused on the rural masses and the vote-buying practices of the politicians. Now they pin their hopes on elections as a means of harmonizing Thai society. However, without a democratic culture of tolerance towards different opinions capable of transforming antagonism into agonism, as mentioned earlier, elections will only serve to intensify the existing "partition of the perceptible" in Thai society. Instead of working as a conflict-management device, elections under this circumstance will only bring more conflict and deepen the political divide in Thai society. The most important question remains how to create "social trust" in such a way that it will heal this great political divide. This is a challenge to all Thais.

NOTES

1. Justin Huggler, "Thai Students Defy Protest Ban to Demand the Return of Democracy", *The Independent*, 25 September 2006.
2. Manop Thip-osod, "Anti-coup Driver Rams Taxi into Army Tank", *Bangkok Post*, 1 October 2006.
3. Saritdet Marukatat, "Rural Folk must Hear Truth about Thaksin", *Bangkok Post*, 4 October 2006.
4. A leading proponent of this argument is Anek Laothammathas, *Thaksina-prachaniyom* [Thaksina-Populism] (Bangkok: Matichon Press, 2006).
5. Sonthi himself later said that this reluctance was simply his strategy to confuse opponents. In late 2007 after his retirement from the army, he assumed a deputy prime minister post in charge of security matters and chaired the national

committee to prevent vote-buying for the 23 December general election. Contrary to media speculation, he did not nominate to contest in the election, nor did he assume any political post after the election.

6. A discussion of the details of events leading up to the coup is provided by James Ockey, "Thailand in 2006: Retreat to Military Rule", *Asian Survey* 47, no. 1 (2007): 133–40. The coup leaders' reasons for staging the coup can be found in the Council for National Security "white paper" entitled "Facts Concerning Governance Reform in Thailand", available at <http://www. cns.go.th/>.

7. Khien Theeravit, "Thailand's 'Coup de Grace' is not Lacking in Legitimacy", *The Nation*, 18 October 2006.

8. Patrick Jory, "Roundtable: September 19th 2006 Coup in Thailand", available at <http://www.ari.nus.edu.sy/showfile.asp?eventfileid=189>, and Justin Huggler, "Royalty and Revolution: The Absolute Monarchy", *The Independent*, 25 September 2006.

9. Pitch Pongsawad, *Karn Muang Khong Phrai* [The Politics of the Subjected] (Bangkok: Open Books, 2007), p. 239. A famous singer, "Bird" Thongchai MacIntyre, composed a song to celebrate his Majesty the King's eightieth birthday and cleverly titled it, "Rup thi thuk ban thong me" (The picture every household must have), which of course means the portrait of the king. The song was first aired on 23 August 2007 and will definitely become popular.

10. The idea of conflict in contemporary Thailand as epitomized by the tussle between these two networks is described in Duncan McCargo, "Network Monarchy and Legitimacy Crises in Thailand", *The Pacific Review* 18, no. 4 (2005): 499–519. See also "A Right Royal Headache", *Far Eastern Economic Review* 165, no. 1 (10 January 2002): 8.

11. "Exclusive Interview: Kingdom 'would not have Survived without Coup'", *The Nation*, 26 October 2006.

12. Kamol Hengkietisak, "His Majesty's Wisdom Shines On", *Bangkok Post*, 10 December 2006.

13. Thitinan Pongsudhirak, "Alarming Rifts in Anti-Thaksin Coalition", *Bangkok Post*, 15 December 2006.

14. This phrase is borrowed from Jacques Ranciere, a French philosopher and political theorist, in his *Disagreement: Politics and Philosophy*, translated by Julie Rose (Minneapolis: University of Minnesota Press, 1999).

15. This kind of argument has been proposed by Thanaphol Eawsakul, *Ratpraharn sip kaw kanya: Ratpraharn pher rabob prachathipatrai un mee phramahakasat throng phen pramuk* [The September 19 Coup: The Coup for Democratic Regime under the Constitutional Monarchy] (Bangkok: Far Diew Gun, 2007).

16. Kultida Sumabuddhi, "After Months of Furious Campaigning on All Sides, Tomorrow the Country Votes", *Bangkok Post*, 18 August 2007, p. 11.

17. Chantal Mouffe, *On the Political* (London and New York: Routledge, 2005), and Chantal Mouffe, *The Democratic Paradox* (London: Verso, 2000).

18. Mouffe, *The Democratic Paradox*, p. 102.

19. Thanong Khanthong, "Pridiyathorn puts His Future on the Line", *The Nation*, 20 December 2006; "Bt 829-billion Blunder", *The Nation*, 20 December 2006; and Atiya Achakulwisut, "Old Ginger seems to be Flip-flopped", *Bangkok Post*, 22 December 2006.

20. Achara Pongvutitham and Petchanet Pratruangkrai, "Blow to Rice Exports as Company Folds", *The Nation*, 24 August 2007.

21. Percharat Pratruangkrai, "Export Growth Falls in July", *The Nation*, 22 August 2007.

22. "Household Debt at Record High", *The Nation*, 24 August 2007.

23. General Saprang, one of the three contenders for the army chief post after General Sonthi's retirement in October 2007, was later appointed permanent secretary-general of the Defence Ministry. The army chief post went to General Anupong Phaochinda, another coup leader who is General Saprang's junior. This caused great disappointment to General Saprang.

24. "Union Demands Sacking of Saprang, Entire Board", *The Nation*, 24 August 2007.

25. Komsan Tortermvasana and Wichit Chantanusornsiri, "Sitthichai: TOT at Risk of Collapse", *Bangkok Post*, 3 August 2007.

26. Saiarun Pinaduang, "Longan Growers Block Road in Protest against Plunge in Prices", *Bangkok Post*, 3 August 2007.

27. "Fruits free-for-all", *Bangkok Post*, 18 August 2007.

28. "South Gets B509m to Buy Anti-rebel Gear", *Bangkok Post*, 8 August 2007.

29. "Thong thiew thai pee 50: took koddun jakpatjai robthid" [Tourism in 2007: Pressures from all Sides]. Available at <http://www.sentangonline.com/sentangthai/index.php?option=com_content> (accessed 11 November 2007).

30. *Bangkok Post*, 30 July 2007.

31. Thitinan Ponsudhirak, "Alarming Fifts in Anti-Thaksin Coalition", *Bangkok Post*, 15 December 2006; "CNS Patting Its Back Too Soon", *Bangkok Post*, 22 December 2006; and "Leadership Needed from Reluctant PM", *The Nation*, 5 January 2007.

32. In early December 2007, General Anupong, the new army chief and one of the coup leaders, publicly responded to reporters on the status of the 19 September coup by stating that the coup did not go wrong [*phid phad*] as many surmised, it was simply distorted [*phid phien*].

33. "Coup Leaders Tighten Grip", *The Nation*, 5 January 2007.

34. Ampa Santimetanedol, "List of Uncooperative Agencies Reaches PM", *Bangkok Post*, 17 February 2007.

35. "Establishing the Rule of Law", *Bangkok Post*, 14 February 2007.

36. "CDRM could Wear out Its Welcome", *The Nation,* 25 September 2006.

37. Wassana Nanuam, "PM: Criticism of Military on Boards Unfounded", *Bangkok Post*, 11 November 2006.

38. Piyanart Srivalo, "Junta Gets Fat-cat Allowances", *The Nation*, 8 November 2006. On 6 June 2007 the Surayud Cabinet approved a 17-billion-baht budget for a new round of salary increases for two million state officials.

39. Full details of the verdict are found in 2550 *KhadeeYubphuk: Avasarn tor ror tor — por chor por phon phid* [The 2007 Dissolution Case: The End of TRT and the Acquittal of the Democrat] (Bangkok: Siam Sport Books, 2007).

40. "King Warns of Trouble", *The Nation*, 25 May 2007.

41. Wassana Nanuam, "Pardon Call Leaves Many Puzzled", *Bangkok Post*, 3 June 2007.

42. "Charnchai to Hand Himself in to Police on Monday", *Bangkok Post*, 11 August 2007.

43. Kamol Hengkietisak, "who Dares to Bribe Judges?" *Bangkok Post*, 11 August 2007.

44. Daniel Ten Kate, "Verdict Sets a Dangerous Precedent", *Bangkok Post*, 9 June 2007.

45. "Amnesty Idea Comes under Fire", *Bangkok Post*, 3 June 2007, and Wassana Nanuam, "Pardon Call Leaves Many Puzzled", *Bangkok Post*, 3 June 2007.

46. Further details on this notion of sovereignty can be found in Carl Schmitt, *Political Theology: Four Chapters on the Concept of Sovereignty*, translated by George Schwab (Chicago and London: The University of Chicago Press, 1985/2005); Giorgio Agamben, *State of Exception*, translated by Kevin Attell (Chicago and London: The University of Chicago Press, 2005); and *Homo Sacer: Sovereign Power and Bare Life*, translated by Daniel Heller-Roazen (Standord: Standord University Press, 1998).

47. "Amnesty Idea Comes under Fire", *Bangkok Post*, 3 June 2007.

48. Wassana Nanuam, "Pardon Call Leaves Many Puzzled", *Bangkok Post*, 3 June 2007.

49. It is widely speculated that leaders of the new Motherland Party [*Puea Paendin*] are these executives who have close connection with General Sonthi and the army.

50. The ASC "Yellow Cover Book", available at <http://www.bangkokbiznews.com/2007/special/yc/yellowcover.pdf>.

51. "ASC Freezes Thaksin's Assets", *Bangkok Post*, 12 June 2007.

52. The ASC "Yellow Cover Book".

53. The court later decided to put the case on hold until the defendants were available in Thailand for trial. The cases were resumed in 2008, as noted in the Introduction.

54. "Songkap thaksin mai khao nguen khai" [Extradite Thaksin not the Case], *Thai Rath Daily*, 17 August 2007.
55. Bancha Khangkhan and Jeeravan Prasomsap, "Samak 'faces Graft Charges'", *The Nation*, 21 August 2007.
56. Thanong Khantong, "A Recirculation of Elites in Thai Politics", *The Nation*, 24 August 2007.
57. Surasak Glahan and agencies, "Thaksin Hires Lawyers in the UK to Battle any Extradition Request", *Bangkok Post*, 18 August 2007. Details of subsequent developments in this case are mentioned in the Introduction.
58. "Anti-coup Protest Thwarted by Riot Cops", *Bangkok Post*, 10 August 2007.
59. Theerawat Khamthita and Kultida Samabuddhi, "Activist's Arrest Fuels Protests", *Bangkok Post*, 8 July 2007.
60. "Taxis Told to Stop Displaying Stickers Critical of Draft Charter", *Bangkok Post*, 10 August 2007.
61. *The Nation*, 28 July 2007, and *Bangkok Post*, 29 July 2007.
62. *Bangkok Post*, 31 July 2007.
63. *Bangkok Post*, 11 July 2007.
64. Wassana Nanuam, Sumeth Wannapruek and *Thai News Agency*, "Second Army Feels Beaten by the Vote", *Bangkok Post*, 21 August 2007.
65. Thitinan Pongsudhirak, "1997–2007: Another Wasted Decade", *Bangkok Post*, 29 June 2007.
66. This is a quotation from General Saprang Kalayanamitr, deputy secretary-general of the CNS and was cited in Matthew B. Arnold, "Justifiable Paranoia over 'Just Cause' Coups", *Bangkok Post*, 16 March 2007.
67. *Matichon Daily*, 20 August 2007.
68. Pravit Rojanaphruk, "Charter's Military-related Articles still Raise Questions", *The Nation*, 13 August 2007.
69. *Bangkok Post*, 20 December 2006.
70. *Bangkok Post*, 29 December 2006.
71. *Bangkok Post*, 7 July 2007.
72. "CNS Accused of Secret Army Operations", *Bangkok Post*, 6 May 2007.
73. "Protesters Clash with Police outside Prem's Residence", *The Nation*, 23 July 2007.
74. "Protester Flare as UDD Leaders are Locked up", *Bangkok Post*, 27 July 2007.
75. "Police Arrest Protest Leaders", *Bangkok Post*, 27 July 2007.
76. "Editorial: Surayud should have Known Better", *The Nation*, 26 July 2007.
77. *Bangkok Post*, 28 June 2007.
78. Pradit Ruangdit and Yuwadee Tunyasiri, "PM Softens Security Law Stance", *Bangkok Post*, 14 July 2007, and "ISOC Bill Needs Careful Study", *Bangkok Post*, 24 August 2007. This act was passed in late 2007, though according to media reports, the prime minister rather than the army head was placed in charge, and court scrutiny of official actions was allowed.

79. "Editorial: Army is on the Wrong Mission", *Bangkok Post*, 24 August 2007.

80. Wassana Nanuam, "Sonthi may see his term extend by six months", *Bangkok Post*, 1 September 2007. However, Sonthi himself denied the report. See Yuwadee Tunyasiri, "Sonthi denies plans to stay on as army chief", *Bangkok Post*, 2 September 2007.

81. As noted above, the extension was not in fact realized. Sonthi became a deputy prime minister in charge of security affairs and chaired the national committee to prevent vote-buying for the 23 December general election.

5
Deconstructing the 2007 Constitution

Vitit Muntarbhorn

Passions are inflamed currently in Thailand for reasons that are self-evident.[1] The drafting of the new constitution has been a polarized rather than consensus-based affair, brought about by the fact that Thailand's sixteenth constitution (1997) — known as the People's Constitution — was overturned by a coup in 2006. Intriguingly, the current text of the proposed new constitution has fewer articles than the sixteenth constitution had, but it is longer in wording. It deserves to be deconstructed to reveal its constituents transparently.

The current draft is the eighteenth, after the seventeenth interim constitution imposed following the 19 September 2006 coup. It reaffirms the central role of the monarchy in the constitutional process. As it now stands, the proposed constitution reads a little better than a draft revealed a few months earlier. It shies away from the idea of a totally selected (appointed) Senate by opting instead for a mixture of selected (seventy-four in number) and elected (seventy-six) members, partly to appease those who feel that a totally selected body would simply not be credible. The earlier proposal to include the possibility of setting up a National Crisis Council, which would have provided even more elbow room for the military to administer the country in times of so-called national crisis, has also been omitted from the current draft.

However, when tested against both the form and substance of the 1997 constitution, there are key challenges at hand. As it stands, the draft is evidently a reaction against the previous government, which was embroiled in perceived or real conflicts of interest, personified by the media-magnate premiership ultimately ejected by military action.

On the one hand, there are some innovations of note. First, there are many limits imposed on the executive branch of government, especially the top-notch of the executive branch. For example, a person elected as prime minister cannot stay in power for more than eight years. The premier, the spouse and under-aged children must declare their assets fully, and they are not allowed to have a hand in companies, especially those in the media and telecommunications industry. A minimum of one-fifth of parliamentarians (Lower House) can propose a no-confidence vote against the prime minister, a lower number than the two-fifths rule under the sixteenth constitution.

Second, there are more detailed provisions concerning human rights in the current draft. For instance, the rights of communities particularly in safeguarding the environment are expanded, and these communities as collectivities will be entitled to take action in courts. The tendency of the sixteenth constitution to subject various rights to the condition that they were to be enjoyed "as stipulated by law" has also been discarded to some extent. That phrasing meant that in order to exercise those rights, one had to look to other laws, for example, acts of parliament, in addition to the constitution, to enjoy those rights in practice. Thus the current draft makes such rights directly applicable in the courts without the need to have other laws.

Third, under the current draft, various independent agencies have more powers to protect people. The National Human Rights Commission will be able to take cases directly to court, in its own name and on behalf of the victims — a power lacking under the sixteenth constitution. The Ombudsperson will be able to scrutinize the conduct of parliamentarians for ethical purposes.

Fourth, the courts will have more power under the draft constitution. High-ranking judges will sit in various selection committees to vet candidates for key organs such as the Senate, and independent agencies including the Counter Corruption Commission and the Election Commission. Given the recent role of the Constitutional Tribunal in dissolving the Thai Rak Thai Party for electoral malpractices and removing the electoral rights of over one hundred of its executives, including the previous premier, for five years in May 2007, judicial power would seem to be on the rise.

Fifth, the ordinary people will be able to question politicians more easily under the new draft as well as to submit laws and seek transparency in government. A minimum of 10,000 people will be able to propose a new law, as compared with 50,000 under the sixteenth constitution. A minimum of 20,000 persons will be able to petition the Senate to dismiss the prime minister and other office-holders. Local government bodies will have to submit their plans and related budgets to the local people, as well as to report their implementation for scrutiny.

On the other hand, there are various grey areas affecting the current draft constitution, inviting deep reflection.

The Typology of Democracy

Clearly, given the circumstances giving birth to the new constitution, the march towards democracy is managed directly or indirectly by the ruling elite. The process is more along the line of "directed democracy" rather than full-fledged democracy of a participatory kind. This is manifested by the drafting process of the new constitution which has avoided the use of broad-based consensus-building techniques which the process leading to the sixteenth constitution used, such as public hearings throughout the whole country. Rather, a select group has been in charge of the current draft and they owe their appointments to the Council for National Security (CNS-composed of the armed forces) which came to power as a consequence of the coup. It should also not be forgotten that the seventeenth constitution, introduced in late 2006, enables the CNS to adopt another constitution if the draft text were rejected by the forthcoming referendum.

The Presence of the Military

An analysis of the draft text cannot be self-contained. While the drafting process has been taking place, the military have been consolidating their power over the country. This has been bolstered by a rise in the national budget allocated to the armed forces as well as replenishment of the secret funds under their control. Uniformed personnel are thus the unwritten power behind the constitutional process and are able to use various intermediaries as their interlocutors. The draft constitution also has a provision giving them blanket amnesty for the events leading to the demise of the previous civilian government.

The Judicialization Process

Interestingly, the role of judges has expanded significantly because of their role in the drafting process as well as in the contents of the text; the draft constitution has thus been "judicialized". There were a large number of judges and lawyers on the thirty-five-member drafting committee. It is likely that they helped to introduce the notion of the "rule of law" which now appears prominently for the first time in a Thai constitution. In addition to the increased powers of the judges in the various selection committees noted above, the judiciary will also be able to propose laws under the new constitution. This poses an intriguing question as to how to balance the functions of the legislature, the judiciary and the executive. From the angle of scrutiny of the assets of parliamentarians, the mandate has been shifted from the Constitutional Court to the Supreme Court (Criminal Division for Politicians). This is a consequence of the unsettling fact that the Constitutional Court under the previous administration found in favour of the media-magnate prime minister in a case where he had been charged with failure to declare his assets.

The Mindset towards Politicians

The draft text clearly shows a degree of mistrust towards politicians, especially those in the executive. In future, all parliamentarians will have to declare their assets and many controls are to be introduced over them. The constitution has a key section on conflict of interests, and measures to address them, such as scrutiny by the Counter Corruption Commission and the Supreme Court. A Code of Ethics will be evolved to test the conduct of politicians. The power of the prime minister in controlling the Cabinet ministers is to be reduced, since in future those appointed as ministers will not lose their parliamentary seats — unlike under the sixteenth constitution whereby those who became ministers automatically lost their seats, and as a result, became more beholden unto the prime minister for further benefits.

However, the rule under the previous constitution which stipulated that a candidate needed to be a member of his/her political party for at least ninety days to be eligible to run as a candidate is now modified; there is an exception in regard to dissolution of Parliament, in which case the candidate need only have been a party member for thirty days or more.

Adjustments of the Political Party System

Under the new text, large-scale parties are likely to be diluted. There is to be a smaller House of Representatives with 480 members of parliament (MPs) — 400 will be elected on a constituency basis and 80 will be elected through proportional representation. This is different from the sixteenth constitution which provided for 500 MPs, out of whom 100 would come through proportional representation. Unlike under the sixteenth constitution, there will no longer be a single candidate, first-past-the-post system. Rather there will be bloc voting in the sense that voters will be electing up to three MPs per constituency.

As for those to be chosen by means of proportional representation, smaller parties will benefit from the abolition of the old rule under the sixteenth constitution whereby each party needed to obtain at least 5 per cent of the total votes in the country (as a single constituency for the purpose of proportional representation) to be eligible to a share of the seats allocated. The country will also be divided up into eight smaller areas under the new constitution for the purpose of computing the seats for proportional representation, thus enabling smaller parties to benefit from the arrangement. The possibility of coalition governments will arise more frequently in future.

The Nature of the Mixed Senate

It should not be forgotten that under the sixteenth constitution, there was provision for only elected senators. This contributed to the country's democratization process, although the quality of senators varied and some were more subjected to political influence from the ruling party than others. The new constitution reduces that process, since out of the projected 150 senators, 74 will be selected by a selection committee with inputs from a variety of professional and other organizations. While the details of the selection procedure will be evolved under a separate Act of Parliament, the possibility of selected/appointed senators lends itself to a greater degree of instrumentalization by the powers-that-be.

Human Rights in Principle and Practice

While it can be claimed that the draft constitution is more detailed in listing a whole series of rights, ranging from those pertaining to non-discrimination to a variety of civil, political, economic, social and cultural rights, the problem in Thai society, as elsewhere, has often been lax implementation and poor quality law enforcement, rather than a lack of stipulations in the constitution and other laws. Conceptually, the current text, as with previous constitutions, also limits the section on rights to the "rights of the Thai people", thus differing from human rights in international law which pertain to all persons irrespective of nationality and other origins. In reality, the safeguards for ordinary people have tended to come from the Criminal and Civil Codes and Criminal and Civil Procedure Codes which have remained constant for many years, rather than the seemingly ever-changing nature of Thailand's constitutions.

The Attitude towards Civil Society

The current text provides for more access by civil society on some fronts in proposing laws and questioning the conduct of politicians. Interestingly, in the future public hearings will need to be conducted before international treaties with key impact on Thai society and economy (such as free trade agreements) are to be concluded, thus enabling the public to have a greater say in international agreements. Yet, there is also a degree of hesitation towards fuller participation by civil society. For example, there is very little space for civil society in the selection committees that will propose candidates to be appointed to the various independent agencies, such as the Counter Corruption Commission. The realities on the streets and in rural areas are also self-evident with a more subdued atmosphere for demonstrations and the enjoyment of freedom of expression, assembly and association through public action to question the power base.

The Accountability Issue

In addition to the various methods for scrutinizing the conduct of politicians noted above, the new constitution will also make national policies and those responsible for them more accountable. While in previous constitutions, there was a tendency to treat national policies (impliedly including National Economic and Social Development Plans) as non-binding and thus exempt from action before the courts, in future these policies are to be backed by laws, with the possibility of the public questioning them through judicial and other processes. On another front, while the right of the public to resist, by peaceful means, attempts to subvert the constitution is recognized, there remains a paradox when a group uses force to overturn a constitutionally elected government, even where the latter is seen to be corrupt. The quandary is furthered by the possibility of an amnesty granted to a group where it is tantamount to self-amnesty.

The Checks and Balances

One of the problems of the previous administration was that not only was it in total control of parliament, but also it was influential in many of the independent agencies which should have acted as checks and balances on executive power. This was seen in the pre-coup phase by the furore facing one group of election commissioners who were seen to be all too close to the executive branch and were ultimately imprisoned for breach of the electoral law. There were also parallel problems facing a group of commissioners under the Counter Corruption Commission.

To the public, under the previous administration, the independent agency which seemed to be most independent from the executive branch was the National Human Rights Commission. Yet, that commission was continually faced with an uphill struggle to get the executive branch to address human rights violations, such as extra-judicial executions in the war against drugs, abductions of human rights defenders, and harsh repression of those opposed to construction of a gas pipeline in southern Thailand, which was built without adequate public participation in an impact assessment. It is thus not surprising that the new draft constitution has adjusted the selection process concerning these independent agencies so as to pre-empt influence from the executive branch. Yet, there lingers the question whether there is to be an effective separation of powers and functions between the legislative, executive and judicial branches of government.

The Rural Mass and the Equity Issue

It is well known that part of the appeal of the previous government among the general populace was its populist policies which gave direct benefits to the rural people and those in the lower economic stratum, such as the 30 baht healthcare for all and one million baht fund for every village in the country. It knew how to exploit the long-standing loophole based on the widening gap, and the lack of equity, between the rich and the poor, the urban and the rural. Part of the opposition to the current draft text from some members of civil society suggests that while the draft text talks of more local participation in decision-making and guaranteeing various rights which will ultimately benefit the poor, not enough is said on how to share wealth more equitably. Much will thus depend on not only the new constitution but also how development policies in the country can aim for greater incentives for the poor and for resource redistribution to nurture an enabling ambiance for pro-poor growth.

The Fluctuating Political Environment

Even without a new constitution, the country is faced with an age-old problem of how to transit towards democracy and ensure that it is led by civilians rather than those in uniform. The current situation suggests that the tide has turned, to a lesser or greater extent, towards a closer coalition of the power base between uniformed personnel and the ruling elite, backed in part by those at the middle stratum of economic development. Government and governance are thus en route to become more vertical than horizontal in their outreach. A disquieting development, side by side with the new constitution, is the proposed draft National Security Act which will confer even more powers on the army chief to act as the focal point on security matters, even to the extent of overriding human rights and protecting officials from scrutiny. The draft law will exempt them from action in the Administrative Court and will constrain other courts from exercising oversight, thus contributing to impunity for official malpractices.[2]

Of critical importance also is the long-standing problem of southern Thailand, a predominantly Muslim region, whose situation has become more aggravated by daily violence. While Prime Minister Surayud's apology to the local population in regard to various excesses committed in the south is welcome, this needs to be advanced by concrete measures such as more decentralization of power and respect for the particular identity of the region. While current law enforcement has been claiming success in pursuing militants and apprehending them, there remains the longer-term aspiration of reconciliation and peace awaiting the region which a merely militaristic approach is unable to fulfil.

In sum, the challenge facing the country is to revert to democracy and to nurture a progressive process of evolving democratic solutions — even imperfect ones — rather than fast-track measures through the use of force. The choice of the country in the march towards a new constitution on 19 August will doubtlessly be influenced by a plurality of factors and social forces — based on faith, fervour, rigour, apathy, scepticism and/or resignation. Whatever the outcome of the referendum, there will be plenty of space for political versatility in the midst of all that volatility — deconstructed.

NOTES

1. This chapter was written just before the 19 August 2007 referendum approved the draft constitution discussed here. A copy of the constitution can be found at <http://www2.nesac.go.th/english/law/pdf/Thai_Constitution2007.pdf>.
2. As mentioned in the previous chapter, this act was passed by the appointed National Legislative Assembly in late 2007, though changes were made to make the prime minister rather than the army head responsible, and allow some court scrutiny of official actions.

6
Thailand's 2007 Constitution and Re-Emerging Democracy: Will Political Polarization Continue?

Suchit Bunbongkarn

The draft constitution which won a majority vote in the referendum on 19 August 2007 has made one thing certain, that is, general elections will be held at the end of the year or early next year at the latest.[1] This indicates that democracy will be brought back to Thailand. The new constitution is supposed to open a new chapter on democratic development in the country. More civil and political rights are recognized, the power and authorities of politicians and public officials will be more restricted, and the system of checks and balances will be more effective. It is hoped that political corruption and the abuse of power by political leaders will be less.

Nevertheless, a pessimistic view remains. Most urban middle-class voters believe that the new constitution cannot make political reforms a reality. Although a majority of them voted for the draft constitution, they believe it cannot prevent those who are loyal to former Prime Minister Thaksin Shinawatra from coming back to power. This is indicated by the outcome of the votes in the referendum.

RESULTS OF THE REFERENDUM

In Thailand's first ever referendum, 57.81 per cent of voters voted for the draft constitution, while 42.19 per cent voted against. What is interesting is that the votes against the draft were very high, and in the north and northeast combined a majority of voters rejected the draft. In the south, which is a strong base of the Democrat Party (a major adversary of Thaksin), a very large majority of the votes were for the draft. A majority of voters in Bangkok and in the central region also were in favour of the new constitution.

What do these outcomes tell us? Most analysts believed that the results of the vote reflected the strong influence and popularity of former Prime Minister Thaksin and his Thai Rak Thai Party in the north and the northeast. There have been quite a number of former politicians still loyal to him working at the grass-roots level to mobilize people not to accept the draft constitution and the military's political role. It worked out very well in the north and the northeast where the people continue to support Thaksin's populist policies. The anti-military campaigners also tried to convince the people that the coup on 19 September last year was unjustified and illegitimate. In sum, those who voted against the new constitution in the countryside still supported Thaksin and perhaps wanted him to come back. They were convinced that the former prime minister was the only leader who really helped the poor despite his corruption while others, who were also corrupt, never made efforts to help them.

As for those who voted in favour of the new constitution, it can be said that people in the south voted for the constitution because they rejected Thaksin and his political allies. If the new constitution were rejected, they believed, Thaksin's cliques would claim a victory and hence increase their chance of coming back to power. A number of Bangkok voters and others in urban areas shared the same view with the southerners. However, it is believed that there were many more who voted for the new constitution not because they were anti-Thaksin, but because they wanted a smooth transition to parliamentary rule.

IMPLICATIONS FOR THE GENERAL ELECTION AND BEYOND

Another question that came out after the referendum was whether the result would be an indicator for the outcome of the next general election. This cannot be predicted with certainty, but what we know is that the referendum result has raised the confidence of the former Thai Rak Thai Party's leading members. It is now certain that they will run in the election under a party called the People Power Party (PPP). Since the Thai Rak Thai Party was dissolved by the order of the Constitutional Tribunal in late May 2007 and is not allowed to be re-established for five years, its leaders did not have any choice except to join one of the small parties and take control of it. The PPP was a small party but became a major party after a number of Thai Rak Thai members joined it. It is believed that Thaksin was behind this move with the intention to make this party the largest after the next elections.

Another party which stands a very good chance to win a large number of seats in the elections is the Democrats. After the dissolution of the Thai Rak Thai, the Democrats became the largest. Known as an anti-Thaksin party, the Democrats have attracted many political aspirants and some former members of parliament. Its leader, Abhisit Vejjajiva, is tipped to be the next prime minister.

Given the possible strength of those two parties, political divisiveness among the Thai public may continue as the anti-Thaksin and pro-Thaksin sentiments will be intensified in the coming election campaigns. Definitely, there will be a number of political parties to project themselves as a third choice, or parties of reconciliation. But they have not yet come out with a policy platform of how to tackle the political polarization. More importantly, most of the politicians who have formed those parties are former Thai Rak Thai members and therefore their independence from former Prime Minister Thaksin is questionable.

In light of the political developments mentioned above, political polarization will continue and it will be difficult for the next government to resolve it. It is believed that the government after the next elections will be a coalition with perhaps the Democrat Party as its core. The government will be a weak one and instability is very likely.

Nevertheless, we cannot underestimate the ability of Thaksin and his colleagues to fight back. It is expected that despite possibly tighter control by the Election Commission, vote-buying will continue. If the PPP or other pro-Thaksin parties get a majority in the election, the country will possibly have Samak Sundaravej or General Chavalit Yongchaiyudh as prime minister.[2] Then we cannot expect any political reform at all.

FUTURE ROLE OF THE MILITARY

Now let us look at the military — will it continue to be in power, or does it want to stay out of politics? I would say that the military is no longer a strong political force. It might be able to launch a coup, but it is unable to rule. After 19 September 2006 it was not able to control the government, the National Legislative Assembly or the Constitutional Drafting Assembly. Due to the increasing political consciousness of the people, both in urban and rural areas, the military has to accept the fact that it is not able to get what it wants. There will be some retired army officers working with some politicians to set up a party but this does not mean that it will be a military party or a party that is backed by the military. Thus I am convinced that the army has no other choice than to withdraw from the political scene after the next election.

In this respect, the constitution is of course not an answer for everything. It simply lays out the rules of the game, and recognizes peoples' rights to liberty and freedom. But this constitution does place strict limits on the political role of the military. If you look at every single clause, there is none that sanctions a political role for the military. This is unlike many constitutions in the past enacted after coups, where the military was able to insert clauses that allowed it a role, such as its members being appointed as senators or as cabinet members.

Some have nonetheless questioned whether the military may be able to exert influence under this constitution. Like any other arm of the bureaucracy, it can exert some influence over the government. But that influence is not necessarily illegitimate. It can ask for an increase in the budget for defence spending, or an increase in personnel, or request that troops be sent overseas to fight in countries such as Iraq. But in the end it will be up to the elected parliament to decide whether it will endorse these requests or not.

THE TROUBLED SOUTH

One area where the situation was extremely dire under Thaksin, and has continued to be, is in the south. The situation has not improved; violence, bomb attacks, and killings of both Muslim Thais and Buddhist Thais, government officials, military and police officers as well as school teachers, remain a regular daily event. What the current government has been doing is to try and contain the violence and build trust with local people. It has been trying to isolate militant terrorists and to win the support of the local people, but it is not easy to achieve.

POLARIZATION — NOT ALL NEGATIVE

Nonetheless not all developments during the Thaksin period were negative. Thaksin's populist policies, and his party's effort to rally rural mass support for his leadership, have increased the political consciousness and the efficacy of the rural people. They know how to articulate their interests, although parochial in nature, and they will continue to vote for parties which respond effectively to their demands.

Rural voters do not care much about corruption or political ethics. It does not mean that they like corruption and do not like political ethics. But when it comes to casting a vote they make their own calculations. If you talk to taxi drivers in Bangkok, many of whom are from the northeast, they will often say they love Thaksin because of the 30 baht healthcare scheme. Drivers speak of relatives who go to hospital for neurosurgery or eye surgery, the real cost of which would be around 10,000 baht, but have had to pay only 30 baht. Such news quickly spread to the whole village, and people were grateful to Thaksin because of this. Rural people do not disregard political ethics or corruption, but weigh these against what politicians do for them — and in the past many promises were not kept. Some taxi drivers even say openly that although there are many more good people, many more honest people contesting the election, they still prefer to vote for Thaksin, because he has helped the rural poor.

In contrast, urban middle-class people are more concerned with corruption among politicians and government officials. What they want is not just a democracy but a democracy with transparency, efficiency, and quality. They believe that good governance and political ethics are needed urgently as a major part of political reform and democratic development.

This polarization can be seen as a natural development of democracy, but it should not lead to political instability and violence. A democracy must be able to reconcile conflicting political forces, and in the case of Thailand the new constitution alone cannot resolve that problem. Institutionalization of the political system and major political organizations, especially the party system, is also necessary. Thai political parties are usually weak and uninstitutionalized. The Democrat Party may stand a better chance of becoming institutionalized than others as it is the oldest party and has been able to survive several crises in the past sixty years, but it has to work harder to win the support of the rural masses in the north and northeast. The new constitution does not have much to say about political parties. The relevant articles are more or less the same as in the previous constitutions, except that if parties commit wrongdoing, like vote-buying or giving money to the people in exchange for votes, this would result in severe punishment. There is no positive attempt to foster parties, but if vote-buying could be reduced, this would be positive for developing democracy.

Thailand will have a period of political instability and a weak government for some time in the future before its political system is institutionalized. In fact, the country has experienced weak and unstable governments before and it was able to muddle through. Thus, if it is going to have this again, it should not be too much of a problem.

I was one of the members of the drafting committee for the 1997 constitution, and in retrospect it went too far in entrenching executive power. Prior to 1997, Thailand had experienced weak government and political instability for so long that it sought to design a constitution that gave more power to the executive. The country made it more difficult for the National Assembly to carry a vote of no-confidence against the government. It made the executive so strong that other so-called checking institutions, like the Constitutional Court, the National Counter Corruption Commission and so on, were powerless. The cabinet controlled parliament, to the point that parliament could not say anything at all, and acted as a rubber stamp for government decisions. The design of the present constitution is to make the government more dependent on parliament. For instance, previously you needed to have the support of 40 per cent of members to table a motion of no-confidence against the prime minister, and 20 per cent to table a motion of no-confidence against other ministers. That is why for five years Prime Minister Thaksin never faced a no-confidence debate or vote, only his ministers. The new constitution has reduced the number of members required to initiate a no-confidence motion against the prime minister and cabinet members to 20 per cent. This has wide popular support because the people want parliament to have more effective control over cabinet.

The role of the monarchy is spelt out in similar terms to earlier constitutions. Thailand is a constitutional monarchy, so the role of the monarch is like that of the queen of England; there is no substantial difference. But Thailand's political situation always fluctuates — sometimes governments are too weak and sometimes too strong. In practice this sometimes means that the monarch has to look into such matters.

Democracy has a cost but no one wants the cost to be too high. Thais do hope that their future democracy will not be too costly. Thailand's democracy will be fragile again but it will survive and another coup will not happen again.

NOTES

1. This chapter is based on an oral keynote address to the National Thai Studies Centre's August 2007 Update.
2. As noted in the Introduction, a PPP government led by Samak was indeed the immediate outcome.

7
Untying the Gordian Knot: The Difficulties in Solving Southern Violence

Chaiwat Satha-Anand

In *We Have Never Been Modern*, Bruno Latour maintains that the intellectual culture in which we live does not know how to categorize. Using different labels such as science, society and technology, there have always been attempts to "retie the Gordian knot" by criss-crossing the divide that separates exact knowledge and the exercise of power.[1] Here I am not moving along Latour's corridor using the Gordian knot as a metaphor for the beginning but rather in its conventional way of solving a difficult problem, so it is not "retying" but "untying the Gordian knot".[2]

But then anyone who is remotely familiar with this Greek legend will certainly notice the "mistake" in my title since it is generally believed that the knot cannot be untied; it needs to be cut. Alexander the Great demonstrated that. The "mistake", however, is intentional because the thesis here will be to prove that Alexander, great as he is, is indeed wrong when it comes to political policy dealing with ethnic majority/minority relations because the Gordian knot cannot be cut but untied — as in the southern Thailand case and perhaps elsewhere in the world. I will return to Alexander later.

THE NRC REPORT AND RECENT DEVELOPMENTS

Let me begin, however, with a few words about my work with the National Reconciliation Commission (NRC) headed by former Prime Minister Anand Panyarachun. The final NRC report was released on 5 June 2006, but unfortunately it came at a time when Thailand was undergoing acute political conflict at all levels. The report was a victim of that.[3] The government of Prime Minister Thaksin Shinnawatra paid little attention to it. After the 19 September coup, when General (Ret) Surayud Chulanont became prime minister, especially during the first six months, he seemed to have done some things in line with NRC suggestions, including going down to the south and offering his apology to victims of violence. He also initiated some policies which underscored the use of reconciliation and nonviolent methods,[4] though there are questions about how much progress has been made on the ground especially following the increasing use of government forces in recent months.

What did the NRC report say? Among other things, Chapter IV contains the NRC's prognosis of the situation.[5] It went something like this:

- Violence will continue;
- Civilian casualties will rise;
- Insurgents will make increasing use of explosives; and
- The economy will go down the drain.

Unfortunately all these predictions have come to pass.

Before looking at some of the data about recent developments let me first warn that it is increasingly difficult to identify what is really going on, even at the level of basic data gained from local sources about the number of people who are killed, or the number of people arrested. Look, for example, at figures given by the mass circulation *Daily News* at the end of last year. It indicated there were already 4,000 deaths, with tens of thousands wounded, after three years of violence, and that 150,000 ethnic Thais had already migrated from the region.[6] The interesting thing about these figures is that they might be really wrong.

What are the correct figures? This is a contentious matter, as all numbers in conflict situations are by and large political. Statistics also become casualties to violence. The latest report from the Issara News Centre, working from Prince of Songkhla University (Pattani campus), indicated that from January 2004 until the end of December 2007, the total number of deaths from southern violence was 2,848, a little more than half of the *Daily News* figure given at the end of 2006.[7]

Migration is even trickier. I have commissioned a researcher to look at how violence impacts upon migration. The results are fascinating, because often it is difficult to say whether people have really migrated or not. For example, a person who still stays in Pattani, or Yala, or Narathiwat, and works there as a teacher, may have already sent his/her family out of the region. Would one say that this family had already migrated? If the official demographic data is used, the person and his/her family would still stay there while in fact, most of the family have already moved.[8] But more importantly, whether this migration was due to the violence is also debatable. Demographic figures show the number of Thai Buddhists dropping even before 2004. Fertility went up, but numbers went down — the explanation is migration. And since migration occurred even before 2004, the recent violence could not have caused this but other factors, including local Buddhists' better education and therefore better economic opportunity outside the region.[9]

What has happened in recent months, from January until July 2007? There is a police report citing 1,292 incidents for this period. This included 608 deaths — 30 policemen, 53 soldiers, 6 teachers, and the rest have been civilians (including civil servants, such as those who work for the post office and the like). In addition, on 31 December 2007, five bombs blasted two hotels in Sungai Kolok, injuring some 32 people.[10] Sadly, as predicted by the NRC, civilians have borne the main brunt of this deadly conflict.

Another interesting fact is that when one looks at all the security-related cases from 2004 until now, there were 4,560 cases being investigated by the state. Of this number only 504 are classified as cases with "known culprits" [*ru tua pu kratham phit*]. In other words, the security forces know the culprits in only 11 per cent of these incidents. For the rest, they are not quite sure.

Does anyone know what insurgent leaders look like? According to Thai security forces, "we" do. The poster in Figure 7.1, with Sapae-ing Basor the centre piece, is one of several which was once publicly displayed, with offers of rewards for information leading to the capture of those featured. Sapae-ing Basor is believed to be behind a lot of violent incidents in the south, and the reward offered for his capture is 10 million baht (just under US$300,000). A reward of 2 million baht was also offered for Romlee Uttarasin. Note the last name of this person, because it happens to be the same last name as a member of the *Wadah* (unity) faction in the former ruling Thai Rak Thai Party, Areepan Uttarasin, elected in December 2007 as a member of the People Power Party. They are reportedly brothers. That is why some of the members of parliament who belong to the *Wadah* group have fallen under the suspicious eyes of the security forces.

This poster was published in Yala, July 2005. It reads:

Separatism movement — These persons have collected weapons, forces and raised money for the unrest in the southern border provinces. Their objective is separatism and they want to set up their own government. If you see these people please contact 1340, 1341 — Southern Crime Hotline. PO Box 1340 Yala 95000. Email: oc_yala@police.go.th. All information will be kept secret and we assure your safety. "We absolutely will not reveal (your identity)."

Figure 7.1
Poster with Offers of Rewards for Information leading to the Capture of those featured
(with Sapae-ing Basor in the centre)

Source: <http://2bangkok.com/posters.shtml>.

In a notice issued by the Department of Special Investigation (DSI) on 18 December 2006, the government declared it was cancelling bounties for arrest of these insurgents. The reason is really interesting. It says the cancellation is "because the government now has a policy to solve the problem by non-violent means, moving towards reconciliation in the area. Bounties on the accused do not positively affect how we could solve the problem, and in fact might pose obstacles to understandings between southern Muslims in the area and government officials".[11] Several notices were sent to the police and other officials. But what has happened on the ground has not reflected this ostensible change of policy.

Despite what has been said about the use of nonviolence, peaceful resolution of the southern conflict, and reconciliatory moves, since June 2007 the government has decided to go into villages and arrest people. Between June and early August they arrested more than 1,900, and from this figure only 300 were believed to be insurgents.[12] This is quite interesting in the context of the officials' ability to identify only 11 per cent of culprits in previous incidents. Now if only 11 per cent of those 1,900 arrested could be identified with some certainty, to what degree will such arrests adversely affect their policy?

An army spokesperson claimed that there was one way to find out whether they had done the right thing or not — if there were no demonstrations or protests against the arrests, it meant they had done the right thing. Since there had been no protests, they must have arrested the right persons. But journalists linked to the National Human Rights Commission visited the south to ask about these arrests. Villagers told them they have been too afraid to protest, because no one could guarantee their safety if they did. So these days, when people get arrested nothing happens.[13] Perhaps, this silence has been misconstrued as support for the present methods used by the government.

Another perception about the conflict emerged from a talk on this topic held at the parliament on the draft Internal Security Act on 16 July 2007. One of the panellists was the secretary-general of the Internal Security Operations Command, General Montri Sangkasap. In defending the government's plan for a revised and tightened Internal Security Act, he mentioned that there have been movements of Cambodian Muslims coming into Thailand. Some 20,000 had come into Thailand, but only about 2,000 returned to Cambodia, so 18,000 were missing. Now this would seem to be a cause for security concern, except for a small fact: most of the Cambodians who had not returned went into Malaysia to get jobs. Why Malaysia and not Thailand? According to Somchai Homla-or, another panellist who is a well-known human rights lawyer, it is because as a Cambodian, one does not need a visa to get into Malaysia; but a visa is needed for getting into Thailand. Therefore it is rational for Cambodians who would come through Thailand to go out into Malaysia to find their jobs. Unfortunately members of the Thai security agencies hastily concluded that in the grand scale of things these non-returning Cambodians might be linked to something larger like a regional network of terrorists, for example. That is one way a terrorist plot could be happily constructed.

WHY IS IT DIFFICULT TO SOLVE SOUTHERN VIOLENCE?

In a new book on the southern violence, Nidhi Eiosriwong, perhaps Thailand's most prominent historian, blamed government policies for failure to end this deadly conflict. Writing in Thai, he used the phrase: *kan jat kan thee mai phrasiphrasa khong ratbarn*, or "foolishly naïve government management". Though some might interpret this as the government's innocent way of dealing with the problem, he maintains that, it is indeed the result of an intention not to learn anything, and of using government officials who are incompetent in dealing with the south. This in turn is the result of ignorance and unwillingness to learn about Thai society as a whole, which comes out of a distorted historical education, the creation of a national culture that does not open up to cultural diversity of a culturally-diverse population, socialization that creates some kind of ethno-phobia and ethnocentrism in Thailand, and biased development that marginalizes ordinary people in the country. All this has taken place in the context of the media and education that blind people to injustice, and public administration that allows government agencies unlimited power.[14]

   Nidhi makes a powerful argument. I will return to some of these themes, but would make the argument slightly differently. In particular three causes are identified to explain the inability to solve the present southern violence.

The Insecurity Industry

What has transpired in the past three years has given rise to something that may be described as an insecurity industry.[15] By that is meant there are people from different sides who benefit from the continuation of this violence and thereby continue to produce and reproduce the industry's rhetoric and rationalization, among other things. There are advantages for all sides, except of course the victims. With continuing insecurity, obviously, increased military budgets for the south can be easily justified with almost no questions asked. There are people interested in creating Islamic funds for some of the Muslim groups in the south, while some on the Buddhist side want to support their own religious interests. Civil servants who chose to go to the south could be "fast-tracked", moved up the bureaucratic pyramid very quickly. Certainly there are some risks involved, but that is true all over the country. Moreover, anyone who is familiar with the Thai scene will wonder about the degree to which corruption might have taken place in the middle of all this violence, but again, no questions have been asked. It would be extremely unpatriotic and even dangerous to question military spending, especially in the midst of such a deadly conflict situation. All these combined create an insecurity industry built upon vested interests in this deadly conflict.

The Southern Security Discourse

Listening to different people talking about southern Thailand, one could hear several conflicting narratives. Some want to connect it with a larger plot of regional or international terrorism. So the question that they normally ask is: "How are these incidents, these groups, connected to regional groups like the *Jemaah Islamiah* (JI)?" They will try very hard to look for incidents that connect the situation in the south with regional groups like that, or even international groups such as *Al-Qaeda*.[16] A close adviser to Prime Minister Surayud who has worked on southern intelligence for many years concludes in his recent book on the subject that there is no evidence of a connection between the insurgency and regional interests.[17] From what I have heard, including from people that I have interviewed on the security side, most analysts see no concrete evidence that the situation is in any way directly related to a regional threat at this time. Of course there are analysts who still focus on this issue. I understand one is writing a book along this line of thinking, perhaps tentatively titled: "The Conspiracy of Silence".[18] This might perhaps be an indictment on how Thai officials and academics have so far been very silent about such issues.

There is another way of looking at regional factors. Instead of looking at the territorial map of the south, an alternative mapping could be conceptualized. For example, if one looks at the cultural map of Southeast Asia and situates southern Thailand in a larger Malay cultural world, then this is an area, a region, where people are already connected by their kin, by their language, by their food, by all kinds of channels. I sometimes tell my friends that as a Bangkok Muslim I have less in common with the people in Pattani than they have in common with people in northern Sumatra, let alone Malay Muslims in Kelantan or Terengganu. I was not brought up that way. My food and culture are different from theirs. So when the area is looked at from a cultural cartographic perspective, instead of the one based on nation-state, then the connectedness among peoples in this area tend to come out "naturally".

Unfortunately, the notion of the national map based on the powerful nation-state ideology is favoured by the security discourse, especially in the context of what has transpired in the south. Crossing borders back and forth become problematic. People with relatives, houses and work in two places across the Thai-Malaysian border, sometimes with dual citizenship, given and received for practical purposes tied to local interests, are considered wrong and even a threat to national security by most in the military.[19] In some countries, one can retain dual citizenship until a certain age when a choice of citizenship needs to be made. Yet in others, for example in Switzerland, more than one citizenship is accepted. If it benefits a lot of people, it is not seen as a threat. But for those who focus on, and at times are restricted by, the nation-state boundary, the distinction between citizens and non-citizens becomes a serious security problem, "flexible citizenship" notwithstanding.[20]

Self-Understanding of Thai Society?

The question of self-understanding of Thai society is annoying to say the least. It has created some kind of complex within because I believe that the story of Thai society in dealing with the others, particularly the ethnic others, has generally been successful. Laotian, Chinese, Vietnamese, even American and Persian are some examples of people who came to the land that is now Thailand at different points in history and then become part and parcel of Thai society. But Malay Muslims in the south seem to be the only group that stubbornly refuse to become like most others. When they refuse to affirm this story, it becomes, to put it mildly, a question mark on the grand narrative of Thai history of successful amalgamation. To put it harshly, some see it as an affront against this success story of Thai society as a society of tolerance, a society that can accommodate all kinds of differences, of othering, and therefore it creates all kinds of complexes within Thai society itself.

Deeper than that, maybe the Malay Muslims' stubborn refusal and the failure of this Thai state project confront Thai society with a history that it does not want to talk about, and that is the history of its own colonial past. Thailand — Siam — prides itself on being a country that has avoided — escaped if you will — the jaws of imperialism, and preserved its independence all these years. But the other side of the coin is to what degree has domestic colonization taken place in the plot of Thai history? And this I think, is something that a lot of people do not want to talk about because, like it or not, the area of southern Thailand has at a particular point in history been involuntarily annexed into Thailand. At least involuntarily by the elites, and probably involuntarily by the rest of the Malay population. Most academics, with some noted exceptions such as Thongchai Winichakul and Craig Reynolds who have begun to address this issue in different ways,[21] do not want to talk about that, because as a history of colonization within it remains a difficult issue to address.

Another research project that I commissioned was undertaken by a military officer. She began her research by posing a simple question to Malay and Thai children: when you grow up what do you want to be? [*Toh kheun yak pen arai?*] Buddhist children said they wanted to grow up to be policemen (women) or soldiers, whereas Muslim children said they wanted to become bandits so they could shoot the soldiers and police.[22] In the research seminar on southern violence held at the Sirindhorn Anthropological Centre on 18–19 August 2006, a researcher told this story to the audience: a four-year-old child went with her mother to the market. Suddenly the little girl shook the hand of her mother when she saw a soldier with guns coming, and then she asked her mother in Malay: "Will the soldier shoot me?" This is fascinating because it reflects how difficult it will be to solve the problems of southern violence in the future. Fear is prevalent in the texture of society at the moment and makes resolution of this deadly conflict very difficult. Talking to the children in some ways means listening to the shape of things to come, and if the shape of things to come is something like this, then it is extremely dangerous.

The danger is not abated when one looks at some security officers working in the field. Another researcher in the project conducted her study on criteria used by security officers in recruiting officers to work in the south. Her focus was on the extent to which criteria such as human rights were used in selecting officers for the south. I wanted to know this because I had heard that one of the criteria used in selecting police officers a couple of years ago, after the eruption of southern violence in 2004, was the number of people the officers have killed in their career. Some claimed to have killed as many as 100 criminals. As someone working in the field of violence and nonviolence, this directly points to disaster. I therefore wanted to see the degree to which they incorporated the notion of human rights, respect for the right to life among other things, as a part of the recruitment process.

There are certain units that use such criteria. The 15th Army Battalion, for example, has very detailed requirements. Though not quite human rights criteria, they come close to this on the behavioural side: officers posted to the south must be good people, free of vices such as excessive drinking and gambling. But then in the case of the para-military Rangers, the criteria are different. Rangers were increasingly relied on by the former army chief General Sonthi Boonyaratglin. Whenever there were problems he sent Rangers, arguing that as local boys and girls they would help lessen the problem. But the advertisement on the Ranger's website reads something like this: preference will be given to those with a history of being victims of violence in the south.[23] This is indeed a recipe for disaster. That is to say, if I want to be a Ranger, I will stand a better chance of being recruited if I claimed that my father was killed by the insurgents. One could imagine the scenario of people with such past histories, armed with guns dealing with "the others" they might believe had something to do with their past atrocities. This is another factor that makes solving the problems in the south much more difficult.

THE FUTURE

I would like to begin a glance towards the future by saying a few words about the constitution. The sad thing about the constitution — the draft constitution that is going on the referendum table on 19 August 2007 — is that it has done nothing to address problems in the south. Nothing whatsoever, despite its supporters claiming that it is championing rights and liberty, transparency, small government (perhaps they mean weak government), and such issues. Thailand has lost an opportunity to at least think about the possibility of political formation that will perhaps lessen the problems of the south.

The second thing which comes to mind is about the period after the 2007 election. Will an elected government respond to the problem of southern violence by the use of peaceful and conciliatory measures? This is a very challenging question. An elected government needs to listen to the rest of the country. It is not at all certain that conciliatory policies will result from this election, as elected political parties will have to respond to the needs of their electorate. Future policy, if formulated by an elected government, will depend on how some crucial questions will be answered: What is the position of southern violence in the imagination of the rest of the country? Do they like the people who live there? How do they feel about it? Do they want to go along with reconciliation moves? Or do they want more of the strong-armed tactics in dealing with the south?

UNTYING THE KNOT

So now we are back to Alexander. I said earlier that by cutting the Gordian knot Alexander was wrong. To say that he was wrong one has to go back a little bit to the myth, and this is called the myth of Gordias. Gordias is the Phrygian king, the father of Midas — the one with the Midas touch who turns everything he touches into gold. Gordias was born a poor peasant, but a divine portent promised him a kingly future when an eagle flew down while he was ploughing and settled on the yoke of his oxen, staying there all day. This portent came true during a period of civil disturbance in Phrygia, when an oracle foretold that a king, who would bring peace to the land, would arrive riding in a cart. Just as the Phrygians were discussing the oracle in assembly, Gordias arrived riding in a cart with his wife and son Midas. At once the people made him their king, naming their city Gordium in Gordias' honour. He dedicated his cart to Zeus, and then hitched the pole of the cart, coupled ingeniously to the yoke with a rope of bark. Another oracle then declared that whoever could undo the fastening would be lord of all Asia. The complicated knot defied all attempts to untie it, until Alexander the Great arrived. He solved the problem by simply cutting through the fastening with his sword. Since then cutting the Gordian knot has become proverbial for resolving a difficulty by decisive or drastic action. And that is the legend of the Gordian knot.

The question then is this, what is the difference between cutting and untying the knot? I would argue that Alexander used something that he is familiar with, and that is the sword. When you use the sword, the logic of the sword dictates that there is not much you can do with it but to use it to cut things. The puzzle of Gordian demands that one uses knowledge and thinking to work out how to untie it, because it could be tied in the first place. Tying the knot essentially indicates a pattern. If this is the case, then a pattern that once was there can again be rediscovered, and perhaps be retraced through the use of knowledge, intelligence, and power to untie the knot, not to cut it. On the other hand, when the knot is cut, the result is there is no longer a connection between the rope and the knot. I am not quite sure whether metaphorically this is something that you really want to do in dealing with southern Thailand. If that is indeed the case, then cutting of the knot, a la Alexander, is not good policy.

How then can we re-invigorate the ties that bind people together? At present, the government, the military, seems to be in favour of using a way to deal with the insurgents by reducing what they call their operational capability. The problem with this understanding of terrorism studies is that it is not only operational capability that needs to be reduced; there are at least two other factors that need to be considered — motivation and affects. How do the methods used by the military to reduce operational capability affect the motivation of others? What does it do to the relationship between people and the state, and among people themselves?

I end this chapter with a small story. One day a wife of one of my students from southern Thailand called me up and said: "My brother-in-law was arrested, can you help?" I asked what had happened. She told me that a young lad, maybe eighteen years old, had been arrested. The security forces came to the house because there were some shootings in the surrounding area. They asked for the lad's identification card, which he could not produce because he had lost it a few days earlier. When the boy could not produce the card he was taken away. The day my friend called was three days after the arrest, and she had heard nothing. The mother was almost growing ill as a result of this. The elder brother was running back and forth trying to find ways to help, but did not know what was happening.

I understand that the military has all kinds of steps, and regulations, to follow on how to deal with a situation like this. But I doubt if they are practised in the field. In *Imagined Land?* a researcher reported a case in which a policeman went to his commander asking permission to kill a Malay Muslim. When the commander asked why, the policeman said because he killed his friends — the police had no evidence, but knew the detainee had done it, and so wanted him dead. This incident, however, was stopped by the police commander who reminded his subordinate of his duty.[24] But for all such incidents stopped, I am sure there were many that went ahead. And if that is the case, then you increase the motivation of people to resort to violence, or support those who do, in the context of deadly conflict in the future. It is a story of pain in an imagined land caused by the centre that refuses to come to terms with reality. And that knotted reality, increasingly complex, is a knot where the use of knowledge and creativity is badly needed to untie it.

NOTES

1. Bruno Latour, *We Have Never Been Modern* (Cambridge: Harvard University Press, 1993), p. 3.

2. This article is a revised version of the talks I gave at Murdoch University in Perth and Australian National University in Canberra (10 and 13 August 2007) and the University of Michigan, Ann Arbor (9 November 2007). It is primarily based on nine research projects on "Violence in Southern Thailand", the first year of a three-year research I directed as Thailand Research Fund's Senior Research Scholar, and has now been published as Chaiwat Satha-Anand, ed., *Imagined Land?: Southern Violence and the State, Thailand* (Bangkok: Matichon, 2008) (in Thai). An English version has just been published in Japan. Chaiwat Satha-Anand, ed., *Imagined Land? The State and Southern Violence in Thailand* (Tokyo: Research Institute for Languages and Cultures of Asia and Africa (ILCAA), Tokyo University of Foreign Studies, 2009). I wish to thank Professor Garry Rodan and the Asia Research Centre and the Security, Terrorism and Counter-Terrorism Program at Murdoch; John Funston and the National Thai Studies Center at ANU; and Professors Linda Lim and Charles Sullivan and the Center for Southeast Asian Studies at the University of Michigan for their kind invitations and excellent arrangements in giving me the opportunities to share my thoughts and research results with distinguished colleagues.

3. See a brief, though critical, discussion of the NRC report in Duncan McCargo, ed., "Postscript: No End in Sight", in *Rethinking Thailand's Southern Violence* (Singapore: National University of Singapore Press, 2007), pp. 168–73.

4. See for example, Prime Ministerial Office Order 206/2549 (2006), signed by General Surayud himself on 30 October 2006, which aims to create a peaceful south with atmosphere conducive to participation in pursuit of reconciliation and justice with claim to adhere to the way of nonviolence in managing conflict.

5. National Reconciliation Commission, *Overcoming Violence with the Power of Reconciliation* (Bangkok: National Reconciliation Commission, 2006), pp. 39–61.

6. *Daily News*, 25 December 2006 (in Thai).

7. *Bangkok Post*, 6 January 2008.

8. Zakee Pitakkhumpol, "Migration and the Violence in the Far South", in *Imagined Land?*, edited by Chaiwat, pp. 165–78.

9. Ammar Siamwalla, "Problems from 'development' and 'underdevelopment'", in *Knowledge and Ignorance in the Three Southern Border Provinces*, edited by Kaew Witoonthian et al. (Bangkok: Social Agenda Working Group and Health Promotion Funds, 2006), p. 114 (in Thai).

10. *Bangkok Post*, 5 January 2008.

11. An official "most urgent" letter from the DSI signed by the Deputy Permanent Secretary of the Ministry of Justice to the Director of Southern Border Provinces Peacekeeping Forces, 18 December 2006.

12. *Bangkok Post*, 30 July 2007.

13. Supara Janchitfah, "Living in the Crossfire", cited in Chaiwat Satha-Anand, "Introduction: Imagined Land? The State and Southern Violence in Thailand", in *Imagined Land?*, edited by Chaiwat, p. 1.

14. Nidhi Eiosriwong, ed., "Editorial Introduction", in *Malayu Studies: Fundamental Knowledge about the Malay Muslims in the South* (Bangkok: Amarin Printing and Midnight University, 2007), pp. 8–9 (in Thai).

15. This is not quite the American "military-industrial complex" as first stated by President Eisenhower as discussed in John Kenneth Galbraith, *How to Control the Military* (New York: Signet Books, 1969); but perhaps more like T.W. Adorno's "culture industry" where rhetoric, seriousness and rationality of the industry need to be taken into critical considerations. See for example, Stephen Crook, "Introduction", in *The Stars Down to Earth and Other Essays on the Irrational in Culture*, edited by T.W. Adorno (London and New York: Routledge, 1994), pp. 14-45.

16. See a critical re-examination of "the alarmist picture" of violence in Southeast Asia in connection with the "Islamist threat", in John T. Sidel, *The Islamist Threat in Southeast Asia: A Reassessment* (Washington, D.C.: East-West Center Washington, 2007).

17. Lieutenant-General Nanthadej Meksawasdi, *Patibatkan Lab Dab Fai Tai* [Secret Operations to Douse the Southern Fires] (Bangkok: Ruamduay Chuay Kan, 2006), pp. 152–54 (in Thai).

18. See Zachary Abuza, *Conspiracy of Silence: The Insurgency in Southern Thailand and its Implications for Southeast Asia* (Washington, D.C.: United States Institute of Peace, 2008).

19. See Jiraporn Ngamlertsuporn et al., *Dual Citizenship: Implications for Thailand-Malaysia Border Security*, a draft research report under "Malaysia: Implications for Thailand" research project (Bangkok: Thailand Research Fund, April 2009) (in Thai).

20. See this concept in Aihwa Ong, *Flexible Citizenship: The Cultural Logics of Transnationality* (Durham and London: Duke University Press, 1999).

21. See Thongchai Winichakul, *Beyond Post October 14 Democracy* [Annual October 14 Public 2005] (Bangkok: October 14 Foundation, 2005) (in Thai); and Craig J. Reynolds, *Seditious Histories: Contesting Thai and Southeast Asian Pasts* (Seattle and London: University of Washington Press, 2005; Singapore: Singapore University Press, 2005).

22. Colonel Pimonpan Ukoskit, "The Internal Culture of Military Units and Its Impact on the Conflict Resolution in Thailand's Far South", in *Imagined Land?*, edited by Chaiwat, p. 98.

23. Rungrawee Chaloemsripinyorat, "The Security Forces and Human Rights Violations in Thailand's Insurgency-Wracked South", in *Imagined Land?*, edited by Chaiwat, pp. 77–78.

24. Ibid., p. 81.

8

Another Country: Reflections on the Politics of Culture and the Muslim South

Michael K. Connors

A country in Southeast Asia: armed soldiers occupy Buddhist temple compounds protected by sandbags and barbed wire to protect themselves from insurgent attacks. The same security forces use sniffer dogs to search the homes and schools of local Muslims, well knowing that this is deeply offensive. Militants, some say inspired by perverted notions of the Islamic faith, behead victims, seemingly in emulation of so-called "jihadists" elsewhere. There appears to be some mercy though — the beheadings take place after death. Young men, suspected of insurgent activity are released from custody and "disappear". The whispered talk of the town in the small tea-shops that populate the main strip is whether there will be "an attack tonight". Welcome to the Malay-speaking "border provinces" of southern Thailand: Pattani, Narathiwat and Yala, where since 2004, over 3,000 people have died in a murky conflict between Malay-Muslim insurgents, criminal networks, and security apparatuses of the Thai state. It feels, in many ways, like another country.[1]

For many outsiders, including myself, the deep south of Thailand has largely been a peripheral concern; studying Thailand has meant studying

Buddhist and nationalist Thailand. For the most part, my own work has been motivated by an interest in how nationalism and ideology bind fissiparous social formations. Integrative and almost religious in their combined power, national identity and nationalism (the weapon and the bullet) continue to confound expectations of a post-national age. Thailand seemed to be a good example of this. This interest has led me to pursuing an overly narrow interest in the "success" of Thai nationalism and its various expressions. Events in the south of Thailand, where some form of struggle for national recognition is underway, has brought home just how misplaced such an assumption regarding Thai nation-building can be. More than that, it has introduced to much of the world, including keen observers of Thailand and Thais themselves, a largely misfitting part of that nation-state (as it is currently constituted): the Muslim majority provinces of the deep south.

On my first visit to Pattani in October 2005 I pursued an interest I was then developing in Thailand's Ministry of Culture. I visited its provincial office on the fourth floor of the Sala Jangwat, the large building that brings together in one provincial location most of the offices of the Thai state. How, I wondered, would a ministry so identified with Buddhism and devotion to the monarchy work in the Muslim south? This is something I am still working on, but my basic finding is that middle-ranking provincial officials — Buddhist and Muslim — can be quite inventive in their interpretation of central dictate, becoming agents of a more sensitive and nuanced cultural policy. This has meant that provincial offices of the Ministry of Culture are now involved in the process of promoting Malay culture, rituals and the preservation of sites that give the deep provinces their distinctive character. And to indicate the complexity of cultural politics in the south, note that as officials from the Ministry of Culture belatedly promote Malay culture (kite flying, dance forms, theatre), supported by cultural networks, they face hostility from Islamic fundamentalists who outwardly reject Malay identity and who see Malay culture as a contaminating influence that preceded the coming of Islam to the region.[2]

Moreover, this seemingly pluralist promotion of Malay culture takes place under the rubric of Thai identity, leaving provincial officials of the Thai state in the deep south caught at the borders of "Thainess"; they end up rhetorically supporting a nation-state project that has little experiential reference in the locality in which they work. This is especially so when they are compatriots of an ethnic grouping (ethnically Malay Muslims) whose diverse ways of life fails to resonate with the triadic ideology of nation (Thai), religion (Buddhism) and monarchy (Buddhist and patron of all religions). With these thoughts in mind — that the south is a cauldron of competing projects, interests, identities — I would like to make some general points about events in the south framed around the question of nationalism.

First, I believe that there is a nationalism in the south, a stateless "nation" (a language and ethnic community) that is in the process of remobilization and regeneration and perhaps still defining its form. The fact of this "nation" will outlive the current insurgency, and any resolution to the current situation will be long-standing only if it comes to terms with this politically-made reality. That requires a will to undertake a critical examination of Thai-centric nationalism (even in its progressive disguise of localism) and to come to terms with a significant second national body (and perhaps others) within the borders of the Thai state. Whether that recognition comes — if it comes at all — from an internal and deliberative process of reform or is foisted through an insurrectionary act cannot be predicted.

Those familiar with Thailand know that it is a deeply nationalist country, and in part this nationalism is refracted through attachments to Buddhism and the monarchy. More recently there has been a progressive evolution of that nationalism into one that has come to valorize local difference as part of the great diversity that makes up the Thais. This has found expression in terms of cultural diversity — now the official policy of the Ministry of Culture.[3] This idea was orthodox by the 1990s and seemingly opened a space in which repressed cultures could be recognized and flourish. This shift was matched, or perhaps driven by, democratic openings in the 1980s that provided an avenue for Muslim elites to enter the political sphere. By the early 1990s it was commonly believed that militant separatist groups were in terminal decline. Signalling this sentiment, in part, was the Thaksin government's dismantling, in 2002, of the Southern Border Provinces Administrative Centre (SBPAC), the chief body that was charged with administration of the region and which incorporated local forces.[4]

The liberalization of policy can be seen in a somewhat schematic way by comparing policy thinking on the south. A 1988 publication by the SBPAC saw insurgent activity as a threat to national security and "... geo-political stability which are chiefly dependent on the integrity of Thailand's national religion, traditions, customs, language and culture, and monarchy".[5] The booklet set out national policy in the south which included the promotion of Thai language, "to use more Thai as the medium of communication", "to enhance positive attitudes toward being their [sic] 'Thainess', not members of a minor group".[6] The organization also noted the centrality of the monarchy to incorporation of the ethnic Malay (or by the preferred nomenclature, "Thai Muslims") into the national body. It notes that the king "appoints a respected Islamic religious leader as *chularajamontri*, or supreme counsellor for Islamic Affairs". And of the king's sojourns at his southern palace, it is said that "the warmth, the supreme happiness, and the charismatic effects always fill up the hearts of all Thai Muslim populace...".[7] A decade later, reflecting the shift in national culture policy, then Deputy Permanent Secretary of the Interior Ministry Phalakon Suwanrat and Director of SBPAC noted:

> In the past the attempt to solve the problems in the Southern border provinces using assimilation has proven to be completely wrong... Today we must change from thinking 'Thai people must be completely the same' or 'Unity is all being the same' to 'Thai people do not have to be the same' and 'Unity can arise in diversity'.[8]

In this spirit, *The National Security Policy for the Southern Border Provinces (1999–2003)* states as its vision for the border areas: "Every person ... will live in happiness, based on their specific religious and cultural identity, especially Thai Muslims."[9] There is evidently some concession to difference here, but it is difficult to locate acceptance of a second national body in official nationalist discourse — hence the endless debates about how to designate the Malay Muslims in the south.[10] What is apparent, and more on this below, is that "Thainess" cannot escape its origins as an ethno-ideology,[11] and while subordinate identities can flourish under it, none can stand equal to it. This surely is a part of the puzzle that continues to confound those seeking an explanation to recent events in the south.

The violence that has escalated since 2003–04 has historic precedents, erupting throughout the twentieth century. The Malay Muslim-majority provinces in southern Thailand (and parts of Songkla) were once home to the Malay sultanate of Patani. Full administrative incorporation into the Thai nation-state in the early years of the twentieth century has led to quite unremarkable economic, cultural and political grievances among Malay Muslims.[12] "Unremarkable" because they inevitably emerge given a situation marked by a predatory and largely chauvinistic state structure, and, more latterly, a pragmatic and opportunistic Muslim political class that has worked with that structure. In this context, no amount of social engineering (read token reconciliation) will eliminate the ebb and flow of separatist or militant-religious inspired politics in the south unless it moves beyond the contradictory strategy of incorporation of opportunist elites and low-level cultural recognition. The 1980s and 1990s is instructive in this regard. During that time, the SBPAC was held to have succeeded in delivering a burgeoning peace in the region, by incorporating Malay-Muslim elements into administrative structures and thus providing for some form of local elite input into governance structures, at a time when the Thai state was heavily centralized. The SBPAC also embodied a two-decades social compact in the south that recognized, integrated and legitimized various interests. Although it was claimed that separatism was quelled by the late twentieth century, one can detect many ebbs and flows through the period. Most startlingly, a read through the Thai-language magazine *Muslim News* from the 1990s reveals that its editors were publishing articles that narrate the history of Siam's encroachment and, ultimately, annexation of "Patani". This nationalist historiography was published under the nose of the SBPAC, while at an ideological level — in the identity-producing agencies of the state at the centre — it was ignored.

The sources for an enduring nationalism in the south are fertile, if currently in flux and perhaps inchoate. But one thing is certain: no can one underestimate the contribution made to nation-formation by the subjective and communal experience of what may be experienced as a form of colonialism. Yes, I am alluding here to the idea that in some ways the experience of the southern provinces is analogous to that of a colony. From this standpoint, nationalism is, in part, worked into shape by the corrosive chisel of humiliation that inheres in the colonial encounter. Take but one example: how some local Muslim civil servants feel about the majority of officials in the region who are largely non-Malay speaking Buddhist Thais from elsewhere. The Thai bureaucracy has always seen itself in a paternal relationship to the rural populations across the nation (although it now embraces the language of clients and modern management shibboleths); in the south this assumes a hyper-civilizing posture, seeing Malay Muslims as a group of people who need to be economically and culturally developed (which includes acquisition of Thai language and culture). That the Thai elite have not similarly experienced a process of colonization by a foreign-tongued conqueror perhaps make some of them incapable of empathy.

Newly arriving officials in the south are presented with primers and manuals outlining the cultural specificity of the region.[13] It is as if they have arrived at a colonial outpost readily armed with manuals providing directives on how to treat the natives. One can imagine that the people-to-civil-servant encounter has affinities to those encounters that characterized colonial trusteeship, and its underbelly of abuse, in the early to mid-twentieth century. Many Muslims are integrated into this system, and so stand in an ambivalent position.

The sketch above is undoubtedly generalized, but it does reflect things on the ground. One informant, a civil servant from Yala, reported that local Muslim officials who came into touch with central Thai bureaucrats were often subjected to the superior airs of their Thai Buddhist colleagues who were armed with the language, education, culture and authority of the centre.[14] The SBPAC put in place cultural and language orientation activities for the constantly rotated band of Thai-speaking and Buddhist bureaucrats. The same informant explained that those local officials charged with the cultural and language orientation of the newly arrived officials often sensed indifference and sometimes contempt for their efforts. The incentive to learn the local language and culture was not great for redeployed bureaucrats: for many the next posting would, hopefully, be elsewhere.

It is from such humiliations that the handmaiden of nationalism often emerges: resentment and anger. Recent events have done much to contribute to a hardening of religious-nationalist sentiment. On 28 April 2004, the proximate anniversary of a brutal crackdown on Muslim dissidents in 1948 that left hundreds dead, over 100 Muslim men, including many teenagers, armed mostly with knives, inexplicably staged attacks on checkpoints and police stations. In one case they retreated into the sacred Krue Se Mosque, where over 30 were killed. In total 107 were killed during the attacks and subsequent retreat. Some of the attackers were summarily executed. On 25 October in Narathiwat Province, security forces arrested over 1,000 protesters, and transported them to an army camp. En route, 78 people died, some by suffocation. This is the stuff from which militant nationalism is strengthened, and from which revenge flows. Military-run re-education camps that suspected insurgents or sympathizers are forced to attend are unlikely to diminish the historical memory of 2004.

The question now being asked is "when will the violence stop"? In June 2006, after a year of deliberation, Thailand's National Reconciliation Commission (NRC) released its final report on the causes and proposed solutions to the violence in the southern border provinces of Thailand.[15] Led by former Prime Minister Anand Panyarachun, the NRC used the problems in the south as a platform upon which to note the deterioration of democratic rule in Thailand under Thaksin Shinawatra (2001–06).[16]

The NRC report notes that the problems that exist in the south also obtain in other regions — poverty, abuse of power, flawed judicial processes. What distinguishes the southern border provinces, and what has thus led to the present low intensity conflict, is that these problems play out in a context marked by religious, language and cultural difference. These provide all the necessary ingredients for a further deterioration if grievances are not addressed.

And, as the NRC notes, these grievances are also mobilized by non-ideological forces who use the opportunity provided by the securitization of the conflict to continue with criminal forms of behaviour such as cross-border trade and drug trafficking. Interestingly, the NRC reports that in close to half of the so-called red-zone villages (where insurgents are held to be operative), conflict over resources is an ongoing issue, thus suggesting that economic issues continue to fuel unrest. Provincial-level statistics showing relative and improved well-being in the south need to be taken lightly and broken down to the district level, to locate pockets of desperation.

While accepting the existence of militant networks, the NRC sees the violence in the south as a consequence of militant, criminal and state-based actors interacting with resource grievances and structural factors such as forms of rule that do not respond to local needs.

Working out who is behind the violence is no easy task.[17] While various organizational names are presented to the media, such as BERSATU, BRN, RKK, PUSAKA, few accounts can be definitive, not least because the intelligence forces offer contradictory accounts. The NRC report notes the lack of consensus among state officials. For example, in the first half of 2005, the Thai police were unable to determine who was responsible for around 80 per cent of the violent incidents on record. Furthermore, the military claimed that only half of the violent incidents in the first quarter of 2004 were attributable to militants.

The key recommendation of the NRC is that an Act of Reconciliation be passed which brings into being three new organizations: the Border Provinces Area Development Council; the Peaceful Strategic Administrative Centre for Southern Border Provinces; and a permanent fund to support reconciliation work.

The proposed Border Provinces Area Development Council which is seen as a response to more radical calls for autonomy, sounds good on paper, but as an advisory body only with no official power, it fails to address local calls for more substantive reform. In not dealing with genuine political reorganization, tensions on the nature of political rule in the deep south will continue. The second body, the Strategic Administrative Centre, essentially recreates the SBPAC that the Thaksin government disbanded in 2002. It is not at all clear that re-establishment of that organization in all but name will end the crisis. SBPAC's success was not simply related to its organizational efficiency. It also embodied a two-decades social compact in the south that, as noted above, recognized, integrated and legitimized various interests. The last five years have seen those interests embroiled in conflict, violence and reconfiguration. The balance of power that held in the SBPAC cannot now be resurrected by simple administrative decree, as evidenced by the post-coup government's limited success in this regard. The NRC report also stresses the importance of working towards increased cultural understanding in the region, including the possible expansion of *shari'a law* (Islamic law). What this means practically will depend on local Muslim interpretation. The NRC also recommended making Malay a "working language" in the region. The significance of such a proposal cannot be underestimated, nor can the immediate rejection of the proposal by the Thaksin government and figures such as Privy Councillor Prem Tinsulanonda. As reported in *The Nation*, NRC member Ahmed Somboon Bualuang called on the state:

> to be more opened-minded and not feel threatened by the Malay language ... Ahmed said Malay was an integral part of the southern community and was used in their daily lives — and in their teaching of Islam. Ahmed said the fact that nearly 300 million people in Southeast Asia speak the Malay language in various dialects should prompt the state to look at the idea as an investment in human capital and in economic prospects.[18]

Thai is a minority language in border provinces, barring Satun, with a dialect of the Malay language spoken by upwards of 60–70 per cent of the population. The trend, according to the Bureau of National Statistics is towards Malay. For example, in 1990 in Pattani, Narathiwat, Yala and Satun, 70.5, 77.9, 62.4, and 2.8 per cent of people spoke Malay respectively. By 2000 the figures had drifted higher (Pattani 76.6; Narathiwat 80.4; Yala 66.1; and Satun 9.9 per cent).[19] The four provinces also experienced a several percentage point rise in the proportion of the resident Muslim population during the same period (this before the current rumours of an exodus of Thai Buddhists from the region). While it is true that many of those who report Malay as their primary language will also speak some Thai, it might be plausible to argue that there is a growing language divide in terms of usage because of two structural features: the first is the rural bias of ethnic-Malay settlement and thus distance from Thai-speaking centres, and the municipal bias of Thai Buddhist settlement. Secondly, there is the continuing presence of Malay-speaking informal schools and religious centres, and the non-presence of many Muslim school-aged youth at Thai-speaking state schools, especially in the rural areas (exacerbated by the current situation). For educational reformers in the south, language is key. A Malay-Muslim educational adviser who is involved in developing a promising bilingual curriculum told me that when he went to primary school in the 1950s, he was hit for speaking Malay.[20] Thai was the language of instruction to an uncomprehending class. The language divide is easily observable. I have attended meetings in Pattani where state officials speak Thai to a Malay-speaking audience. People leave those meetings or sit indifferently, as they cannot comprehend what is being said.[21]

Culture is lived through language. Devaluing the language spoken by the majority of the people in the southern border provinces in the name of promoting national integration has bred resentment and antagonism, entrenching a sense of alienation towards the state among some Malay Muslims in the south. The NRC language recommendation has the potential to provide a long-term solution to the anomic violence that may, in part, flow from social exclusion. If you cannot speak in your own voice, how can you be a citizen? The introduction of a new language policy would be an expansion of citizenship rights in Thailand.

The response to language from the government and figures such as Prem points to a more general point: the inability to imagine that a "nation" may warrant some form of autonomous rule. This has proved a stumbling block for the NRC too, as its report failed to raise the question of autonomy for the south. In so doing, the Bangkok liberal elite and their Muslim interlocutors were incapable of working on a political solution, thus reducing the likelihood of halting the downward spiral of fear and hopelessness that, in turn, breeds insecurity, mistrust and violence.

Indicative of just how prevalent mistrust is in the region, a respected Muslim senator we met from one of the three provinces in April 2006 told us that the government, pursuing repressive measures with abandon, had alienated even the most moderate elements in the south. Even those working with state agencies had been rounded up and taken in for questioning. Asked what solution he foresaw, he resolutely called for United Nations intervention. The call makes sense from the perspective of human security. To be a Muslim and a Malay speaker involved in community life is enough to get a person on one of the various blacklists that circulate among security forces — and if worse comes to worst that person becomes one of the "disappeared". The head of a private Islamic College in Pattani province explained that even though he sits on various government committees and has a good relationship with state officials, the military still interrogated him. "If they can't trust people like me, who can they turn to?" he asked.[22] It is precisely because of this indiscriminate suspicion that anger and mistrust grow, and the presence of a neutral peacekeeping force grows more urgent.

Police and security forces regularly carry out surveillance. An *ustad*, a religious teacher, in a so-called "red zone" of alleged insurgent activity, told us how the police regularly visit his *pondok*, an Islamic boarding school, "just to introduce themselves". He says he is neutral in the ongoing conflict and all he wants to do is provide his students with Islamic guidance. The school is surrounded by basic brick huts that the students have built themselves. He wants to give them skills that they can take to the outside world.[23] For the moment, religious teachers and students are high on the list of suspected militants.

Hundreds of citizens from the south have been charged on various counts only to be released or acquitted because of lack of evidence. Some see the arrests as pure intimidation, bereft of legal purpose. A prime example is that of Waemahadee Waeda-oh who was jailed in 2003 while awaiting trail for *Jemaah Islamiyah* (JI) membership and plotting to bomb Bangkok. In 2005 he was acquitted and then went on to win a seat in the now aborted Senate election of 2006. His victory was not an endorsement of JI politics. Waemahadee symbolized a defiant rejection, by a mobilized population, of repressive government measures, including an emergency decree which virtually suspends due legal process in the southern border provinces, and which the United Nations has judged to be in violation of human rights.[24]

Fear, of course, works both ways. Muslims who work closely with the state also fear attacks from militants — and indeed many of those killed by militants are officials or associates of local government with a Muslim background.[25] A high-level Muslim civil servant who works for the government in Pattani province told me that he never travelled at night, fearful of being targeted by militants as a collaborator.[26] Lots of people carry private guns for protection with good reason: the insurgents have proven to be callous and monstrous in their effort to carry out symbolic killings as a means of coercing non-cooperation with the state.[27]

There is also the under-reported story of mass graves. In November 2005 news surfaced of hundreds of unidentified corpses being found in unmarked graves in the southern border provinces. News on this has been surprisingly sporadic. Conflicting reports in the Thai language press suggest that there are 200 unidentified bodies in Yala and over 300 in Pattani Province.[28]

Kraisak Choonhaven, then caretaker senator, and chair of the House Committee on Foreign Affairs, speaking at a public rally in Bangkok in May 2006 against Prime Minister Thaksin Shinawatra, claimed that the graves may be linked to "missing" Muslims.[29] In Melbourne, in late July

2006, Kraisak spoke to me about unofficial death squads targeting alleged militants. He claims that "people who complain have also disappeared". Kraisak says that the corpses in the mass graves are of recent origin, and indicate "that indiscriminate suppression has become acceptable". Not everyone agrees. In March, the Bangkok-based *The Nation* reported a source saying that the bodies may well be those of Cambodian immigrants who locals described as having a "tendency to get drunk and fight",[30] a claim Kraisak described as "preposterous".

Islamic Councils in the provinces have indicated that exhumation of the deceased for the purposes of autopsy would be acceptable, but Thai forensic scientists' efforts to undertake an investigation have been frustrated by government and bureaucratic stonewalling over budget allocation and jurisdiction.[31]

The majority of the bodies seem to have been deposited in the graves by a local burial foundation, with little regard for registration. Kraisak told me that in 2004 security forces had a "semi-open policy" of notifying the relatives of those it killed. This led to hatred and hostility among those relatives who came to collect the bodies. Now, death squads are simply leaving the body to be collected by foundations: "They [the killers] would prefer the families to have doubts about where they [the missing relatives] have gone to. ..." While some of the bodies may well be a legacy from the ruthless war on drugs of 2003, there is a widespread belief that some of the deceased are "the disappeared".[32]

Which brings us back to the question of cultural politics and the status of this "other country". When life is so cheap (both ways), why should anyone imagine cultural policy will make any difference? Indeed, a cultural policy that envisages diversity as a source of unity — as proclaimed national policy — is at odds with the very real political mobilization of nationalist sentiment by security and political forces and the mobilization of nationalist and religious myths by insurgents.

In a country where the nationalist establishment (the monarchy, palace patronized foundations, state agencies, etc.) are intent on inculcation of Thainess, and where the population would seem to have largely embraced many of its elements, especially the "monarchy" as the soul of Thainess, the Malay Muslims may well constitute an identity dilemma for the normative Thai. Consider a hypothetical Thai person: having been taught what Thainess is, and having internalized such notions as part of a personal identity, how does such a person confront a Thai citizen who speaks a different language, worships *Allah*, and who does not fully participate in rituals associated with elevating the embodiment of Thainess — the king?

If they are not Thai, are they Malay? Are they trouble-makers? While means of cooperation and co-existence, and indeed shared life, have been found at the local level among mixed Buddhist Thai and Muslim communities (as enduring periods of peace testify), the centralized highly ideological state currently provides no such means for co-existence as equals at the national level. Indeed the mechanisms of the state, and the actions of insurgents, are driving a wedge between communities — the stuff of communal resentment and ultimately an endless cycle of violence. This takes shape in stories that are passed from person to person — for example, stories that Buddhist shopkeepers must employ Muslims to work in shopfronts otherwise no Muslim customers will enter; or stories of Thai civil servants humiliating Malay Muslim men by speaking down to them, so that Muslim women take on tasks involving contact with the state. Other stories point to the possibility, in a distorted way, of shared fate and identity — the story of a Buddhist vocational teacher who is repeatedly warned by several of her Muslim students to avoid certain areas "tonight or tomorrow night" because an "incident" is planned.[33]

It is unclear what lies ahead. Should the current flow of violence ebb and the insurgency move to a latent phase, either as a result of a transitory political or military solution, it will be tempting for many strategic actors to put aside the difficult task of recognizing that another nation of language and culture exists in the south. In so doing, they will be preparing the ground for a future insurgency or instability of some kind. Better to make the recognition of another nation (in whatever political form) the starting point of any process of peace-building. Yet, as Thailand-based scholar Patrick Jory has observed "within official discourses of Thainess while there is a place for Muslims, it appears there is no place for Malays."[34] Indeed, if one returns to documents prepared by the SBPAC under the auspices of the Interior Ministry, one finds an explicit prohibition of recognizing the Malay Muslims as Malay:

> Civil servants and officials of the state in the border provinces should avoid the following behaviour: the use of words that create dissatisfaction or which create division between people who hold different religions. For example, calling Muslims "Khaek" or using words that make Thai Muslims understand that they are Malay, such as saying "orang maleyu".[35]

The question remains of whether official Thai nationalism and its custodians can entertain some kind of autonomy or national federation in the long term. That starts with the Malay question in its national sense.

NOTES

1. This is an edited and expanded version of a talk given at the Thailand Update in September 2006. I owe many thanks to Duncan McCargo who introduced me to the "border provinces" by persuading me to overcome my initial reluctance to visit Pattani during his year-long stay in the province (2005–06). The observations made in this article benefitted greatly from discussions with him. I have made a number of subsequent trips and I have been the beneficiary of much kindness from many people. Some of the fieldwork and research contained in this text was made possible by the provision of an Australian Research Discovery Grant (DP0664126), and by supportive colleagues at La Trobe University. For reasons of anonymity some persons and place names have been changed.

2. Author's field notes, October 2005, and January 2006.

3. See discussion in Michael Connors, "Ministering Culture", *Critical Asian Studies* 37, no. 4 (2005): 532–35.

4. For an overview, see Duncan McCargo, ed., *Rethinking Thailand's Southern Violence* (Singapore: Singapore University Press, 2007), pp. 35–68.

5. Southern Border Provinces Administrative Centre, *Thai Muslims in Southern Border Provinces* (Yala: SBPAC, 1988), p. 10.

6. Ibid., p. 11.

7. Ibid., p. 20.

8. Southern Border Provinces Administrative Centre, *Ekkhasan prakob kanprathumnithet jangwat chai daen pak tai pi 2542* [A Primer on the Southern Border Provinces, 1999] (Yala: SBPAC, 1999), p. ii.

9. Office of the National Security Council, *Naiyobai kwammankhong haeng chat kieo kap jangwat chai daen pak tai* (2542–2546) [The National Security Policy for the Southern Border Provinces (1999–2003)], 1999. Mimeograph, p. 4.

10. Patrick Jory, "From Patani Maleyu to Thai Muslim", *ISIM Review* 18 (2006): 40–43.

11. Kasian Tejapira, "Globalizers vs Communitarians: Post-May 1992 Debates among Thai Public Intellectuals", paper presented at "Direction and Priorities of Research on Southeast Asia" at the Annual Meeting of the U.S. Associations for Asian Studies in Honolulu, 11–14 April 1996.

12. For background, see M. Gilquin, *The Muslims of Thailand* (Silkworm: Chiang Mai, 2005).

13. See SPBAC 1999; Interior Ministry, *Khu Mue kanpatibatrachakan nai jangwat chai daen pak tai* [Civil Service Manual for the Southern Border Provinces] (Bangkok: Interior Ministry, 2002).

14. Author's field notes, April 2006.

15. National Reconciliation Commission (NRC), *Overcoming Violence Through the Power of Reconciliation* (Bangkok: NRC, 2006).

16. The section detailing the NRC report is based on Michael Connors, "Addressing the Southern Conflagration", *Bangkok Post*, 13 June 2006.

17. See Marc Askew, *Conspiracy, Politics, and a Disorderly Border: The Struggle to Comprehend Insurgency in Thailand's Deep South* (Washington, D.C.: East-West Center; Singapore: Institute of Southeast Asian Studies, 2007); Michael K. Connors, "War on Error and the Southern Fire: How Terrorism Experts Get it Wrong", *Critical Asian Studies* 38, no. 1 (2006): 151–75; Duncan McCargo, ed., *Rethinking Thailand's Southern Violence* (Singapore: Singapore University Press, 2007).
18. *The Nation*, 20 June 2006.
19. Figures calculated from provincial census reports from 1990 and 2000 by the author.
20. Author's field notes, January 2006.
21. Author's field notes, October 2005.
22. Ibid.
23. Ibid.
24. *Matichon*, 20 July 2006. *Yu en chee pho. ro. ko. lamaet sithi 'human right'* [UN says the Emergency Degree Violates Human Rights], Matichon (online).
25. See Srisompob Jitpiromsri and Panyasak Sobhonvasu, "Unpacking Thailand's Southern Conflict: The Poverty of Structural Explanations", *Critical Asian Studies* 38, no. 1 (2006): 95–117.
26. Author's field notes, August 2006.
27. See Human Rights Watch, *No One Is Safe. Insurgent Attacks on Civilians in Thailand's Southern Border Provinces*, 2007. Available at <http://hrw.org/reports/2007/thailand0807/>.
28. *Prachathai*, "Mo Phonthip daen na phisut 300 sop rai yat yeu fai tai" [Dr Phonthip Makes Progress on the 300 Unidentified Victims of the Southern Fire], 24 November 2005.
29. *Prachathai*, "Kraisak phoei phop lumsop niranaam … 3 jangwat tai" [Kraisak Exposes Unmarked Graves in the Three Southern Provinces], 28 May 2006.
30. *The Nation*, 24 March 2006.
31. *Phujatkan, Ko. Ko. Isalam* [Islamic Committee], 30 May 2006. I was also informed in early January 2008 by a former member of the National Human Rights Commission that the graves remain unexamined because of security concerns.
32. *Prachathai*, "Kammakaansithi.-Mor Phonthip buk susaan pattani Prachathai" [Human Rights Committee-Dr Phonthip heads to Pattani Graveyard], 4 June 2006.
33. Author's field notes October 2005 and January 2006.
34. Patrick Jory, op. cit., p. 43.
35. The term *khaek* (meaning guest, also refers to people from India, Malaysia, Indonesia, Pakistan, etc.) in Thailand can sometimes carry derogatory meaning when used against people from the south. *"Orang Maleyu"* may be translated as Malay person.

⑨
Governance in the South: Is Decentralization an Option?

John Funston

At the beginning of September 2006, army chief General Sonthi Boonyaratglin called for a change of policy on the south, to allow negotiations with insurgent leaders and give him freedom to act as he saw fit without political interference.[1] These remarks contradicted the government's public refusal to negotiate, and marked a very open falling out with Prime Minister Thaksin Shinawatra. Only two months earlier, Thaksin had declared he was handing General Sonthi absolute decision-making power in the south, saying that as a Muslim (albeit from Bangkok rather than the south) he would understand the situation. On 16 September five people were killed and sixty wounded when suspected insurgents exploded six bombs in the southern business centre of Hat Yai. It was the most destructive attack on this city hitherto, and the first time in the conflict that a Westerner (a Canadian) was among the fatalities. Several journalists saw Sonthi's dissent on southern policy, and apparent escalation of this conflict, as closely linked to the 19 September coup.[2]

Nonetheless, discussion of the south did not appear prominently in official justifications of the coup. Initially the focus was on four issues — severe rifts and disunity among the Thai people (more a reference to the mass public rallies in the streets of Bangkok than problems in the south); signs of rampant corruption, malfeasance and nepotism; interference in independent institutions; and actions verging on *lèse-majesté*. Nor did coup leaders have the south in mind when they later added problems of social injustice, and the existence of a situation that if left unattended could adversely affect security and the economy — this was a claim that violent clashes were about to break out in Bangkok between supporters of Prime Minister Thaksin and the opposition. Coup leader General Sonthi made no direct references to the south, other than on 20 September when he said there would be no change to strategies there.[3]

Still, in a broad sense problems in the south did undoubtedly contribute to the pre-coup opposition to Thaksin. Although Thaksin's heavy-handed policies were popular among a majority, they met with growing opposition from human rights advocates and others in Bangkok's middle class. Their concerns also extended to Thaksin's inability to contain the conflict. September's differences between Thaksin and Sonthi, and the violence in Hat Yai, would have reinforced this consensus against Thaksin. The *Bangkok Post* also reported a source close to General Sonthi as confirming that "finding an efficient way to tackle the southern unrest was one of the reasons behind the coup since the Thaksin government had repeatedly hampered peaceful solutions to the prolonged southern violence."[4] And, as Gothom Arya notes in this volume, an early announcement of the military coup group established a twenty-six-member Advisory Group on Reconciliation and Social Justice, which included no less than seven who were members of the former National Reconciliation Commission (NRC) established in March 2005 to advise the government on alternative ways to resolve the southern violence.

September's problems also highlighted the intractable nature of southern violence. The conflict is undoubtedly multifaceted, and an array of prescriptions have been advanced ranging from Thaksin's security first approach, to others that give priority to matters of justice, or economic assistance. All are undoubtedly important, but yet another approach has focused on decentralization. One advocate has been the southern Thai academic, Wan Kadir Che Man, author of the seminal *Muslim Separatism: The Moros of Southern Philippines and the Malays of Southern Thailand*.[5] Based mainly in Malaysia, in the early 1990s Wan Kadir joined the resistance through Bersatu, an umbrella group bringing most of the separatist groups together. After maintaining a low profile for many years, in May 2004 he attended a public seminar in Kuala Lumpur declaring he no longer wanted independence for the south, but would accept greater autonomy. In June 2005 he called on the Thai government to "truly and effectively implement articles 282 to 290 of the 1997 Thai constitution, which makes allowances for local government and limited self-control".[6]

The NRC also emphasized the importance of decentralization in its report, submitted June 2006. Rather than look to constitutional proposals for local government, this report sought to build on what amounted to a *de facto* form of decentralization developed over many years — though reduced under Thaksin — in the culturally distinct Malay-majority provinces.[7]

Before looking at these two decentralization proposals, the particular circumstances of the south need to be placed in context.[8]

SOUTHERN DIFFERENCES

At the beginning of the twenty-first century, the integration of Thailand's Muslim minority in the south appeared to be a success story. After a troubled period in the 1960s and 1970s, armed insurgency quietened in the next two decades. Malay Muslims achieved high office in the central government — such as Wan Muhamad Nor Matha, who held several full ministerial portfolios and the post of parliamentary speaker between 1995 and 2005; and Surin Pitsuwan, deputy foreign minister in the early 1990s and foreign minister from 1997 to 2001. Compared to other countries, Thailand's integration of its Muslim minority appeared exemplary.

Violence resumed on Christmas Eve 2001 with coordinated attacks on police posts in Pattani, Yala and Narathiwat, killing five police and one defence volunteer. In the next two years, around fifty were killed in this tri-border area, though most were members of the police force in what was largely an intra-security agencies dispute. Conflict escalated after a raid on a weapons armoury on 4 January 2004, during which 413 weapons were seized, and four soldiers killed. In the next five years more than 3,000 lives were lost in a tragic and often brutal conflict.

Thailand's three southern provinces, and four districts in Songkla, are very different from the rest of Thailand. Around 80 per cent of the population in these areas are Malay Muslim, in a state where over 90 per cent of the population are Buddhist. The area, known as Patani from around the fifteenth century, became a trading power, one of the leading centres of Islam in Southeast Asia, and a major player in the politics of the Malayan peninsula. Even after it was incorporated in Thailand in 1902, the region retained a separate cultural identity, particularly through continuing use of Malay as the primary language and institutions such as traditional Islamic schools known as *pondok*. Muslims in this region thus differ from other more assimilated Muslims throughout Thailand, and even those in the neighbouring province of Satun, which also has a Malay majority. Satun was previously linked to Kedah and not Patani, and its more integrated, Thai-speaking population has never been the centre of violent resistance to Bangkok.

Unlike any other area in Thailand, there have been a number of practical arrangements in the deep south which are unique in Thailand, and constitute a *de facto* form of decentralization. These include special security-administrative structures and special administrative and educational arrangements for southern Muslims.

Special administrative and security arrangements have existed for many years, but gained greater coherence with the establishment of the Civilian-Police-Military Task Force 43 on 6 November 1980 and the Southern Border Provinces Administrative Centre (SBPAC) on 5 April 1981. The writ of both organizations extended to five southern provinces (also including Satun and Songkhla). Task Force 43, under the command of the Fourth Army, coordinated security activities in the region. The SBPAC came largely under the interior ministry, and addressed a wide range of responsibilities that included issues related to culture, the local economy and administrative practice. It established mechanisms for consulting Malay Muslims, listened to their concerns, and acted both to convey these to Bangkok and national policies to the region. The two organizations were closed down by Thaksin in May 2002, but a military-dominated replacement, the Southern Border Provinces Peace-building Command (SBPPC), was established in March 2004. This was reorganized several times but remains in existence, even after the post-coup government reinstated Task Force 43 and the SBPAC.

Since the deep south was brought under direct Bangkok administrative rule in 1902, special arrangements have existed for its Muslim population. Except for a brief period in the early 1940s, Islamic courts have existed alongside (though subordinate to) secular courts in the four southern provinces. *Pondok* schools — teaching in Malay or Arabic — are also largely confined to the deep south. These were for many years tolerated alongside national schools. In the 1960s the government of Prime Minister Sarit sought to replace them with state-assisted "Islamic private schools" which taught in Thai and often included secular subjects. These are now the main form of education in the region, though in 2004 the government registered remaining *pondok* schools (around 300, catering to 15,000 pupils) in an exercise that has conferred some legitimacy on them.

In addition, the preponderance of Muslims in the south has meant that the state-recognized Islamic bureaucracy is also of particular relevance for the southern region. This includes a top official known as the *chularajamontri*, assisted by an elected National Islamic Council at the top, elected organizations at the provincial level (Provincial Councils for Islamic Affairs) and committees for all mosques. These organizations are integrated into the Thai bureaucracy under the ministries of interior and culture. The provincial councils in particular enjoy high prestige, but that has not been true of national institutions, in particular that of the *chularajamontri*. There never has been a *chularajamontri* from the south as the voting system provides all provinces with an Islamic Council (currently thirty-six) equal voting rights.

WAN KADIR'S PROPOSAL — DECENTRALIZATION UNDER THE 1997 CONSTITUTION

As noted above, Wan Kadir urged greater autonomy based on articles 282–290 (Chapter 9) of the 1997 constitution.[9] The constitution gave strong emphasis to representation of local interests and decentralization, in several different provisions. First, it created single-member constituencies in the House of Representatives, and the first-ever elected Senate (based on provinces). Second, in several provisions it emphasized the importance of civil society and local initiatives. Thirdly, it mandated the establishment of elected local assemblies. Section 78 stipulated that "the State shall decentralise powers to localities for the purpose of independence and self-determination of local affairs ... as well as develop into a large-sized local government organisation a province ready for such purpose". Chapter 9 referred to by Wan Kadir required the government to clarify the relationship between central and local authorities with "particular regard to the promotion of decentralization". Legislation should set out how this would be achieved, and ensure a review every five years. Local government organizations had to have an elected assembly and an elected administrative organization (either directly elected, or by the assembly) — with elections held every four years. Assemblies were empowered to pass local ordinances, and the public could petition them to pass such ordinances if half of the eligible voters expressed support. Assemblies were specifically empowered to "provide education and professional training in accordance with the suitability to and the need of that locality. ... [having] ... regard to the conservation of local arts, custom, knowledge and good culture", and to promote and maintain "the quality of the environment". (Similar proposals to Chapter 9 have been incorporated as Chapter 14 in the 2007 constitution.)

Building on these provisions, and supported by several new acts in 1999, current arrangements are as set out below:

Figure 9.1
Local Organizations

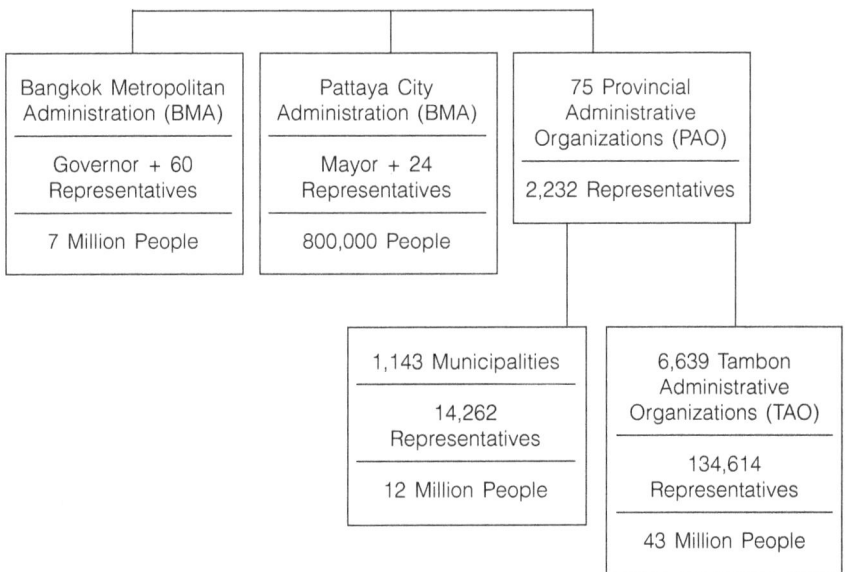

Bangkok Metropolitan Administration (BMA)	Pattaya City Administration (BMA)	75 Provincial Administrative Organizations (PAO)
Governor + 60 Representatives	Mayor + 24 Representatives	2,232 Representatives
7 Million People	800,000 People	

1,143 Municipalities	6,639 Tambon Administrative Organizations (TAO)
14,262 Representatives	134,614 Representatives
12 Million People	43 Million People

Source: Promotion of Local Administration Foundation, *Summary of Important Matters Relating to Local Government Administrators*, Bangkok, 2004, p. 5 (in Thai).

Under legislation passed in 1999, 35 per cent of the national budget should have been passed to these local bodies by 2006. This target was not reached, but a figure of around 20 per cent was.

As far as I am aware, the Thai government never responded to Wan Kadir's suggestion to strengthen local administration. Even his offer to help mediate a resolution to the conflict was passed over following resolute opposition from then Deputy Prime Minister Chavalit Yongchaiyut.

NATIONAL RECONCILIATION COMMISSION
RECOMMENDATIONS

In February 2005 Prime Minister Thaksin announced the appointment of an independent NRC, chaired by respected former Prime Minister Anand Panyarachun. Anand then selected members, and a forty-eight-member body (later increased by two) came into being on 28 March. NRC members were tasked with pooling "their mental and physical energies to find a long-term solution to the problem, in order to bring about true reconciliation, peace and justice".[10] Besides Anand and his vice-chairman, respected civil society activist Dr Prawet Wasi, the NRC comprised 17 members from the southern border provinces, 12 from civil society outside the area, 7 from politics (government, opposition and the Senate) and 12 civil servants. While less than one-third were Muslim, it did include high profile southern leaders including the heads of the Islamic Councils for Pattani, Narathiwat and Yala, the rector of the Yala Islamic University Professor Ismail Lutfi Japakiya, and respected Bangkok academics Dr Chaiwat Satha-Anand and Professor Ammar Siamwalla.

The NRC report issued in June 2006 made recommendations at three levels: "individual" or "group" (referring particularly to the insurgents), "structural" and "cultural".[11] Its main focus is on the peaceful resolution of conflicts and implementing justice, sometimes, though not always, related to decentralization. Recommendations to address problems at the first level include entering into dialogue with insurgents — in effect, recognizing a form of local power. To address underlying structural causes, the report recommends local control over natural resources, upgrading and strengthening Islamic law and Islamic education, and amending the 1997 Act on the Administration of Islamic Religious Organizations to give greater influence to the southern provinces. To address "cultural" problems, the NRC controversially urged recognition of Malay as a "working language".

To help tie all these proposals together the NRC proposed a new act — an *Act on Peaceful Reconciliation in the Southern Border Provinces* (Calming the South Act). This would establish two key institutions, the most important being the Southern Border Provinces Peace Strategy Administration Centre (SBPPSAC), with powers very similar to those of the former SBPAC. Unlike the SBPAC, however, the new body's importance would be enhanced by establishing it under a parliamentary act, rather than an order of the Prime Minister. This would be supported by a Council for the Development of the Southern Border Provinces Area, an advisory body "selected and appointed from religious leaders, local scholars, highly qualified persons and an appropriate proportion of representatives from professions".[12] The council would advise the SBPPSAC, Parliament and Cabinet on all aspects of policy in the southern provinces. This is seen as consonant with Section 76 of the 1997 constitution, which endorses the support of civil society in national affairs.

The report was issued at a time when the government was preoccupied with the prolonged crisis that occupied most of 2006. Government leaders made it clear that they were not enthusiastic, and the two government ministers who were NRC members (Deputy Prime Minister and Minister for Interior Police General (ret) Chitchai Vanastidya and Deputy Prime Minister Chaturon Chaisang) did not come to its defence. When Privy Councillor Prem Tinsulanonda criticized it for proposing to make Malay an "official" language — a misrepresentation of the proposal for a working language — government leaders were quick to reject it on similar grounds.

The post-19 September coup leaders have been more forthcoming in supporting NRC proposals. The government adopted some policy changes that are similar to NRC recommendations, including reinstating Task Force 43 and the SBPAC. However they have not systematically set out to implement the report.

COULD DECENTRALIZATION WORK?

Could either of these decentralization proposals help alleviate tensions in the south? On paper, local organizations would appear already to be powerful entities. In practice this has not happened. There are several reasons for this, but among the most important have been the influence of local elites (expressed particularly through vote-buying) and reluctance on the part of central authorities to relinquish financial controls.[13] Decentralization was never a priority for the Thaksin administration — indeed Thaksin's policy of creating CEO provincial governors directly responsible to the prime minister increased central control. Nonetheless there have been some cases where local authorities have effectively defended local interests, and if Bangkok were prepared to offer support much more could be done.

What about NRC proposals to build on forms of *de facto* decentralization that have been developed over many years? In retrospect most analysts agree that attempts by the Thaksin administration to centralize control over the south — particularly its dissolution of the SBPAC — were a major cause of subsequent unrest.[14] Another important factor was Thaksin's heavy-handed security policies, but this in turn might have been at least partly contained if southern interests were able to make themselves heard through institutions such as the SBPAC. It is indeed probable therefore that establishment of a body similar to the SBPAC, and the related advisory council to coordinate southern Malay/Muslim views, should prove beneficial. The subsequent re-establishment of the SBPAC late in 2006 shows that this alone is not a panacea — the level of violence has continued to remain high. However, the new SBPAC remains subordinate to military authorities, and is still in its infancy, awaiting passage of enabling parliamentary legislation. It may be, also, that the conflict has now reached a level of intensity that precludes any quick turning back of the clock. In the long run it should prove helpful, particularly if other NRC recommendations on pursuing a peaceful settlement of the conflict are heeded.

On cultural matters, NRC proposals for reform of Islamic education and administration would certainly be welcomed by southern Muslims. These recommendations have not yet attracted government attention.

Neither Wan Kadir nor the NRC specifically address the possibility of bringing three or more of the southern provinces together as an administrative unit. A survey of 1,200 southerners commissioned by the NRC did find strong support for this — 41.8 per cent said they would like a special administrative body, while a further 41.4 per cent said they did not want a new body but saw the need to develop a form of local administration better suited to local needs. Media reports said that the issue was not, however, included in the main report of the NRC, due to fears that conservative officials would misinterpret this as support for southern independence.[15]

A form of regional administration has, however, been contemplated by government officials in the past. The first policy statement of the Thaksin government suggested that a number of provinces might group together to coordinate their efforts and form special areas.[16] And in June 2004 Deputy Prime Minister Chavalit proposed the creation of *Maha Nakhon Pattani* [Pattani Metropolis], also encompassing Yala and Narathiwat. Chavalit envisaged

> progressive steps with the Pattani provincial administrative organisation starting out as a special governing entity similar to that of Pattaya City. The three provinces would ultimately be upgraded to take the form of Bangkok Metropolitan Administration when Pattani Metropolis would be able to oversee its own administration, collect its own taxes, and elect its own governor.[17]

Prime Minister Thaksin expressed reservations but did not rule it out, and Chavalit reiterated his proposal a little over a year later.[18]

A separate Pattani (or Patani) Metropolis would undoubtedly be welcomed by many southern Malays, and would seem desirable in the long term. However it is not difficult to understand why many Thais, educated to place the highest priority on the country's indivisibility, might worry that this would be a first step towards southern independence — as NRC caution on this matter reflects. However serious efforts to implement proposals by Wan Kadir and the NRC would provide the south with a degree of control over its own affairs, without threatening national unity, and should be an acceptable starting point for all.

NOTES

1. "Sonthi Slams Meddling", *Bangkok Post*, 2 September 2006.
2. See for instance three articles in *The Australian*, 21 September 2006 — Greg Sheridan, "A Coup for the Better"; Andrew Drummond and Sian Powell, "Thailand's Bloodless Coup Ousts Thaksin"; and the AFP report, "Muslim Veteran Clashed with PM". See also Michael Sheridan, "Thai Coup Sparked by Failed War on Islamists", in *The Sunday Times*, 24 September 2006, and reproduced in *The Australian*, 25 September 2006.
3. Sopaporn Kurz, "Sonthi: Civilian Govt in 2 Weeks", *The Nation*, 21 September 2006.
4. Wassana Nanuam, "Fourth Army Chief Believes Rebels will Halt Major Attacks", Bangkok Post, 22 September 2006.
5. W.K. Che Man, *Muslim Separatism: The Moros of Southern Philippines and the Malays of Southern Thailand* (Singapore: Oxford University Press, 1990).
6. "Dr. Farish A. Noor Interviews the Head of the Patani BERSATU Movement", *Malaysia Today*, 15 June 2005. Available at <http://www.malaysia-today.net/Blog-e/2005/06/dr-farish-noor-interviews-head-of.htm>.
7. For a more recent, excellent examination of decentralization issues, see Srisompob Jitpiromrsi and Duncan McCargo, "A Ministry for the South: New Governance Proposals for Thailand's Southern Region", *Comtemporary Southeast Asia*, vol. 30, no. 3 (2008): 402–28.
8. The following section draws on John Funston, *Southern Thailand: The Dynamics of Conflict* (Washington, D.C.: East-West Center, 2008; Singapore: Institute of Southeast Asian Studies, 2008).
9. Foreign Law Division, Office of the Council of State, *Constitution of the Kingdom of Thailand, B.E. 2540 (1997)* (Bangkok: Office of the Council of State, 1997).
10. National Reconciliation Commission (NRC), *Overcoming Violence Through the Power of Reconciliation* (Bangkok: NRC, 2006), p. 37.
11. NRC, *Overcoming Violence Through the Power of Reconciliation*.
12. Ibid., p. 108.

13. See Michael H. Nelson, ed., "Thailand: Problems with Decentralisation?", in *Thailand's New Politics*. *KPI Yearbook* (Bangkok: King Prajadhipok's Institute & White Lotus, 2001); and Daniel Arghiros, "Political Reform and Civil Society at the Local Level: Thailand's Local Government Reforms", in *Reforming Thai Politics*, edited by Duncan McCargo (Copenhangen: Nordic Institute of Asian Studies, 2002).

14. Marc Askew dissents from the view that dissolving the SBPAC was important in the resumption of southern violence. He makes some telling points about the ineffectiveness of the SBPAC in the years before it was closed. However he does acknowledge that the institution may have had an important symbolic role for southern Muslims, and does not address the importance of giving the police rather than the military the dominant security role in the south. See Marc Askew, *Conspiracy, Politics, and a Disorderly Border: The Struggle to Comprehend Insurgency in Thailand's Deep South* (Washington, D.C.: East-West Center, 2007; Singapore: Institute of Southeast Asian Studies, 2007).

15. Supalak Ganjanakhundee, "Admin Body Urged for South", *The Nation*, 15 June 2006.

16. Michael H. Nelson, "Thailand: Problems with Decentralisation?", p. 249.

17. Wassana Nanuam, "Metropolis Plan for Pattani", *Bangkok Post*, 30 June 2004.

18. "Revise History, Chavalit Says", *The Nation*, 10 November 2005.

10
Tradition and Reform in Islamic Education in Southern Thailand

Joseph Chinyong Liow

INTRODUCTION

There is much literature on Islamic education in the south. Most of it identifies a major disconnect between how Islamic schools are perceived by the state and by the Malay-Muslim community. From the state's perspective, a number of assumptions inform their understanding of Islamic schools in the south: schools encourage separatism by perpetuating Malay culture in an insular and exclusivist manner; the system of education privileging religious over academic and vocational training does not prepare students for modern Thai society, thereby widening the gulf between Malay (communal) and Thai (national) identities; and, schools teach a radical brand of Islam that legitimizes violence against the state.

On the other hand, in the eyes of the local Malay-Muslim community, Islamic education is seen to be central to Malay-Muslim identity based on a historical narrative that speaks of the greatness and independence of the Patani kingdom. To them, the centrality of Islamic education is expressed in the institution of the *pondok*, the traditional Islamic school that remains a key institution in Malay communal life, and the prominence of the Malay language as the language of Islam.

Notwithstanding the significant gulf in perceptions enumerated above, the tendency in both perspectives is to view the Muslim community and Islamic education as a monolithic entity. In doing so, the literature that spawns from such perspectives paper over some major shifts and trends in Islamic education in the southern provinces that have important implications for how we understand the conflict in the south. This chapter aims to flesh out some of these shifts and trends, and suggest how they might inform our thinking of developments in the south in relation to questions of Malay-Muslim history and identity.[1]

ISLAM, HISTORY, AND TRADITIONALISM

Historically, the Kingdom of Patani consisted of the area that today roughly coheres geographically to the provinces of Pattani, Yala, and Narathiwat in southern Thailand, and was known between the sixteenth and eighteenth centuries as a *Dar' al Islam* (abode of Islam). At the same time, Patani was also a flourishing centre of commerce and trade, where traders from Southeast Asia met and transacted with counterparts from elsewhere on the Asian continent as well as Europe.

More specifically, for our purpose here, it is important to note how Patani Darussalam was during this time emerging as a major centre for Islamic learning in Southeast Asia — to the extent that scholars would later describe it as the cradle of Islam in Southeast Asia.[2] The *pondok* schools of southern Thailand, a traditional institution of Islamic education that was in its heyday ubiquitous across the Malay world, played a particularly important role in establishing and sustaining this reputation.

By the early twentieth century, just as a re-awakening of religious consciousness was underway across the Muslim world, the Patani region had the largest number of *pondok* schools in the Malay Peninsula, drawing students from all over the Southeast Asian region. Following the administrative consolidation of Siamese rule over the territories of the traditional Patani kingdom in 1909 after the signing of the Anglo-Siamese Treaty, southern resistance was led by feudal Malay elites displaced as a result of these changes. Indeed, it would be this feudal Malay elite who would lead Malay-Muslim resistance to Bangkok for the first half of the twentieth century. Yet despite the recognizable role of this traditional feudal leadership in the early stages of the Malay-Muslim rebellion against Siam, religious leaders have always played a key role in articulating resistance and challenging the hegemony of the central state. The Siamese government's attempts to exert control over traditional institutions such as the *pondok* and *shari'a* (Islamic law) courts, the educational and judicial backbone of Malay society, ensured that disenchanted religious teachers and jurists provided a fertile source of intellectual leadership and religio-cultural legitimacy for movements opposing the incorporation of the southern provinces into the Siamese central state. Religious leaders were further emboldened by the Islamic reformist movement of the early twentieth century that swept through the Malay world. As will be seen later, this reformist tide witnessed the influx of ideas from Muslim scholars that transformed Muslim mindsets and assertiveness, placing them further at odds with central authorities who in any case never fully comprehended the implications of Islamic reformism on Thai-Muslim consciousness.

RISE OF THE REFORMIST MOVEMENT IN THE SOUTH — HAJJI SULONG ABDUL KADIR

The first stirrings of the reform movement in Thailand were felt not in the southern provinces, but in Bangkok. This reformist tradition was brought to Thailand by Ahmad Wahab, a Sumatran member of the Indonesian modernist organization Muhammadiyah, who had studied and sojourned in Mecca and was subsequently exiled by the Dutch colonial authorities for his political views. After settling in Taman Tok, Bangkok, Wahab slowly expanded his following and established Ansorisunnah, the first Islamic reformist organization in Thailand. His following included Direk Kulsiriswasd (Ibrahim Qureyshi), who would eventually be responsible for the translation of the *Qur'an* into the Thai language. Under Wahab's leadership, Bangkok soon became the centre of reformist thinking among the Muslim intelligentsia and middle class.[3] Additionally, a South Asian variant of reformist influence soon found its way to Thailand with the formation by Pakistani migrant workers of the *Jami-yatul Islam*.

The reform movement in southern Thailand was led by Hajji Sulong Abdul Kadir.[4] Hajji Sulong attended Pondok Hajji Abdul Rashid in Kampung Sungei Pandang, Patani, for his early Islamic education before proceeding to Mecca's Ma'ahad Dar al-Ulum, then a well-known institution set up for Malay-speaking students in the vicinity of the Holy Ka'abah. The years which followed were the most consequential and formative for Hajji Sulong in terms of his pursuit of Islamic knowledge and his subsequent emergence as the progenitor of reformist and modernist Islamic education and thought in southern Thailand. It was during these early years in Mecca that Hajji Sulong established a firm grounding in formal religious studies, particularly in the classical texts. At Ma'had Dar al-Ulum, Hajji Sulong was trained in the traditional science of *tafsir* [Qur'anic exegesis], *hadith*, *usul al-fiqh* [principles of jurisprudence] and *nahwi* [Arabic grammar]. However, it was also during this time that he was exposed to, and began to explore, reformist ideas as a result of normative influences through socialization, interaction, and discussions with eminent Arab *alim* [religious scholars] who were followers of Muhammad Abduh.

In Mecca, he was introduced by Malay *alim* to, and subsequently joined, the Malay-speaking *halaqah* [scholastic circles] in the Masjid Al-Haram. Among the *alim* closest to Hajji Sulong were Syeikh Wan Ahmad bin Mohamed Zain al Fatani, a famous Patani scholar, and Tok Kenali, a renowned Islamic scholar from the northern Malayan state of Kelantan which bordered Patani. Both Syeikh Wan Ahmad and Tok Kenali were known in the circle of Muslim scholars in Mecca as "*Ulama Jawi*", a title that recognized their stature as distinguished scholars of Islam from the Malay world. In 1927, Hajji Sulong joined the ranks of his distinguished mentors and became a junior lecturer on Islamic jurisprudence of the Shafi'i school.

Additionally, while participating in the Malay *halaqah* in Saudi Arabia, Hajji Sulong also came into contact with and socialized among Egyptian scholarly circles during the time of the *hajj* (pilgrimage), many of whom were prominent reformists and modernists. Hajji Sulong's previous exposure to anti-colonial Malay-Muslim nationalism sparked in him further interest in the Arab nationalism that was at the time sweeping across the Arabian Peninsula, and which was distinctly captured in Islamist thinking emanating from Egypt. He became more intimately acquainted with the reformist ideas of Abduh, as well as the thought of Jamaluddin al-Afghani (1839–97), also popularly known as the "Awakener of the East", through these exchanges with Egyptian Islamists and intellectuals, and witnessed on a daily basis how *ulama* [religious leaders] led the struggle to bring justice to the *ummah* [Muslim community] on the Arab socio-political scene.

Coupled with his active interest in Malay-Muslim nationalism, Hajji Sulong increasingly began to see his role as an *ulama* extending beyond the teaching of religion and into the socio-political sphere. In turn, this generated in him an abiding interest in political and social activism which was to preoccupy him for the rest of his life, and catapulted him to a position of prominence as a leader of southern Thailand's Malay-Muslim community from the late 1920s. He was imprisoned for urging greater autonomy for Malays in 1947 (the famous seven demands), released in 1952, then died while under police custody in 1954.

THE CONTEMPORARY REFORM MOVEMENT — PROFESSOR ISMAIL LUTFI JAPAKIYA

The contemporary reformist movement is led by Ismail Lutfi Japakiya, who graduated in 1986 from the Islamic University of Imam Muhammad bin Saud in Saudi Arabia with a doctorate in *shari'a*. Ismail Lutfi is widely seen as the leading reformist/modernist Muslim educator in Thailand today, and on the back of his connections with various Saudi-based interests, it would not be an exaggeration to say that he has single-handedly charted the course and directed the expansion of the contemporary reformist movement in Thailand.[5] A popular reformist scholar not unlike Hajji Sulong in his heyday, Lutfi's appeal has undoubtedly been facilitated by the influx of large amounts of financial support from the Saudi government and Saudi-linked charities that have overseen the establishment of a number of mosques and modernist Islamic schools modelled on *madrasah* [modern Islamic schools], therein accounting for the widely-held belief that he is the conduit for Wahhabism into Thailand.

Ismail Lutfi is the rector of the Yala Islamic University, which boasts modern educational facilities in both its campuses in Pattani and Yala. Lutfi is also principal of Bamrung Islam Mukim Pujud, an Islamic private school in Muang Pattani, where he teaches and conducts weekly lectures for the general public from its mosque, often in front of audiences in excess of a thousand people. On top of his profile as an *ulama* and educator, Lutfi holds a number of other prominent positions as well, serving as the chairman of the Consultative Committee of the Foundation for Islamic Education in Southern Thailand, and was an appointed member of parliament under the military appointed administration (2006–07). Beyond these local activities, Lutfi is also a popular speaker in Islamic scholarly circles in northern Malaysia, though he told the writer that since September 9/11 his speaking engagements in Malaysia have been markedly reduced. The intensity of his preaching and forcefulness of his personality, not to mention personal charisma, has ensured that while certain aspects of Lutfi's reformist dogma which challenge long-held traditional beliefs are met with caution by the traditionalist custodians of the faith, he himself has emerged as one of the most popular religious scholars in Thailand. His competence and fluency in Arabic is clearly his *forte* for it allows him to demonstrate a deep knowledge and access to "authentic" scripture that few among Thailand's Islamic religious intelligentsia can match. Because of this, Lutfi is viewed as a scholar who has the ability to simplify complex concepts of Islamic thought, a factor which has proven critical to his appeal.

Ismail Lutfi's overall popularity has been enhanced by his embrace of modern technology. His transmission of knowledge is often facilitated by the latest communication devices such as microphones, cassette recorders, and CDs, clearly distinguishing him from traditional religious teachers. Aside from his religious credentials and oratorical skills, Lutfi's popularity is further augmented by his access to substantial amounts of Saudi financial support, which he manages and disburses through his Islamic charity, *Islah*, with branches in each of the three Malay-Muslim provinces. The Saudi government has also been instrumental in setting up the Yala Islamic University. That said, while Ismail Lutfi is no doubt an immensely popular and respected *ulama* in Thailand and his public lectures attract audiences in the thousands, his pool of committed followers — those who imbibe his reformist ideas to the extent that they are prepared to critique their traditional religious leaders — is significantly smaller, probably because most Muslims in southern Thailand remain respectful of the latter and followers of long-held practices.

There is no question that Ismail Lutfi views his reformist agenda for transformation of Islamic education in Thailand as part of the advancement of Islamic knowledge in the region. Be that as it may, his vision has also been a source of some disquiet to mainstream traditionalist Islamic circles. Reminiscent of their reaction to Hajji Sulong when he attempted to transform traditionalist Islamic education practices decades earlier, Lutfi's charisma and communicative skills have raised concerns in certain circles among the traditionalist religious establishment who fear that his brand of Islam will appeal to the younger generation. The root of this disquiet can perhaps be traced to his perspective of Patani's place in the history of Islamic knowledge in Southeast Asia.

Contrary to conventional wisdom that portrays Patani as a centre of excellence in Islamic studies, Lutfi argues controversially that earlier epochs of Islam in Thailand (for which he means periods prior to the advent of the current wave of reformist thinking) were in fact marked by a lack of *ilmu* [knowledge]. To his mind, the advent of reformist Islam was both a basis and consequence of an increase in *ilmu*. In Lutfi's own words, "Islamic knowledge in Thailand used to be weak, and traditional Islam was based on this lack of knowledge. But it (*ilmu*) has improved over time. This leads to a deeper understanding of Islam."[6]

Despite his message on the need to transform Islamic education, which would no doubt resonate with government authorities who have always been of the view that resistance to change on the part of Islamic schools in the south has been a constant source of provocation, Ismail Lutfi continues to be demonized in media and counter-terrorism circles as a "hard line Wahhabi cleric", as some pundits and analysts have taken to calling him. His agenda for the transformation of Islamic education in Thailand has likewise been dismissed as nothing but a cover for a more insidious programme to radicalize the Muslim population of southern Thailand. Many of these allegations come from sceptics who cast a suspecting eye on Salafism, often equating it to Wahhabism, the highly politicized fundamentalist offshoot of broader Salafi dogma which has admittedly enjoyed a chequered history both as a reform as well as militant Muslim movement, which has captured the attention of the terrorism studies community since 9/11. Ismail Lutfi's training in Saudi Arabia (where he attained his Bachelor's and Doctoral degrees) and continued ties with both government and private interests in the kingdom have been mustered by these detractors to corroborate their accusations. Further underlying these suspicions is an ideological reading of Wahhabism not only as an austere and strict genre within Salafism, a reading which enjoys widespread consensus, but more so a militant and uncompromising brand of Islam. Notwithstanding these perceptions that typify conventional wisdom, under more careful interrogation interesting anomalies emerge that cloud the erstwhile "clear" picture of the impact of Lutfi's "indoctrination" in Saudi Arabia as described by these analysts. Concomitantly, Lutfi appears a considerably more complex figure than their analysis often implies.

Though Ismail Lutfi studied at the Islamic University of Imam Muhammad bin Saud, a university with known Wahhabi links, those who enjoyed the most influence on his intellectual and religio-ideological development were in fact not conventional Wahhabi ideologues or educators at all. Rather, his tutor and supervisor was Shaykh Said Hawwa, a Syrian lecturer and member of the *Ikhwanul Muslimin* [Muslim Brotherhood] who taught in Saudi Arabia during Lutfi's stay there. Notwithstanding the identity and ideological proclivity of his mentor, it is Lutfi's own ideas that are intriguing insofar as they speak to the complexities surrounding his doctrinal inclinations. For instance, in his dissertation on *shari'a*, Lutfi in fact argued for the importance of time, space, and context when applying precepts of Islamic law.[7] In so doing, his views certainly appear at least on the surface to echo what many Muslim scholars who are today deemed "progressive" are propounding when discussing the question of the rigidity in the application of Islamic law, though the actual substance of Ismail Lutfi's understanding of jurisprudence itself may depart fundamentally from the views of liberal-progressive Islamic scholars.

Given Lutfi's perceived Wahhabi credentials, it is perhaps apropos to note here that while many have criticized Wahhabism for its doctrinal conservatism and rigidity, the importance of context is also a typical intellectual trait of Wahhabi thought which believes, at least in theory, that the doors of *ijtihad* [independent interpretation] remain open. What is perhaps more important to register though, is the fact that whether Lutfi is indeed the scripturalist, literalist Muslim scholar that he is often made out to be, his emphasis on context speaks of an appreciation of the complex and multifaceted nature both of the challenges confronting Islam, as well as the avenues of response available to the Muslim community.

Some other aspects of Ismail Lutfi's activities draw into further question his "Wahhabi" credentials. For instance, while mainstream Wahhabism rejects *Mawlid* (celebration of the Prophet Muhammad's birthday), in 2006 Lutfi contributed to an annual collection of essays compiled by Thai Islamic scholars and published by the Islamic Centre of Thailand on the occasion of the prophet's birthday to "propagate the valuable teachings of the great Prophet Muhammad Sal Allahu Allhi Wa Salam to all human beings".[8] Ismail's contribution to the 2006 volume is titled "Status and Roles of *Ulama* in the *Holy Qur'an* and *Sunna*", and is remarkable both for its reiteration of distinctively Salafi beliefs and practices as well as departure from patently orthodox Wahhabi perspectives. In his discussion on the role and status of *alim* in Muslim society for instance, while acknowledging that they are to be respected and sought out for their wisdom, Lutfi also cautioned, in characteristic Salafi fashion, that "esteem and respect from any society for *alim* should not be frenetic and indulgent. The love and respect has to be based on the foundation of the *Qur'an* and *Sunna* and in accordance with the level of his *imam* to Allah and His Messengers." He goes on further to elaborate that this is because "however high the status of an *alim*, he is also a human being who will have defects and errors".

Lutfi's view here accords with the practice of Salafi teachings to caution against excessive celebration of human capabilities, even those of noted religious scholars. On the other hand, compared to some Wahhabi and Salafi scholars, Lutfi appears to demonstrate a more sophisticated appreciation for Shi'ism. While more orthodox Salafi and Wahhabi scholars tend to make sweeping accusations of Shi'ism as apostasy, in his discussion on "bad" and "wicked" *ulama* and the act of *fitnah* [lies], where he alludes to key events in Islamic history associated with the rise of Shi'ism, Lutfi reserves his harshest criticism for the *Kharawij*[9] as well as those who rejected the peace treaty between Ali, whom Shi'a Muslims believe to be the fourth "Rightly Guided Caliph", and Muawiyyah. While Islamic scholars continue to discuss the impact of the Battle of Siffin (from which the armistice between Ali and Muawiyyah arose) on how the office of Caliph (supreme ruler) evolved, it appears that embedded in Lutfi's message is an expression of concern for the unity of the *ummah* as a whole rather than the polemics and hubris that is sometimes found in Islamic historiography.

Finally, while much is made of the financial support that Ismail Lutfi's Yala Islamic University has received from the governments of Saudi Arabia and Kuwait, little is said of the vast contributions that the government of Qatar, not normally known for its scripturalist position on matters of religion, has committed. In this regard, even more astonishing is the fact that the university has applied to the U.S.-linked Asia Foundation for a grant in support of English language training for its faculty and study trips to Malaysia.

It is also important that we consider Lutfi's position on violence. While accused in several terrorism studies circles of not speaking out against violence, Lutfi has in fact been one of the most vocal critics of the ongoing conflict in southern Thailand. In fact, Lutfi is the author of *Islam Penjana Kedamaian Sejagat* [Islam as the Pathway to Peace], a major treatise that seeks to explain the place of the use of force in Islam, a religion of peace. In it, Lutfi draws attention at several junctures to the close relationship that Muslims and Christians enjoyed during the classical era. He cites, for example, how Christians in Syria had enjoyed a close relationship with Muslims. He further suggests that Islam encourages the values of "*tolong-menolong*" [mutual assistance] and "*berkenal-kenalan*" [dialogue towards the fostering of familiarity and understanding] across cultures and religions that go beyond the superficiality of mere familiarity with a neighbour's name and status.

ARENAS OF CONTESTATION

Schools associated with Ismail Lutfi's reformist agenda in southern Thailand are predominantly run by Saudi-trained teachers who do not subscribe to the traditional emphasis of Shafi'i Mazhab that characterizes the jurisprudential inclinations of the vast majority of Malay Muslims. Indeed, such has been the deviation of the reformist template from the norms of

Sufi and Shafi'i Islamic traditionalism in southern Thailand that it has
been opined in certain quarters that some of these teachers returning from
Saudi Arabia are introducing a new school of *fiqh* [Islamic jurisprudence].
To say that these reformists reject the Shafi'i school, the dominant legal
tradition in Southeast Asia, is however a mistake, for these schools do
provide Mazhab instruction. More appropriately, these reformist scholars
do not consider Shafi'i Mazhab, or any of the other traditional schools of
Islamic law for that matter, to be the blanket authoritative statement of
Islam on any given issue.

Epistemologically, while reformists schools do indeed also provide
instruction in Mazhab Shafi'i (as they do with the other three traditional
schools of jurisprudential thought), what distinguishes them from their
traditionalist counterparts is the markedly reduced emphasis accorded to *fiqh*
in general, and the reluctance to privilege a specific Mazhab in particular.
This approach is premised on their belief that the emphasis of Islamic
education should be centred on *tawhid* [the unity of God], from which
all else flows, and that the *Qur'an* and *hadith* are the only binding sources
of law. The fact that the reformists by and large also generally deny *qiyas*
[analogy] has reinforced the perception among certain observers that they
are scripturalists, literalist, and puritans. Yet, while in some respects clearly
fundamentalist in theological and epistemological orientation, they are also
reformist in how this orientation is challenging the legalist-traditionalist
culture of Islam in southern Thailand.

Three reasons are commonly cited to underscore this reformist position
on Islamic jurisprudence among its proponents in southern Thailand.
First, it has been argued that because *fiqh* is not primarily rooted in the
Qur'an (*bukan berasal Qur'an*), it should not command the intellectual
and exegetical primacy that should rightly be reserved for the *Qur'an* and
hadith. Second, it has been suggested that *fiqh* is highly contextual, and
the question of the relevance of the respective schools of jurisprudence is
dependent on circumstances surrounding a particular situation. Consequently,
it is from this intellectual elasticity (that is, focus on context) in the
realm of Islamic jurisprudence that they derive their reformist credentials.
Finally, reformists follow epistemological traditions that reject *taqlid*, the
unquestioning acceptance of established interpretations that is a feature
of conventional Islamic education, and argue for individual interpretation
[*ijtihad*] based on a return to the *Qur'an* and *hadith*, the scriptural sources
of Islam, rather than reliance on classical jurisprudence.

The intellectual challenge posed by the reformists on traditional Islamic
thought and praxis is best illustrated in texts that deal not only with *fiqh*,

but *aqidah* [faith, belief], *tassawuf* [mysticism], and *aklak* [morals, ethics] as well. One such text is *Kifayah Al-Muhtadi*, a popular Islamic studies textbook currently being used in many Islamic schools in the southern provinces that calls attention to many of the intellectual tensions alluded to earlier between the reformist Islam being introduced by Salafis and traditionalist Sunni and Sufi ideas and conventions. A similar distinction is drawn by Ismail Lutfi in his discussion of al-Anfaal: 24, found in *Hayat Tayyibah: Dari Kalimat Tayyibah Hingga Masakin Tayyibah* [The Good Life: From A Good Word to A Good Abode], where he defines the injunction "and know that Allah comes in between a person and his heart" as indicating that it is Allah who "prevents an evil person from doing anything (presumably evil acts)".[10] This distinction regarding how Sufis and Salafis understand the human heart as human intention is further captured in the different local textual exegeses on the topic of theology. Whereas *Kifayah* represents how reformists understand the question of spirituality and theology (with its emphasis on forms and literal interpretations as described above), Sufi texts such as *Hidayatul Salatin*, a traditionalist text on *aqidah* and *tassawuf* written by Syeikh Samad al-Palimbani, a renown Malay Sufi scholar, and which remains popular in the region, emphasizes the cultivation of the heart and love for the divine.

While not entrenched, reformist influence has continued to expand gradually in Thailand on the back of Saudi funding for various religious schools. As the discussion has thus far illustrated, this funding is often followed by active involvement in curriculum. As was the case in the 1930s with Hajji Sulong's Madrasah al-Maarif al-Wataniyyah, the presence of these schools has been viewed as a challenge to the traditional Sunni institutions and ideas, and has at times been viewed negatively by religious teachers from the latter. One *tok guru* [traditional headmaster] interviewed assailed the reformists as *Kaum Muda* [young group] who were "*sangat takbur*" [very arrogant] in their attitude towards more established schools of Islamic thought. Others described the residual tension between the *Kaum Muda* and *Kaum Tua* [traditionalists] as being that between those who thought themselves "faultless" [*yang merasa sempurna*] and traditionalists who resist change. Numerous traditionalist *ustaz* [Islamic teachers] have berated their reformist counterparts who condemn local beliefs and practices as part of Islamic education. While these reformists justify their attack on tradition as "improving the community's understanding of and adherence to Islam", traditionalists have retorted that the former are, in the words of a *tok guru* from the famed Pondok Dalor, "self-righteous". Others see this influence as incompatible with local *adat* [customary law] which remains an important institution in Malay culture. There are, of course, traditionalists who adopt a more measured approach. The following opinion for instance, captures this more conciliatory mood: "*fiqh* starts with Qur'an and Sunnah, and then some lean towards Shafi'i but not too much. Traditional practices are left for individuals to decide, especially when they go home. There is no condemning the locals' beliefs and practices."[11]

CONCLUSION

The multifarious and fluid nature of contestations within Thailand's Muslim community addressed thus far has meant that Muslim identities defy easy categorization. In particular, the imprint of Ismail Lutfi and his followers on Islamic education in southern Thailand is further instructive of the difficulties associated with capturing and labelling the essence of Islamic movements. As far as I have been able to ascertain, Lutfi's agenda is at once reformist, modernist, and fundamentalist. It is reformist in that it acknowledges the limitations of traditional Islamic education and the need for reform in order to make it relevant to modernity. Beyond this, the movement is also modernist in how it aims to integrate secular subjects such as science, technology, business, and finance into the curriculum of Islamic schools as part of reform efforts. Yet this agenda is also fundamentalist in how it locates Islam, and in particular the *Qur'an* and *hadith*, which the reformists believe carry the essential principles of modern knowledge, at the heart of their reformist movement.

The re-emergence of reformist Muslim *ulama* and *ustaz*, primarily though not exclusively in the Malay-Muslim provinces, has fostered a concern about the influx of Wahhabism into Thailand. Indeed, analysts have tended to lump reformists together as Wahhabi, with the insinuation being that the reformist agenda is ultimately political — the Islamization of southern Thailand by force, and the integration of the region to the larger entity of the *Daulah Islamiyah* as declared by regional radical groups such as *Jemaah Islamiyah* (JI), to which southern Thailand's Wahhabis are purportedly aligned. Evidence mustered to support this assertion include Ismail Lutfi's meeting with JI's operational head in Southeast Asia, Hambali, and the former's alleged participation in Rabitatul Mujahideen meetings that plotted the terrestrial boundaries of a Southeast Asian Islamic state. Concern for the reformist conduit for radicalism stems further from its Saudi connection. Since the 9/11 terrorist attacks, the causal argument has often been made that exposure to Saudi education would open the gates to Wahhabi indoctrination, which, given its literalist reading of scripture and negative predisposition to prevailing Muslim traditions, is often seen in turn to be a channel for Islamic radicalism and militancy.

Against this conceptual backdrop, the present account of Islamic education in Thailand contests several facets of this correlation between foreign education (especially in Saudi Arabia), radicalism, and militancy. First, the teleological fashion in which the transfer of knowledge and shaping of worldviews is considered, that is, that by implication a Saudi education will lead to radicalization and militancy, renders it tenuous. Consider, for example, the absence of Nasserist ideology among the Muslim population in Thailand despite the vast numbers of Thai Muslims who were sent to Egypt to further their religious and secular education in the 1960s. Second, the epistemological basis to this argument is also questionable. For instance, if encounters with the West actually reinforced the radical leanings of Muslim militants such as Syed Qutb or JI leader Azahari Hussein rather than moderating them, on what basis should we expect the radicalization of erstwhile "moderate" Muslims upon encounters with "hardline" Wahhabism (which by the way, is a fundamentally different environment from Afghanistan during the Mujahideen resistance) to be something pre-determined? Indeed, such structuralist arguments often bracket out contexts and intervening variables that are vital to explaining social and political phenomenon. Finally, such claims simply do not stand the empirical test. In the wake of ongoing violence among the Malay-Muslim community in the south, Ismail Lutfi, the personification of militant Wahhabism according to these accounts, has in fact played an active role as an interlocutor between the Thai government and the Malay-Muslim community.

This is not to say however, that the rise of the reformist movement in Thailand has not generated tensions within the community. Their ideas on epistemology, methodology, culture, and identity have been greeted with circumspection, if not outright hostility, in many traditionalist quarters that harbour misgivings about reformist dogma. This has particularly been so in the realm of Islamic education, where debates over authenticity and legitimacy within the Muslim community define much of the terrain of Islamic thought and praxis.

Scholars who study Muslims in Thailand have accurately maintained that Thai Islam has enjoyed a long and vibrant tradition, and that the country itself has been home to a wide variety of representations of Muslim identity. Muslim heterogeneity however, has also generated multifarious patterns of dissonance and contestations of late, which have been profoundly captured in the realm of Islamic education. While differences between the state and Muslim society, as well as Malay and Thai identities, have sparked considerable press and academic interest and coverage lately, the question of contestations that have emerged within the Muslim community itself as it seeks to negotiate identity and authenticity, have yet to come under substantive scrutiny and analysis.

Islamic education is proving to be a dynamic realm where Muslim identities and authenticities are contested and negotiated. The current fixation among scholarly and policy communities with Malay-Muslim violence has ignored these deeper currents in Islamic education that will likely have significance consequences for Muslim identity, community, and authenticity in Thailand on the whole. In their obsession with solving the Muslim "problem" in southern Thailand, Thai policy-makers would do well to pay greater attention to the gradual dislocation of traditional Muslim society with the influx of reformist ideas and ideology, and the impact this may have on Muslim identity and community.

NOTES

1. Sections of this chapter draw from Joseph Chinyong Liow, *Islam, Education, and Reform in Southern Thailand: Tradition and Transformation* (Singapore: Institute of Southeast Asian Studies, 2009).
2. See Hasan Madmarn, *The Pondok and Madrasah in Pattani* (Bangi: Penerbit University Kebangsaan Malaysia, 1999).
3. For a discussion on the emergence of reformist Islam in Thailand during this period, see Raymond Scupin, "Muslim Accommodation in Thai Society", *Journal of Islamic Studies* 9, no. 2 (1998): 229–58.
4. The major scholarly works that address the legacy of Hajji Sulong on Muslim culture and education in the southern border provinces include Surin Pitsuwan, *Islam and Malay Nationalism: A Case Study of the Malay-Muslims of Southern Thailand* (Bangkok: Thai Khadi Research Institute, Thammasat University, 1985); Wan Kadir Che Man, *Muslim Separatism: The Moro of Southern Philippines and the Malays of Southern Thailand* (Singapore: Oxford University Press, 1990); Mohd. Zamberi Abdul Malik, *Umat Islam Patani: Sejarah dan Politik* [The Patani Muslim Community: History and Politics] (Shah Alam: HIZBI, 1993); Ahmad Fathi, *Ulama Besar dari Fatani* [Prominent Ulama from Patani] (Kelantan: Pustaka Aman, 2001); Numan Hayimasae, "*Hj Sulong Abdul Kadir (1895–1954): Perjuangan dan Sumbangan Beliau Kepada Masyarakat Melayu Patani* [Hj Sulong Abdul Kadir: Struggle and Contributions to the Patani Malays]", M.Sc. dissertation, Universiti Sains Kebangsaan Malaysia, 2002.

5. Unlike Hajji Sulong, the writings and teachings of Ismail Lutfi have not been subjected to scholarly analysis except for Liow, *Islam, Education, and Reform*, Chapter 4. The information here was gleaned from three interviews with Ismail Lutfi, in January 2005, August 2005, and October 2006.

6. Interview with Ismail Lutfi, Pattani, 14 January 2006.

7. See Ismail Lutfi al Fatani, *Ikhtilaf Ad-Darain wa Atsaruhu fi Ahkam Al-Munakahat wa Al-Muamalat* [The Effect of Two Dars (Dar Al-Islam and Dar Al-Harb) on Islamic Personal and Transaction Laws] (Cairo: Dar As-Salam, 1990).

8. See Ismail Lutfi Japakiya, "Status and Roles of Ulama in the Holy Qur'an and Sunna", in Maulid Klang Organizing Committee of Thailand, *Holding Fast to the Ideology of Harmony Among Thais* (Bangkok: Islamic Committee of Thailand, 2006).

9. The earliest Islamic sect, which began during a religio-political controversy over the caliphate. It upheld a radical, fundamentalist theology based on the *Qur'an*, which recognized the right to rebel against an unjust ruler, and considered many moderate Muslims "hypocrites" and "unbelievers" who could be killed with impunity.

10. Ismail Lutfi Japakiya, *Hayat Tayyibah: Dari Kalimat Tayyibah Hingga Masakin Tayyibah* [The Good Life: From A Good Word to A Good Abode] (Pattani: Majlis Al-Ilm Fattani, 2001), pp. 38–39.

11. Interview at Narawi Islam School, Narathiwat, 2 August 2006.

11
The Economy Under the Thaksin Government: Stalled Recovery

Peter Warr

The Thai Rak Thai government of Prime Minister Thaksin Shinawatra was elected in February 2001, promising rapid recovery from the financial crisis of 1997–98 and the speedy eradication of poverty. In September 2006 a military coup dislodged the Thai Rak Thai government, forcing Thaksin himself into exile. This chapter reviews the economic performance of the five-and-a-half years of the Thaksin government. This exercise seems especially relevant because the promises of the Thaksin government were focused on economics. On taking office, Thaksin promised a return to the double-digit growth rates of the boom decade of 1987 to 1996 and to eradicate poverty within a decade. To what extent were these promises fulfilled?

THE THAI ECONOMY IN LONG-TERM PERSPECTIVE

We begin with some long-term context. Thailand's growth performance from 1951 to 2006 is summarized in Figure 11.1, showing the level of real GDP per capita in each year (vertical bars) and its annual growth rate (solid line). The figure identifies four periods of the country's recent

Figure 11.1
Thailand: Real GDP per capita and Its Growth Rate, 1951 to 2006

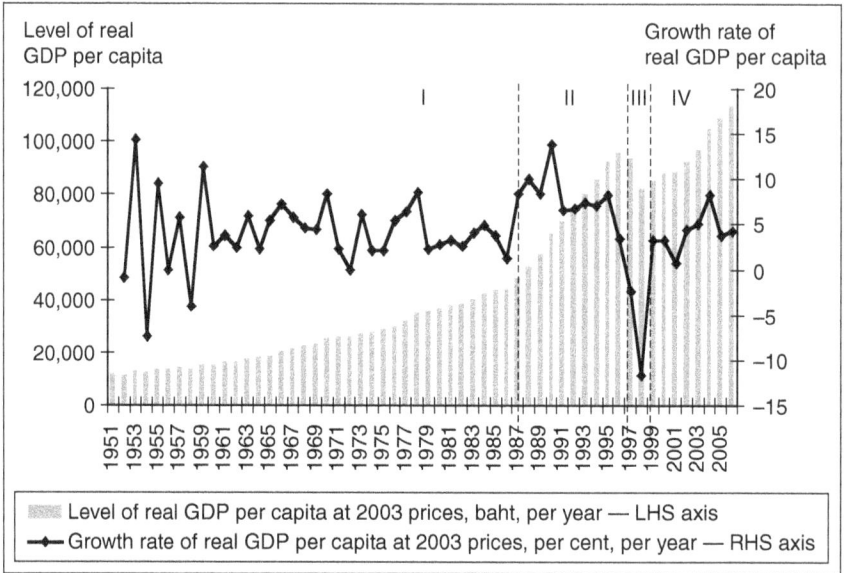

Source: Author's calculations, using data from National Economic and Social Development Board.

economic history: Pre-boom (until 1986); Boom (1987 to 1996); Crisis (1997 to 1999); and Recovery (2000 to 2006).

Table 11.1 shows that over the period 1968 to 1986, the average annual growth rate of real GNP was 6.7 per cent (almost 5 per cent per person), compared with an average of 2.4 per cent for low and middle-income countries over the same period. Then, over the decade 1987 to 1996, the Thai economy boomed and it was the fastest growing in the world. The twin currency and banking crises of 1997–99 ended this boom, eroding some, but definitely not all, of the gains that had been made over the preceding decades.[1]

As we shall see below, Thailand's boom was driven by very high levels of investment, both domestic and foreign, in physical capital. Even more remarkable than the rate of growth over this long period was the stability of the growth. Not a single year of negative growth of real output per head of population was experienced over the four decades from 1958 to 1996, a unique achievement among oil importing developing countries.

Table 11.1
Thailand: Growth of GDP and Its Sectoral Components, 1951 to 2006
(per cent per annum)

	Pre-boom	Boom	Crisis	Recovery	Whole period
	1968–86	1987–96	1997–99	2000–06	1968–2006
Total GDP	6.7	9.5	–2.5	5.0	6.4
Agriculture	4.5	2.6	0.1	2.7	3.3
Industry	8.5	12.8	–1.7	6.2	8.4
Services	6.8	9	–3.6	4.3	6.1

Sources: Bank of Thailand, data for 1951 to 1986; National Economic and Social Development Board, data from 1987.

Thailand's performance was often described as an example others might emulate. Its principal economic institutions, including its central bank, the Bank of Thailand, were often cited as examples of competent and stable management.

The crisis of 1997–98 reversed these assessments. Domestically, the economy was in disarray: output and investment were contracting; poverty incidence was rising; the exchange rate had collapsed, following the decision to float the currency in July 1997; the government had been compelled to accept a humiliating IMF bailout package; the financial system was largely bankrupt; and confidence in the country's economic institutions, including the Bank of Thailand, was shattered. Internationally, Thailand was now characterized as the initiator of a "contagion effect" in Asian financial markets, undermining economic and political stability and bringing economic hardship to millions of people.

The economic damage done by the crisis of 1997–99, and the hardship that resulted, were both substantial. The crisis eroded some of the gains from the economic growth that had been achieved during the long period of economic expansion, but it did not erase them. At the low point of the crisis in 1998 the level of GDP per capita was almost 14 per cent lower than it had been only two years earlier, in 1996. Nevertheless, because of the sustained growth that had preceded the crisis, this reduced level of 1998 was still higher than it had been only five years earlier, in 1993, and was seven times its level in 1951. Since the crisis, Thailand's economic recovery has been moderate. The rate of growth of real GDP has been somewhat below its long-term trend rate and it was not until 2003 that the level of real GDP per capita had recovered to its pre-crisis level of 1996. Foreign direct investment has declined dramatically since 1998 and private domestic investment has remained sluggish. In 2006 the level of real economic output per person was 19 per cent above its 1996 pre-crisis level and almost ten times its level fifty-five years earlier. The average annual rate of growth of real GDP per person over this entire period of five-and-a-half decades was 4.2 per cent.

Figures 11.2 and 11.3 place the last two decades in a comparative East Asian perspective. Data on real GDP are presented for eight East Asian economies, including Thailand. The pre-crisis period of 1986 to 1996 is covered in Figure 11.2, with each country's 1986 level of real GDP indexed to 100. The crisis and post-crisis periods of 1996 to 2006 are shown in Figure 11.3 with 1996 real GDP this time indexed to 100. Figure 11.2 shows that Thailand's boom was the largest of the countries shown, but only marginally so. Singapore, Malaysia, Indonesia, Korea and Taiwan were not far behind.

Figure 11.3 shows that in 1998 serious contractions occurred in Korea, Malaysia, and Indonesia, but that, relative to 1996, Thailand's initial contraction was the most severe. Along with Indonesia, its contraction has

Figure 11.2
Real GDP in East Asia, 1986 to 1996

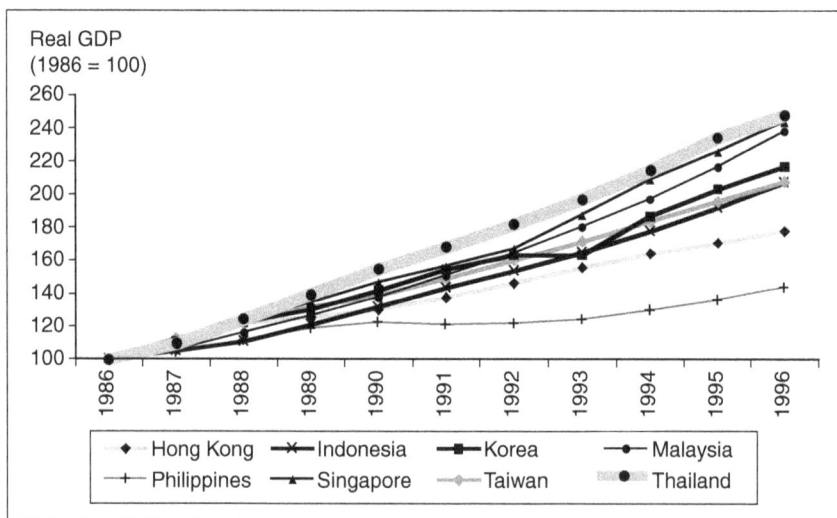

Source: Asian Development Bank, Development Indicators, various issues.

Figure 11.3
Real GDP in East Asia, 1996 to 2005

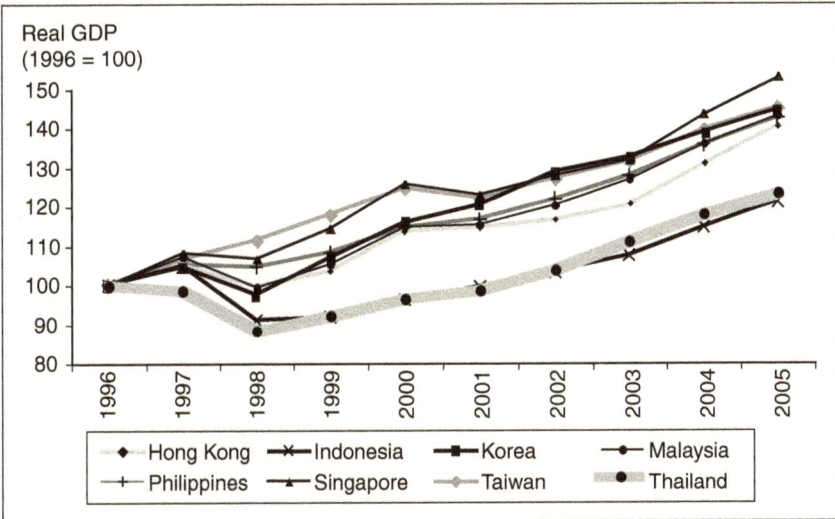

Source: Asian Development Bank, Development Indicators, various issues.

also been the most long lasting. Thailand's contraction was initially larger than Indonesia's, but Indonesia did not experience a recovery as large as Thailand's in 1999. It is commonly said that Indonesia's economic crisis was more severe than Thailand's, but these data reveal a somewhat different story. Using the pre-crisis year of 1996 as a base, their time paths of real GDP, relative to that 1996 base, were remarkably similar. The main difference is that since 2002 Indonesia's recovery has been marginally slower.

During the immediate post-crisis period (1998 to 2001) Thailand's rate of recovery was moderate and this description broadly characterizes the period of the Thaksin government as well. Its recovery has been only marginally superior to Indonesia's.

SOURCES OF AGGREGATE GROWTH

Where did Thailand's economic growth come from? Explaining long-term growth involves distinguishing between the growth of the factors of production employed and the growth in their productivity. We now discuss a growth accounting exercise for Thailand, covering the years 1980 to 2002.

The present section presents this analysis at an aggregate, economy-wide level and the following section disaggregates the analysis by major sector.

The assumption being made in this kind of analysis is that during the period covered output was primarily supply-constrained; aggregate demand was not the binding constraint on output. This assumption seems reasonable for the period prior to the Asian crisis of 1997–99, but the crisis and recovery periods from 1997 onwards were characterized by a deficiency of aggregate demand. A growth accounting framework, which focuses on the determinants of aggregate supply, is therefore of limited relevance for such periods. The data relating to that period are included here mainly for completeness.

Data on labour inputs are adjusted for changes in the quality of the workforce by disaggregating the workforce by the educational characteristics of workers and weighing these components of the workforce using time series wage data for the educational categories concerned. Data on land inputs are similarly adjusted for the changing quality of land inputs by disaggregating by irrigated and non-irrigated land and then re-aggregating these components using data on land prices. In Table 11.2, the resulting estimates of factor growth rates are contained in the first column. The second column provides average factor cost shares over time, compiled from factor price data. These factor cost shares impose the assumption of

Table 11.2
Thailand: Aggregate Growth Accounting, 1980 to 2002

	Annual growth rate (per cent per year)	Average cost share (per cent)	Contribution to total growth (per cent per year)	Contribution to total growth (per cent)
Output	6.01	n.a.	n.a.	100
All factors	5.41	100	5.41	90.0
Raw labour	2.19	40.2	0.88	14.7
Human capital	46.9	4.24	70.6	4.6
Physical capital	1.8	0.02	3.3	
Agricultural land	n.a.	0.60	10.0	
Aggregate TFP growth	n.a.			

Note: n.a. means not applicable.
Source: Author's calculations, using data from National Economic and Social Development Board.

constant returns to scale. The factor cost shares used in the calculations vary over time. The summary data shown in the table are the averages of these shares.

The third column on factor contributions to growth weighs the growth rates of factors by their cost shares, producing an estimate of the degree to which the growth of output (6.01 per cent) is attributable to growth of each component. These data are then used to calculate total factor productivity growth as a residual. The final column shows the estimated percentage contribution of each component to the overall growth rate.

The outstanding point is the rapid growth of the physical capital stock. The capital stock grew more rapidly than output in both the pre-boom and boom periods. This growth of the capital stock accounted for 70 per cent of the growth of output. Growth of the size of the labour force contributed about 15 per cent of the growth of output, but improvements in the quality of the labour force made only a modest contribution, explaining less than 5 per cent of overall growth. Indeed, the performance of its educational sector has been among the weakest in East Asia. Secondary school participation rates were low and did not improve greatly during the pre-boom and boom periods.[2] Similarly, since the 1960s the expansion of the cultivated land area has been small. Growth of the stock of land was not the source either. Total factor productivity (TFP) growth was only moderately important, accounting for 10 per cent of output growth.

It is perhaps unsurprising that the explanation for Thailand's impressive growth lies primarily with growth of the physical capital stock. Both domestic and foreign investment grew rapidly, but the growth rate of foreign investment was larger, from about 1987.[3] Foreign investment plays an important role in introducing new technology and in the development of export markets. Nevertheless, the quantitative importance of foreign investment in Thailand's capital stock accumulation is easily exaggerated. Figure 11.4 makes this point by decomposing Thailand's total annual level of investment into three components: domestic private, public and foreign direct investment (FDI). It does this for each of these four years — 1975, 1985, 1995 and 2005. Of these three components, domestic private investment is by far the largest and FDI by far the smallest. In 2005 their percentage contributions to the overall level of investment were: private domestic — 69.5 per cent, public — 26.8 per cent and FDI — 3.7 per cent. Private investment by Thais themselves was the dominant contributor to overall capital accumulation.

How was the investment financed? Did the funds come from domestic savings or borrowed from abroad? Table 11.3 presents an accounting of this

Figure 11.4
Thailand: Composition of Net Annual Investment, 1975 to 2005

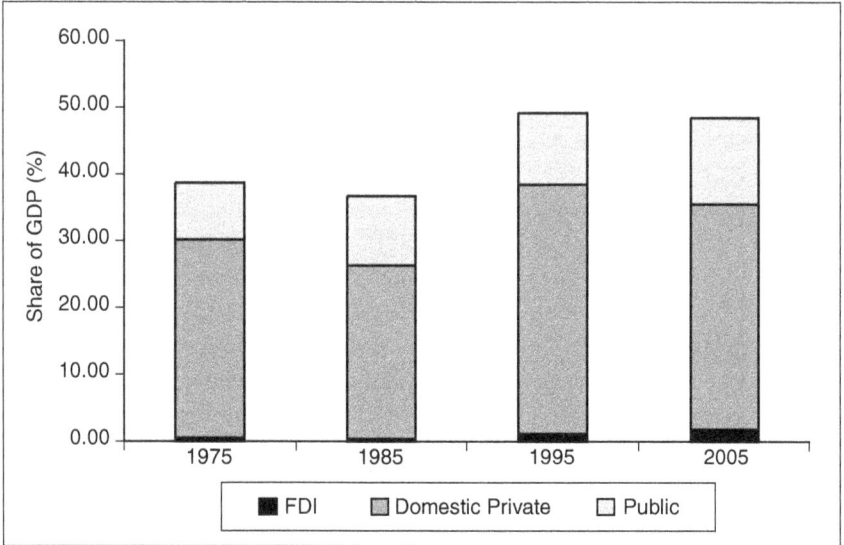

Source: Author's calculations using data from National Economic and Social Development Board.

issue based on the identities that: (i) total investment = household savings + government savings + foreign savings; and (ii) foreign savings = long-term capital inflow + short-term capital inflow — change in international reserves of the central bank. By far the most important source of finance was the private savings of Thais themselves.

Contrary to the common perception that Thailand's boom (1987 to 1996) was financed largely by foreign capital, this source, consisting of private foreign direct investment (FDI) plus foreign government investment (ODA), accounted for an average of only 5 per cent of total investment. During the pre-boom period, FDI accounted for about 61 per cent of this inflow of long-term foreign capital and ODA accounted for the other 39 per cent. During the boom period, these proportions were 73 and 27 per cent, respectively. Short-term capital inflows, consisting of borrowing from abroad plus portfolio inflows plus domestic bank accounts held by foreigners were a more important source, accounting for 23 per cent of total investment. During the boom, government dis-saving (budget deficits) reduced the funds available for investment by 11 per cent and increases in

Table 11.3
Thailand: Financing of Aggregate Investment, 1973 to 2002

| | Private savings | Government savings | Foreign savings | | | | Total savings = total investment |
| | | | Average share of each component (per cent) | | | | |
			Total	L-term capital inflow	S-term capital inflow	Decline in reserves	
1973 to 1986 Pre-boom	112.9	−16.7	3.8	5.1	2.1	−3.4	100
1987 to 1996 Boom	93.1	−11.4	18.2	4.1	22.8	−8.7	100
1997 to 1998 Crisis	160.9	−23.2	−37.7	17.3	−70.4	15.4	100
1999 to 2002 Post-crisis	142.3	−6.4	−36.2	11.3	−35.4	−12.1	100

Source: Author's calculations, using data from Bank of Thailand and National Economic and Social Development Board.

the international reserves of the Bank of Thailand reduced it by a further 9 per cent. It is instructive to compare the boom period (1987 to 1996) with the pre-boom period (1973 to 1986).

The major difference between the pre-boom and boom periods was in the proportion of total investment that was financed by short-term capital inflows. This proportion increased from 2 per cent before the boom to 23 per cent during the boom. It financed investment, but it also sowed the seeds of the crisis of 1997–99. The accumulated stock of mobile foreign-owned capital grew to levels far exceeding the stock of the Bank of Thailand's foreign exchange reserves. If the owners of these funds chose to withdraw them from Thailand, the Bank of Thailand would be unable to defend its fixed exchange rate. It has been demonstrated[4] that this is precisely what happened in July 1997.

In summary, growth of the physical capital stock was the most important contributor to Thailand's aggregate growth, accounting for 70 per cent of all growth over the period 1981 to 2002. Most of this investment was financed from Thai domestic private savings. The notion that Thailand's accumulation of physical capital was financed by foreign direct investment (FDI) and/or foreign aid is a myth. Total foreign capital inflows, FDI plus Overseas Development Assistance (ODA) accounted for only about 5 per cent of total investment. ODA was less than one third of this foreign capital inflow. That is, the quantity of ODA explains only 1.5 per cent of total investment over this period, and thus under 1 per cent of total growth.

Before leaving the subject of Thailand's aggregate economic performance, one further topic requires discussion. Why has Thailand's recovery been so slow? As noted above, the crisis was a contraction in aggregate demand, rather than a contraction in productive capacity. Labour and capital were under-utilized because there was insufficient demand for Thai output. Where did this contraction in demand come from? Table 11.4 addresses this point. The upper section of the table shows the composition of expenditure on GDP in Thailand during the pre-crisis boom (1987 to 1996), the crisis (1997 to 1999) and the post-crisis recovery period (2000 to 2005). During the crisis the share of investment in GDP collapsed by 13 percentage points. Investor confidence was severely damaged by the events surrounding the crisis and during the post-crisis recovery period, this share did not recover sufficiently to restore Thailand's long-term rate of growth.

Why has this occurred? High interest rates are not the answer. Figure 11.5 shows that although Thailand's interest rates increased during the crisis, they have been at historically low levels since 2000. A clue is provided by Figure 11.6, which shows the relationship between the Stock

Figure 11.5
Thailand: Real and Nominal Interest Rates, 1994 to 2006

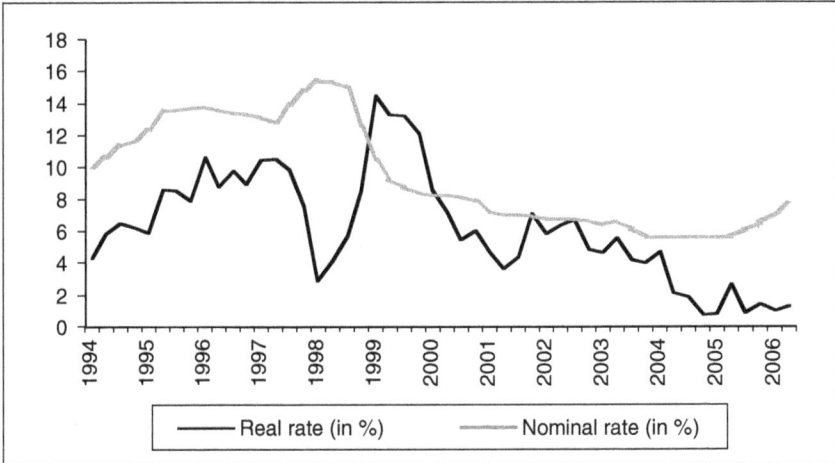

Source: Bank of Thailand.

Figure 11.6
Thailand: Private Investment and the Stock Exchange Price Index

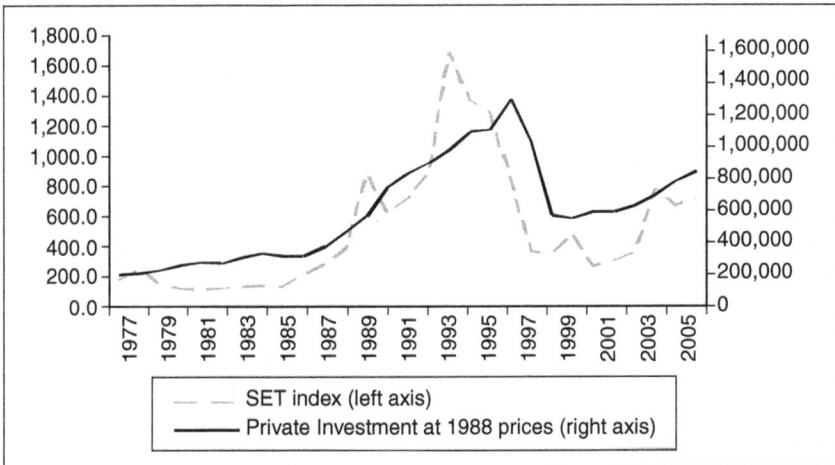

Sources: National Economic and Social Development Board and Stock Exchange of Thailand.

Exchange Index for Thailand (SET) and the level of private investment. Investment follows the SET, but with a lag. The Stock Exchange Index may be viewed as an indicator of investor confidence. Investors have lost confidence in the capacity of the Thai economy to generate a satisfactory return on their investments.

This problem is not unique to Thailand. Table 11.4 shows similar calculations for two other crisis-affected economies, Indonesia and Malaysia. The pattern is very similar. Finally, Figure 11.7 shows annual data on the share of investment in GDP in five crisis-affected East Asian economies: Thailand, Indonesia, Malaysia, the Philippines and Korea. Although the contraction of private investment in Thailand is at least as large as any other (Malaysia is similar), the figure shows that the problem of sluggish recovery of investment is shared by several East Asian economies. It would not seem appropriate to look for country-specific causes. The decline of investor confidence is region-wide. The point is that under the Thaksin

Table 11.4
Thailand, Indonesia and Malaysia: Contributions to Expenditure on GDP,
1987 to 2005

Country/ Period	Consumption	Investment	Government	Net Exports	Total
Thailand					
Pre-crisis (1987–96)	54.8	38.9	9.9	–5.0	100
Crisis (1997–99)	54.9	25.7	10.9	9.9	100
Post-crisis (2000–05)	56.9	24.8	11.2	4.9	100
Indonesia					
Pre-crisis (1987–96)	55.0	27.8	9.1	0.4	100
Crisis (1997–99)	76.1	29.1	8.5	7.5	100
Post-crisis (2000–05)	60.6	20.8	8.7	6.2	100

Table 11.4   (*Continued*)

Country/ Period	Consumption	Investment	Government	Net Exports	Total
Malaysia					
Pre-crisis (1987–96)	48.8	37.2	12.8	1.2	100
Crisis (1997–99)	42.8	30.5	10.5	16.2	100
Post-crisis (2000-05)	43.6	23.0	12.9	20.6	100

Source: Author's calculations, using data from World Bank, World Development Indicators.

Figure 11.7
Investment Shares of GDP in East Asia, 1993 to 2005

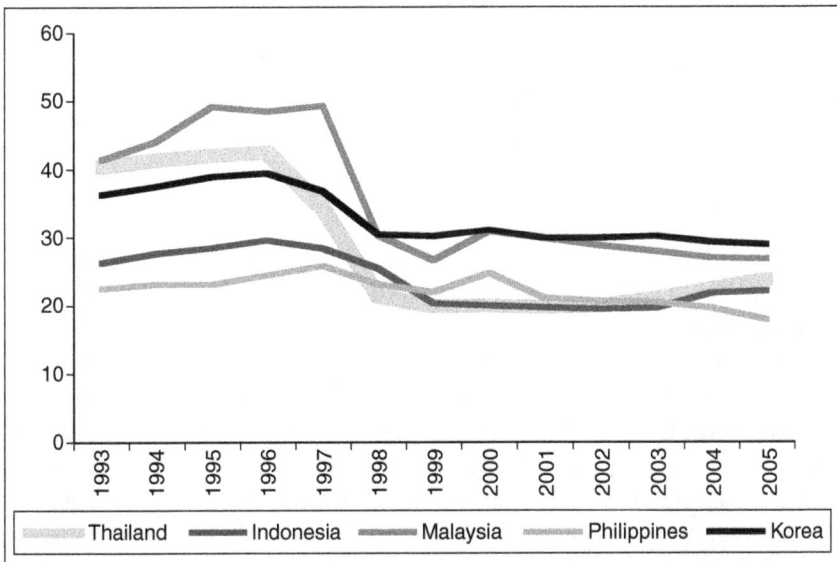

Source: Author's calculations, using data from World Bank, World Development Indicators.

government Thailand performed neither better nor worse than most of its crisis-affected regional neighbours in restoring the willingness of the private sector to invest.

POVERTY INCIDENCE AND INEQUALITY

Is economic growth really so important? Do the poor actually benefit from it, or only the rich? Many observers, mostly non-economists, seem to believe the latter. Within Thailand, as elsewhere, there is considerable debate about these matters. Before turning to the relationship between poverty incidence and economic growth in Thailand, some characteristics of poverty in Thailand will be reviewed. Despite much dispute about measurement and conceptual issues, all major studies of poverty incidence and inequality in Thailand agree on some basic points:

- Poverty is concentrated in rural areas, especially in the northeastern and northern regions of the country.
- Absolute poverty has declined dramatically over the last four decades, but inequality has increased.
- The long-term decline in poverty incidence was not confined to the capital, Bangkok, or its immediate environs, or to urban areas in general, but occurred in rural areas as well. Since 1988, the largest absolute decline in poverty incidence occurred in the poorest region of the country, the northeast.
- Large families are more likely to be poor than smaller families.
- Farming families operating small areas of land are more likely to be poor than those operating larger areas.
- Households headed by persons with low levels of education are more likely to be poor than others.

The following discussion draws upon the official poverty estimates produced by the Thai government's National Economic and Social Development Board (NESDB) which, like all other available poverty estimates, are based upon the household incomes collected in the National Statistical Office's Socio-economic Survey (SES) household survey data. Despite their imperfections, these are the only data available covering a long time period. These survey data have been collected since 1962. The early data were based on small samples, but their reliability has improved steadily, and since 1988 the raw data have been available in electronic form. Table 11.5 summarizes the available official data for the four decades from 1988 to 2004.

The table focuses on the familiar headcount measure of poverty incidence: the percentage of a particular population whose household incomes per person fall below the poverty line. The data confirm that most of Thailand's poor people reside in rural areas. Until recently, the SES data were classified according to residential location in the categories of municipal areas, sanitary districts and villages. These correspond to inner urban (historical urban boundaries), outer urban (newly established urban areas) and rural areas, respectively. Poverty incidence is highest in the rural areas, followed by outer urban, and lowest in the inner urban areas. When these data are recalculated in terms of the share of each of these residential areas in the total number of poor people and then the share of the total population, as in the last two rows of the table, respectively, a striking point emerges. In 2004, rural areas accounted for 93 per cent of the total number of poor people but only 64 per cent of the total population.

The final column of Table 11.5 shows the Gini coefficient of inequality. This index takes values between 0 and 1, with higher values indicating greater inequality. The index rose significantly over the forty years shown. Combined with the reduction in absolute poverty which also occurred, this means that the real incomes of the poor increased with economic growth, but the incomes of the rich increased even faster.

The data summarized in Table 11.5 reveal a very considerable decline in poverty incidence up to 1996, an increase over the following four years to 2000, and then, over the ensuing four years, a resumption of something like the pre-crisis pattern of steady poverty reduction. Over the eight years from 1988 to 1996, measured poverty incidence declined by an enormous

Table 11.5
Thailand: Poverty Incidence and Gini Coefficient, 1988 to 2004
(headcount measure, percentage of total population)

	Poverty incidence (headcount measure, per cent of population)			Inequality (Gini coefficient)
	Aggregate	Rural	Urban	Aggregate
1988	44.9	52.9	25.2	0.482
1990	38.2	45.2	21.4	0.520
1992	32.5	40.3	14.1	0.541
1994	25.0	30.7	11.7	0.522
1996	17.0	21.3	7.3	0.518
1998	18.8	23.7	7.5	0.515
2000	21.3	27.0	8.7	0.525
2002	15.5	19.7	6.7	0.501
2004	11.3	14.3	4.9	0.499

Note: Higher values of the Gini coefficient indicate greater inequality.
Source: National Economic and Social Development Board website: <http://poverty.nesdb. go.th/poverty_new/doc/NESDB/wanchat_20041220041907.ppt>.

27.9 per cent of the population, an average rate of decline in poverty incidence of 3.5 percentage points per year. That is, each year, on average 3.5 per cent of the population moved from incomes below the poverty line to incomes above it. Over the ensuing four years ending in 2000 poverty incidence increased by 4.3 per cent of the population.

Alternatively, over the eight years ending in 1996 the absolute number of persons in poverty declined by 11.1 million (from 17.9 million to 6.8 million); over the following four years the number increased by around 2 million (from 6.8 to 8.8 million). Thus, according to the official data, measured in terms of absolute number of people in poverty, the crisis and its immediate aftermath reversed just under one fifth (18 per cent) of the poverty reduction that had occurred during the eight-year period of economic boom immediately preceding the crisis. Over the four years to 2004, this crisis-induced increase in poverty incidence was erased. The number of people in poverty was then around 5 million, well below the number in 1996, prior to the crisis.

From Figure 11.8, it is apparent that the northeast region dominates poverty incidence in Thailand. This one region accounted for 51 per cent of Thailand's poor people in 2004, but only 34 per cent of the total population. Every other region's share of the total number of poor is smaller

Figure 11.8
Thailand: Poverty Incidence by Region, 2004

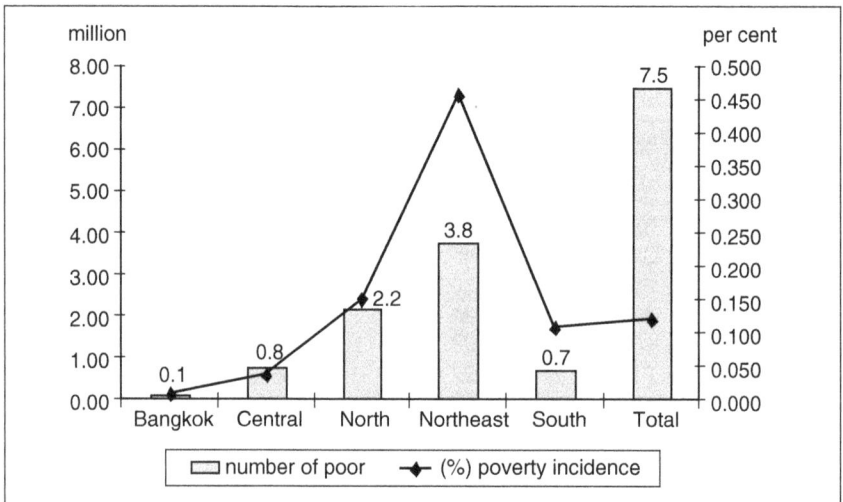

Source: Author's calculations, using data from National Economic and Social Development Board.

than its share of the total population. Poverty is an especially important issue for rural people, particularly in the northeast.

More dramatic than any of these data, however, are recently released data on the relationship between poverty incidence and education. According to the National Economic and Social Development Board's data, of the total number of poor people in 2002, 94.7 per cent had received primary or less education. A further 2.8 per cent had lower secondary education, 1.7 per cent upper secondary, 0.48 per cent had vocational qualifications and 0.31 per cent had graduated from universities. Thailand's poor are overwhelmingly uneducated, rural and living in large families. But they are not necessarily landless.

What caused the long-term decline in poverty incidence? It is obvious that over the long term, sustained economic growth is a necessary condition for large-scale poverty alleviation. No amount of redistribution could turn a poor country into a rich one. Long-term improvements in education have undoubtedly been important, but despite the limitations of the underlying SES data, a reasonably clear statistical picture also emerges on the short-term relationship between poverty reduction and the rate of economic growth. The data are summarized in Figure 11.9, which plots the relationship

Figure 11.9
Thailand: Poverty Incidence and Economic Growth

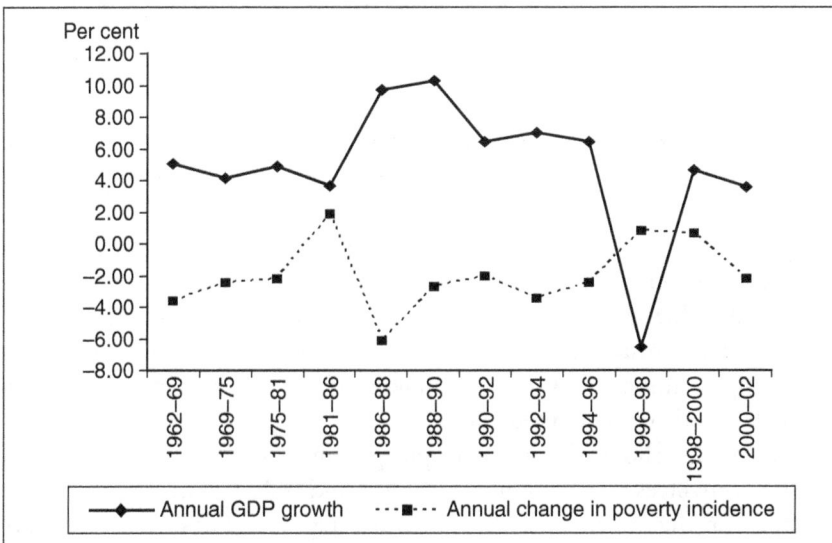

Source: Author's calculations using poverty data as in Table 11.5 and GDP data from National Economic and Social Development Board.

between changes in poverty incidence, calculated from Table 11.5, and the real rate of growth of GDP over the corresponding period.

Although the number of data points is small, the implications seem clear. Periods of more rapid economic growth were associated with more rapid reductions in the level of absolute poverty incidence. Moderately rapid growth from 1962 to 1981 coincided with steadily declining poverty incidence. Reduced growth in Thailand caused by the world recession in the early to mid-1980s coincided with worsening poverty incidence in the years 1981 to 1986. Then, Thailand's economic boom of the late 1980s and early 1990s coincided with dramatically reduced poverty incidence. Finally, the contraction following the crisis of 1997–98 led to increased poverty incidence. The recovery since the crisis has been associated with significant poverty reductions.

On the other hand, no such simple short-term relationship can be found between the change in inequality over time and the rate of growth. The rate of growth does not seem to be a significant determinant of short-term changes in the level of inequality. Other social factors have undoubtedly played a role, but research on this issue remains inconclusive.

ECONOMIC ORIGINS OF THE SOUTHERN CONFLICT

Over recent years, the unrest in Thailand's three southern-most provinces has claimed many hundreds of lives. The conflict has a number of sources, including religious intolerance, but socio-economic deprivation in these three provinces is a genuine source of grievance. The economic basis of the conflict is frequently denied, drawing on the fact that the southern region of the country is relatively well off, compared with other regions. Table 11.6 confirms this point by comparing average incomes per person in Bangkok, the central, northern, northeastern and southern regions. Incomes per person are highest in Bangkok, followed by the central region and then the south. Incomes per person in the north and northeastern regions are considerably lower. These facts are well known and are frequently used to portray the southern conflict as simply a problem of terrorism, with a policing solution. This was the stance of the Thaksin government in particular, with tragic consequences.

Table 11.6 shows that incomes per person in the three southern-most Muslim provinces — Narathiwat, Pattani and Yala — are similar to the average for the north and the northeast regions. These three Muslim provinces are heavily agricultural and much poorer than adjacent southern provinces. The high average level of income in the south is attributable to

Table 11.6
Thailand: GRP per capita and Share of Agriculture, 2001,
and Household Income per capita, 2002
(Baht per person, current prices, and per cent (share of agriculture))

	GRP per capita, 2001	Share of Agriculture in GPP (%), 2001	Household income per capita, 2002
Bangkok Metropolitan	239,207	0.6	28,239
Central Region	78,588	10.7	14,128
North Region	40,352	20.1	9,530
Northeast Region	27,381	18.9	9,279
South Region	54,176	33.9	12,487
Narathiwat	31,412	37.1	7,603
Pattani	47,690	50.8	9,703
Yala	44,160	28.5	10,018
Phuket	225,060	10.5	26,363
Songkhla	62,544	35.1	14,192
Thailand	81,435	10.4	13,736

Source: National Economic and Social Development Board, Bangkok, and Thailand in Figures, 8th ed. (Bangkok: Alpha Research Co. Ltd., 2005).

the high incomes in the tourist areas of Phuket and Songkhla, very different areas from the three Muslim provinces. When aggregate statistics are relied upon, these high income areas mask the low levels of income in the three southern-most rural provinces.

Data on poverty incidence reinforce these conclusions. These data are shown in Table 11.7. Poverty incidence in the three southern-most provinces is three times the average for the southern region as a whole and well above even the average for the northeast region, known for its poverty. It is true that the south as a region is not poor, but this point does not apply to the three southern-most Muslim provinces. There, agriculture dominates, incomes are low and poverty incidence is more than double the national average. Clearly, there are genuine law-and-order problems in these three provinces but a long-term solution to the areas' problems cannot be based on policing alone. It must address the socio-economic basis for the grievances that genuinely exist.

Table 11.7
Thailand: Poverty Incidence by Location, 1990 and 2000

	1990		2000	
	Population shares	Poverty incidence	Population shares	Poverty incidence
Bangkok Metropolitan	10.13	2.41	6.66	0.18
Central Region	17.18	22.52	26.71	3.54
North Region	20.22	24.67	22.49	6.92
North East Region	35.82	44.47	27.18	16.46
South Region	13.78	30.03	16.96	7.31
Three Muslim Provinces	2.99	45.78	3.39	21.07
Phuket + Songkla	2.36	16.85	0.04	1.28
Others	8.44	28.14	0.48	4.65
Thailand	100	29.29	100	8.23

Note: These calculations are based on the National Economic and Social Development Board's "old" poverty line and thus differ from the calculations shown in Table 11.5, which uses the National Economic and Social Development Board's revised poverty line. The revised poverty line is higher and thus indicates a higher level of overall poverty incidence. This difference in poverty lines does not affect the comparison across regions, which is the point of the table.
Source: Calculated from Socio-economic Survey (SES) 1990 and 2000, National Statistical Office, Bangkok.

WAS THAKSIN GOOD FOR THE RURAL POOR?

Thaksin Shinawatra's political support was concentrated in the north and northeast regions, especially in rural areas. The 30 baht health card, farmer debt forgiveness and the village fund scheme were immensely popular and conferred on Thaksin the image of a leader who actually did something for the poor, especially the rural poor. Thaksin's achievements in this respect were genuine and have rightly been continued since the demise of his government. But was Thaksin really good for the rural poor? Was his government more effective in reducing poverty than its predecessors, as it had promised to be? Table 11.8 addresses this question.

The first column compares the average rate of poverty reduction over various periods. Under Thaksin (2002 to 2004), poverty incidence declined

Table 11.8
Thailand: Poverty Incidence and Growth, 1988 to 2004

Period	Annual reduction in aggregate poverty incidence (per cent of population per year)	Annual rate of real GDP growth (per cent per year)	Aggregate poverty reduction per unit of real GDP growth	Rural poverty reduction per unit of real GDP growth
1988–96	3.5	9.2	0.380	0.429
1996–2000	−1.1	−2.9	*0.372*	*0.491*
2000–02	2.9	3.4	0.853	1.073
2002–04	2.1	6.6	0.318	0.409
1988–2004	2.1	6.1	0.344	0.389

Note: Since growth was negative from 1996 to 2000 and poverty incidence increased, "poverty reduction per unit of real GDP growth" means the increase in poverty incidence per unit of GDP decline, both expressed in percentage terms. The calculations are shown in italics to emphasize this point.
Source: Author's calculations based on Table 11.5 and growth data from National Economic and Social Development Board, Bangkok.

at 2.1 per cent per year, while the average for the sixteen years from 1988 to 2004 was 2.4 per cent per year. This difference arose despite the fact that the average rate of GDP growth was slightly higher during Thaksin's tenure than the longer-term average rate, including the crisis years (the second column). The poverty-reducing power of the growth that occurred under Thaksin (the third column) was lower than the long-term average rate (0.32 vs. 0.39) and this difference still arises if we focus only on rural poverty, as shown in the fourth column. These data provide no support for the notion that Thaksin was better at reducing poverty than his predecessors.

CONCLUSION

Thaksin Shinawatra's Thai Rak Thai government successfully convinced large numbers of rural people that it represented their interests. Some of this reputation at least was justified. Thai Rak Thai delivered genuine benefits to Thailand's poor. The 30 baht health card, the farmer debt forgiveness programme and the village fund scheme were all important in this respect. However, the Thaksin government performed similarly to, and certainly no better than, most other crisis-affected East Asian countries in restoring growth. The problem which Thailand shared with its neighbours was that of restoring private investment and in this Thaksin was no more successful than his regional counterparts. Thailand's growth rate during the Thaksin period was below the long-term growth rate from 1968 to 2006 of 6.4 per cent and the poverty-reducing power of this growth was also below the long-term average rate. In economic terms, the Thaksin government was nothing special.

NOTES

1. Peter Warr, ed., "Boom, Bust and Beyond", in *Thailand Beyond the Crisis* (London: Routledge, 2005): 3–65.
2. Sirilaksana Khoman, "Education Policy", in *The Thai Economy in Transition*, edited by Peter Warr (Cambridge: Cambridge University Press, 1993), pp. 325–54.
3. Peter Warr, ed., "The Thai Economy", in *The Thai Economy in Transition*, pp. 1–80.
4. See Peter Warr, "What Happened to Thailand?", in *The World Economy* 22 (July 1999): 631–50; and Warr, "Boom, Bust and Beyond", op. cit.

12

The Thai Economy after the Coup

Bhanupong Nidhiprabha

INTRODUCTION

When the Thai Rak Thai (TRT) party won a landslide victory in 2005, Thaksin obtained an absolute majority in Parliament. Still, from early 2006 there were demonstrations against Thaksin, demanding that he step down. He was accused of being corrupt and abusing his administrative power. Political turbulence was further aggravated when opposition parties boycotted the April 2006 general election, which was later declared invalid by the courts. The Thaksin administration was in turmoil until the 19 September military coup in 2006. The military-installed government that succeeded the Thaksin government turned out to be weak, indecisive, and inconsistent in policy implementation. It was not able to lead the country effectively through difficult times.

The tourism industry, representing 6 per cent of GDP, was also badly affected by Thailand's internal problems. There were many incidents in 2007 that discouraged tourists. The New Year's Eve bombings, southern violence, and high oil prices had an adverse impact on the tourism industry. While the number of tourists increased by 20 per cent in 2006, the first quarter of 2007 witnessed a sharp decline with the growth rate dropping to

5.8 per cent. By the second quarter, tourist numbers increased by a meagre 0.4 per cent. A small increase of 2.2 per cent was observed in the third quarter. For the whole of 2007, the tourism industry experienced a slump, although other Asian countries enjoyed boom times.

There is no doubt that these problems depressed the Thai economy, resulting in slow output expansion compared with the rest of the world. The Thai economy in 2007 was one of the slowest growing in the region (see Figure 12.1). In this globalizing era, when countries are competing to raise standards of living, any economy that expands at a rate lower than the world average will have difficulty catching up with more advanced countries. The income gap between Thailand and Malaysia is widening, while the income gaps between Thailand and other fast-growing economies like Vietnam, China, and India are narrowing. The Thai economy was a laggard in 2007; it failed to take advantage of the expanding world trade.

Since high level of income is an outcome of cumulative growth in the past, a small per cent difference in the growth rate, if maintained for a decade, would result in substantial difference in per capita income. On

Figure 12.1
GDP Growth in 2007

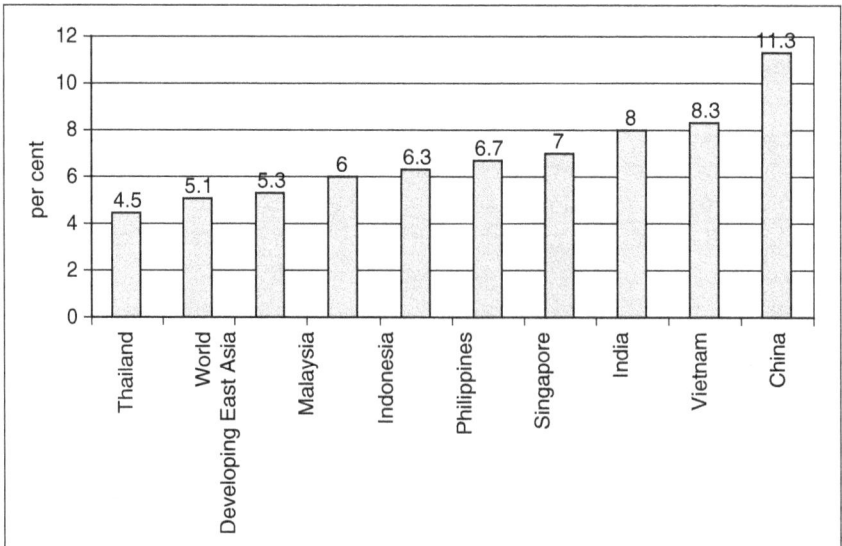

Source: Asian Development Bank, National Economic and Social Development Board (NESDB).

the other hand, any country that maintains its growth rate at more than 7 per cent for a decade would double its income level. That was exactly what Thailand did in the period before the financial crisis in 1998.

Low growth implies that poverty reduction would slow down and unemployment would rise.[1] There has been a fashionable wisdom that the Thai economy should grow moderately at around 5 per cent to avoid social malaise and environmental degradation. Regrettably, that view ignores the importance of maintaining the potential long-term growth. If the economy expands below the normal growth path, unemployment would ensue. Unemployment can be considered as a social cost and a threat to social stability.[2] Thailand had been a country with price stability and low unemployment, because the economy was able to expand at a rate sufficiently high to provide jobs. But that changed in 2007.

It is true that excessive growth is harmful to sustainable development, because it creates macroeconomic imbalances: inflation and current account deficit. The boom-bust cycles can be observed in Figure 12.2, indicating that output was 25 per cent above the long-term path in 1996.[3] But the actual output in 2007 was more than 20 per cent lower than the potential path. To be able to maintain its growth path, the economy must grow above 7 per cent in order to regain its potential path. Otherwise, the Thai people will have to forgo the relative living standard once achieved in the period before the financial crisis. How can a sudden shift of the Thai economy

Figure 12.2
Deviation from the Long-Term Income Path
(per cent)

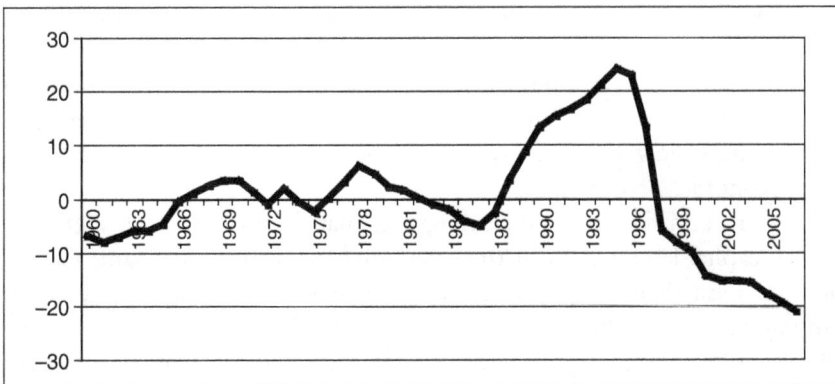

Source: International Financial Statistics, NESDB.

from good to bad performance be explained? This chapter addresses the issue of deviation from the long-term income path and discusses its long-term consequences.

As we can see from Figure 12.2, the Thai economy could have performed with growth and stability as it had achieved between 1960 and 1988. The growth could have oscillated along the trend path had the economy been rid of political disturbances. It seems that the instability could be explosive. What factor could bring the economy back to the original trend path? What happened to the traditional stabilizing mechanism that used to work so well in the period before the crisis? What went wrong?

The following section discusses the causes of the economic slump after the coup. Next, the controversial capital controls of the Bank of Thailand (BoT), which aimed to slow down baht appreciation is examined. The following section analyses the relationship between poverty and political inclination in various parts of the country. The last section provides concluding remarks and suggests the future long-term trend of the Thai economy.

INSUFFICIENT DOMESTIC DEMAND

The Thai economy expanded below its potential level because of shortfalls in consumption and investment. It was not the lack of foreign demand for Thai exports that caused a lacklustre performance of the Thai economy in 2006 and 2007. It was not a supply constraint that precluded Thailand from growing to its full potential level. This was a new phenomenon: poor economic performance was related to a poor political environment.

The spectacular performance achieved in past decades was due to a high investment rate. Figure 12.3 shows an excessive investment rate above 40 per cent of GDP in the late 1990s, leading to overheating and an unsustainable current account deficit. On the other hand, an under-investment episode was evident after the economy recovered from the financial crisis. Low investment rate results in low productivity, loss of international competitiveness, and poor economic performance.

Figure 12.4 reveals the disturbing fact that since the crisis in 1997, the overall capital-labour ratio of the economy has remained stagnant. Capital accumulation therefore expanded at more or less the same rate as labour employment. Since the high capital ratio implies high marginal productivity of labour, a constant capital-labour ratio indicates problems with labour productivity growth. If output does not expand sufficiently, demand for labour will not be able to absorb the growing numbers entering the job market.

Bhanupong Nidhiprabha

Figure 12.3
Long-Term Capital Formations

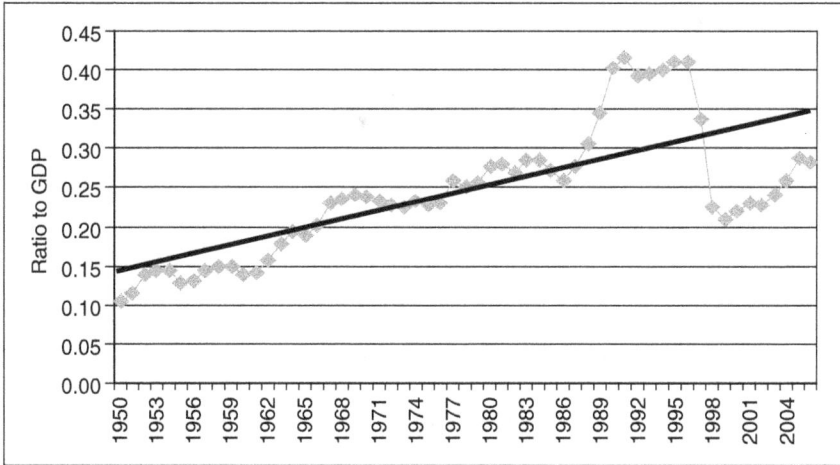

Source: International Financial Statistics.

Figure 12.4
Stagnant Capital-Labour Ratio

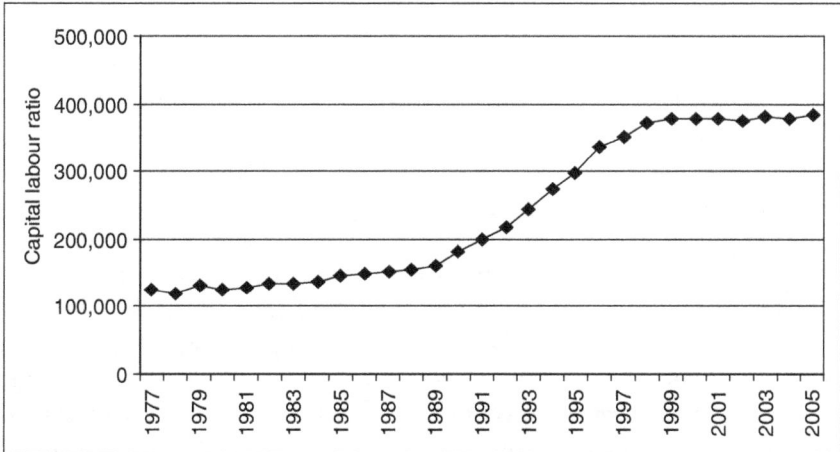

Source: NESDB.

The process of transferring rural labour to the urban sector will slow down, leaving labour remaining in the agricultural sector. Although agricultural output expanded by 4.5 per cent in 2007, this would not be effective in reducing poverty in rural areas as the non-agricultural sector is more capable of transforming low-productivity agricultural labour into higher productivity labour. Furthermore, rural poverty and low farm productivity are consequences of economy-wide under-investment. A country with higher capital intensity is likely to have a higher standard of living than countries with low capital intensity. It is evident that the living standard of the Thai people will be lower in the long run if there is no capital deepening to push up the productivity of labour.

Productivity growth is also due to other factors besides capital intensity. Improvements in technology, human capital investment, and good governance institutions can also enhance growth. But improvement in these factors cannot yield immediate results due to lag effects. In the short run, growth must be propelled by capital accumulation in such a way that the economy on the average remains on the long-term growth path.

Capital accumulation is best effected by leaving it alone to be determined by market forces. Intervention by the government can lead to increased uncertainty and risk as a result of restricted freedom of entrepreneurship. Recently there have been many incidents during the military-appointed regime that have created uncertainties. The military-backed government tightened the foreign investment criteria. Ownership in protected sectors is determined by share of voting rights instead of shares as before. This was a move in reaction to Thaksin's family's sale of Shin Corp to Singapore's Temasek. There were also attempts to change Thailand's 1999 Alien Business Act. The private sector and foreign investors are worried about the changing policy environment and the policy inconsistency of the interim government. The investment climate was destroyed as socio-economic and political risks remained high.

The year 2001 witnessed a decline in investment and consumption spending as a result of the slowdown in world trade. The Thai economy expanded only 2 per cent in 2001, as a result of external shocks. However, the economy showed its resilience by rebounding through the expansion of consumption and investment, buoyed by the political stability in the aftermath of the general election. As the Thaksin government started implementing policies favourable to growth, investor and consumer confidence returned. Output growth increased to 5.3 per cent in 2002, reaching a peak of 7.1 per cent in 2003 before it petered out to 6.3 and 4.5 per cent in 2004 and 2005 respectively.

Consumption and investment began to slow down again in 2005, as the political turmoil gradually developed and intensified into a military coup in September 2006. Consumer confidence and business confidence were eroded, reflected in a sharp decline in private consumption and investment in 2006 and 2007 (see Table 12.1).

A similar collapse of consumption occurred before the economic crisis in 1998, when the Thai economy's output declined by 10 per cent. Since consumption expenditure is the largest component of aggregate demand, a contraction in consumer spending produced a large contractionary impact on output in 2006 and 2007.[4]

Negative consumption shocks are related to decline in investment. Delay in purchasing consumer durables reflects uncertainties about future income and job security. As consumers revised downward their expected income, they postponed consumption and started saving for the future. As investment spending in capital goods collapsed, production capacity was increasingly under-utilized. Except for energy and high capital-intensive industry such as petrochemical and chemical products, excess capacity in other sectors remains high.

It turns out that exports in 2007 grew by 16 per cent, higher than the Ministry of Commerce expectation of 12.5 per cent. Evidence indicates that exports are affected more by the income of trading partners than the exchange rate. Imports grew only 7 per cent, resulting in an US$11,000 million trade surplus in 2007. Despite this positive development, the

Table 12.1
Changes in Consumption and Investment

	Private consumption (y-o-y)	Private investment (q-o-q)	Public investment (q-o-q)	Total capital formation (q-o-q)
2006 Q1	4	2.7	3.6	2.9
Q2	3.1	0.6	13.5	3.5
Q3	2.8	−10.4	22.2	−2.3
Q4	2.7	10	−29	−2.1
2007 Q1	1.3	−1.5	3.8	−0.3
Q2	0.8	2.3	14	5.1
Q3	1.9	−8.8	25.8	0

Note: Private consumption (% y-o-y); Investment (% q-o-q).
Source: NESDB.

economy continued to weaken. In the first eleven months of 2007, the number of newly registered companies declined by 12 per cent. Similarly, during the same period, automobile sales dropped by 5 per cent.[5] In 2004, the economy expanded at 6.3 per cent, while domestic credit rose by 4.2 per cent. However, when the GDP increased by 4.5 per cent in 2007, domestic credit expanded only 1.2 per cent. The low growth of bank credit contributed to the unwillingness of investors and consumers to purchase capital goods. Many Thai business people adopted a wait-and-see attitude because they were not sure about the scheduling of the general election at the end of 2007 and whether a new democratic government could be formed.

For the Thai economy, a 4 per cent growth rate can be considered a mild recession, because it is a growth rate below the trend of the path that would guarantee near full employment. The problem basically stemmed from insufficient domestic demand. Neither supply constraints nor external oil shocks can be blamed for the lost opportunity. Although Malaysia and Singapore experienced sharp currency appreciation, both countries were able to grow faster than 6 per cent in 2007, due to strong domestic demand. It is therefore not true that countries with currency appreciation cannot grow rapidly. On the contrary, currency appreciation can be a result of strong economic growth. In Thailand, however, currency appreciation was due to capital inflows and balance of payments surplus, and the weakening U.S. dollar, rather than strong economic growth.

CAPITAL CONTROLS: A POLICY *FAUX PAS*

Except for Indonesia, Asian currencies appreciated against the U.S. dollar in 2007. As a result, exports decelerated throughout Asia. However, lower export demand from the United States and the appreciation of the Asian currencies did not preclude their economies from expanding. Note that the Philippines' peso, the Malaysian ringgit, and the Indian rupee appreciated at a larger per cent than the Thai baht. These economies grew in spite of strengthening currencies because of domestic demand expansion, enhanced by business and consumer confidence.

Conventional wisdom is that strong economic growth must be led by good exports, which in turn require weak currencies. The BoT opted to maintain a weak baht to stimulate exports. Moral hazards usually follow any attempts to bail out weak commercial banks and inefficient exporters. Because of the failure to see the big picture of the economy, the BoT imposed a 30 per cent Unremunerated Reserve Requirement (URR) on short-term capital inflows on 18 December 2006, three months after the

Bhanupong Nidhiprabha

Figure 12.5
Currency Appreciation against the USD
December 2007 (y-o-y)

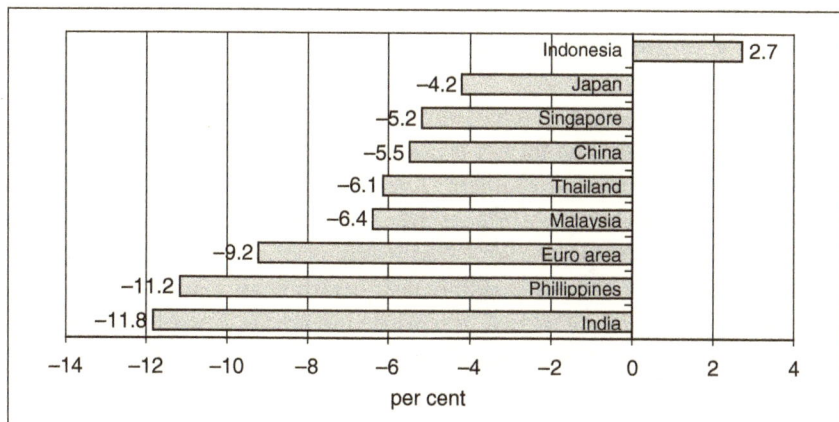

Note: Negative (positive) indicates appreciation (depreciation).
Source: *The Economist*.

coup took place. A 10 per cent withholding tax was imposed on capital inflows that leave the country before one year. The measure led to panic and a stock market crash.[6] The BoT had to reverse its policy the following day to cool down the panic and since then gradually relaxed measures on capital controls, allowing exceptions for foreign portfolio investment. The abandonment of stringent capital controls bodes well for the policy blunder that ignored wide-economy impacts of the capital controls. The BoT argued that the monetary authorities do not want to reverse the course of baht appreciation, but aim to slow down fast appreciation to allow exporters time to adjust with the strengthening baht. The minister of finance supported capital controls, arguing that the extraordinary situation required special measures to guard against adverse impacts of baht appreciation.

The central bank argued that URR would remain until the economy recovered and that the economic recovery would have been much slower without the URR. The BoT presumed that the robust export growth in 2007 was the result of URR slowing down baht appreciation. This kind of argument ignores the fact that other countries experienced strong export growth despite the fact that their currencies appreciated at a substantially higher rate. It is the expansion of world trade that drove export growth of countries in the region, despite the fact that their currencies appreciated considerably against the U.S. dollar. The economic slump was due to the failure of the BoT to stimulate the economy through interest rate policy. Sterilization by the BoT prevented the interest rate from falling; it was unable to stimulate consumption and investment during the downturn of the economy.

Capital controls lead to separation of foreign exchange markets: onshore and offshore markets. The former is protected by high tariffs, while the latter is freely traded in foreign markets. The controls gave rise to differentials in the price of the baht (see Figure 12.6). The gap between the two rates widened with rising speculation of baht appreciation. Like many markets that offer the same products at different prices, there is opportunity to profit from price differentials. The BoT essentially intervenes in the foreign market by targeting a certain foreign exchange level. From 2003 to 2007, the baht appreciated against the U.S. dollar by 16.6 per cent, from 41.5 to 34.6 baht to the dollar. During the same period, the international reserves rose by US$41.1 billion to US$84.6 billion, the swap obligations rose by 3.5 times, from US$5.2 billion to US$18.3 billion. The BoT has intervened heavily to resist strengthening of the baht since 2003. This is against the essence of inflation targeting which required that no target, except inflation, be used as a monetary strategy after floating the baht in 1997.

Figure 12.6
Market Separation

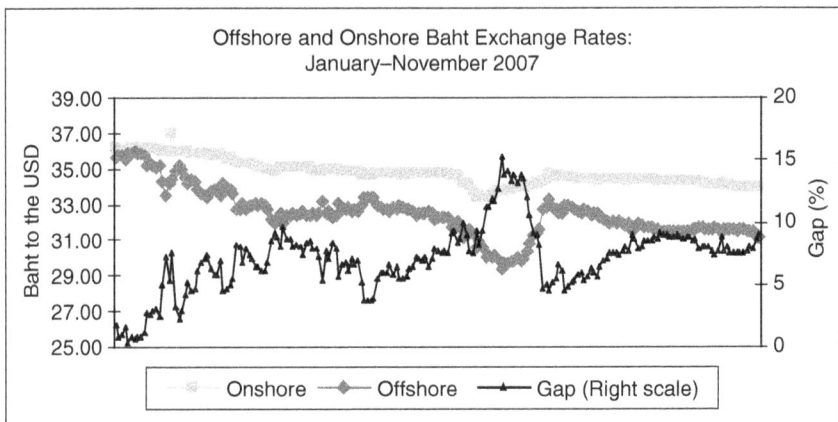

Offshore and Onshore Baht Exchange Rates:
January–November 2007

Onshore ——— Offshore ——— Gap (Right scale)

Source: Bank of Thailand.

After a year of capital control implementation, the BoT further relaxed measures by waiving Thai companies with less than US$1 million of external debt with over one year of maturity from observing the withholding reserves of 30 per cent and fully hedged requirement. In sum, the BoT is repeating mistakes it committed a decade ago — albeit in the opposite direction in terms of the value of the baht. The result remains the same: huge financial losses and ineffective outcomes. The BoT suffered financial losses of 170 billion baht in 2006.

The BoT also sterilizes the inflow of capital by issuing BoT bonds to mop up liquidity in the financial markets. This measure is not effective in the long run in preventing money supply from growing, because higher interest rates offered by the BoT bonds give rise to more capital inflows in response to interest rate differentials. At the beginning of 2007, the BoT asked the Ministry of Finance for permission to issue 900 billion baht in BoT bonds, and an additional 500 billion baht at the end of 2007. The sterilization is ineffective and costly, because the BoT must use the proceeds from selling the bonds to invest abroad to be able to pay BoT bond holders. If the baht keeps on appreciating, the BoT ends up losing more money. The question is therefore whether the loss of billions of baht is worth the outcome of sterilization. Would it not be better to spend the same amount of money on projects with a higher social rate of return?

A panel study of 96 countries between 1970 and 2000 provides evidence that capital controls deter foreign direct investment (FDI).[7] Capital account on the other hand promotes FDI in emerging markets. If changes in laws and policies are unpredictable, the risk of policy reversal undermines the credibility of the government. The BoT's capital controls measure reversed the policy of an open capital account. The perception of policy inconsistency damaged investors' confidence in Thailand's open-door policy for foreign investors. Imposing controls on short-term capital sends a bad signal to all foreign investors. It should be noted that the structure of maturing of capital inflows in 2007 was totally different from the structure in 1996. Capital controls can change the structure of maturity but they cannot prevent capital inflows. It did not reduce the total volume of aggregate flows moving into Thailand. It has not deterred the baht from appreciating, nor has it reduced stock market instability.

During a period of high oil prices, baht appreciation can reduce inflationary pressure from the price of imported oil. By resisting baht appreciation, price distortions were created in favour of foreign markets against domestic markets. Firms that invest in purchasing imported capital goods had to pay higher prices than they should have. Consequently, capital formation was adversely affected by the unrealistically low value of the Thai baht, delaying the process of regaining the investment growth path.

POVERTY AND POLITICAL RAMIFICATIONS

Economists have been blamed for paying too much attention to economic growth. It seems that Thais have taken growth for granted. Social problems intensify as growth slows down below 5 per cent. The crime rate went up in 2007 in spite of an empowered military overseeing national security. Unemployment rises as economic growth decelerates. In particular, new job seekers have difficulty finding jobs related to their training. The number of university graduates who have been looking for jobs for more than two years after graduation has increased. From a survey of the National Statistical Office (NSO) in May 2007, 36 per cent of the unemployed were university graduates, 24 per cent had finished high school, 22 per cent secondary school, and 18 per cent primary school. The higher the level of education, the higher the probability of being unemployed. Although this is a long-term problem of the Thai education system, which has been unable to produce labour corresponding to market demand, sluggish economic activity does not have the strength to employ many new graduates even if they are in the right discipline.

Official figures show an unemployment rate of 1.6 per cent in 2007, suggesting that Thailand had the lowest unemployment rate among countries in the region. This is hardly plausible if we consider how the economy has drifted from its potential growth path. The capacity utilization of the whole economy was 76 per cent on average for 2007.[8] The NSO survey in May 2007 indicated that there were 580,000 unemployed, 30 per cent of which were in the northeast, 26 per cent in the central region, 21 per cent in the north, 14 per cent in the south, and 9 per cent in Bangkok.

Poverty is related to unemployment. If output growth is high, the fast-growing economy can generate employment in urban areas. In consequence, unemployed people from rural areas can be put to work in non-agricultural sectors. As the Thai economy expanded by 15 per cent from 2003 to 2006, the number of poor was reduced from 7 million in 2004 to around 6 million in 2006, while the per cent of the poor who lived below the poverty line declined from 11.2 per cent to 9.6 per cent. It should be noted that the per cent of the extreme poor reduced from 0.56 to 0.53 per cent during the same period. Evidently, economic growth can eradicate the type of poverty that kills to almost zero. However when the economy stagnates, unemployment increases, making it difficult to speed up the process of poverty reduction.

There were a series of policies adopted by the military-installed interim government that shook the confidence of investors: compulsory licensing of pharmaceuticals; amendment of the alien business law; and capital controls. In January 2007, the government bypassed patents of anti-Aids and heart drugs. Compulsory licensing by the interim government, though cheapening the cost of HIV and Aids treatment, raised questions of property rights and damaged the foreign investment climate. The interim government allocated budgetary resources to purchase a submarine. The budget could have been used for research and development in producing generic drugs to fight new diseases. Thailand is not so poor that it cannot afford to pay for expensive medicine.

There is a trade-off between obtaining low-cost medicine and loss of the country's investment climate and abandoning adherence to rules of international property rights. Some of these policy measures were made less stringent to cool down the panic of investors, but perceptions of policy uncertainty, an unfriendly business environment, and political instability have driven foreign direct investment to other neighbouring countries such as Vietnam. According to the *International Business Report 2007*, conducted by Grant Thornton International, Thailand has lost its investment opportunities to Vietnam and Malaysia due mainly to political turmoil and uncertain economic policy.

The Japan External Trade Organization (JETRO) reported in December 2007 that Japanese companies are relocating production bases to Vietnam to take advantage of lower operating costs and to avoid political turmoil in Thailand. Foreign direct investment in the manufacturing sector depends also on how the domestic market can expand to absorb production by multinational corporations. Neighbouring countries are growing rapidly because of strong domestic demand. Economic growth therefore is crucial for attracting foreign direct investment that can create spillover effects of technology transfer. Thailand's economic slump led to lost opportunity to obtain foreign direct investment.

There has been a vicious cycle in Thailand's politics: general elections are usually followed by weak elected governments, a military coup takes place and abolishes the old constitution, then a new constitution is drafted and the country temporarily returns to democracy until a new coup takes place. In the short history of the nascent Thai democracy, there have been eighteen constitutions in total since 1932. An unusual and peculiar aspect of the 2006 coup is that the business sector has been affected. The military-installed government has engineered a policy that derailed investment sentiment and destroyed consumer confidence.

Except for Bangkok, where poverty incidence is close to zero, there was a positive correlation between poverty and the per cent of "no" votes for the new constitution drafted by a committee set up by the military regime. As people become poorer, they value more the populism policy package previously offered by TRT. There has been a view in Bangkok that voting cannot be considered democratic as long as voters can be bought. The victory of TRT in general elections was considered fraudulent as there was rampant vote-buying. The poor in Thailand associated voting "no" to the constitutional draft with saying "yes" to the return of TRT.

Bangkok is different from the rest of the country (see Figure 12.7). With the lowest poverty level, the "no" vote should have been low. A "no" vote does not imply voting in favour of TRT, but a vote against dictatorship. However, "yes" votes overwhelmed "no" votes in Bangkok. Voting was not dictated by economic reasoning. People in Bangkok voted "yes" because they wanted the country to return to normalcy through the election process. That is why they voted to approve the draft constitution.

Figure 12.7
Poverty and Political Inclination

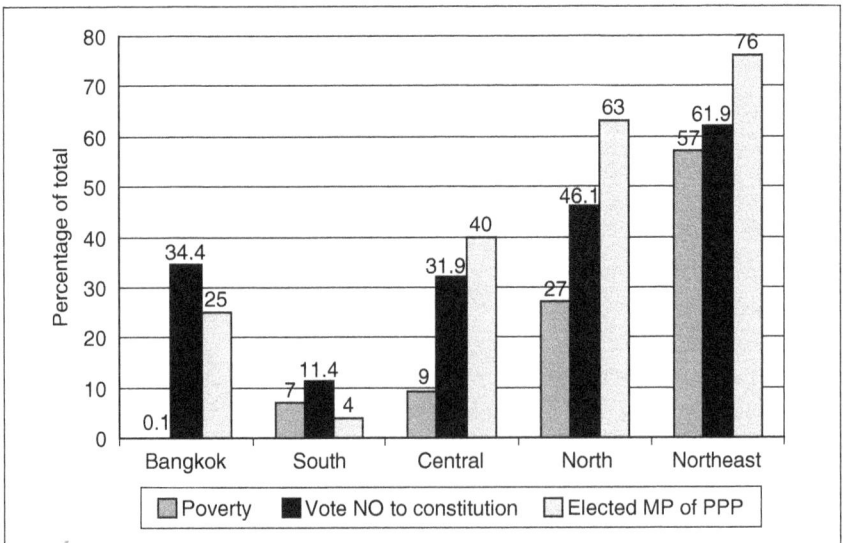

Source: Election Commission and NESDB.

Note that there were no accusations of fraud in voting down the constitutional draft, but the outcome of the general elections on 23 December 2007 resembled the pattern of rejection of the new constitutional draft (see Figure 12.7). The People Power Party (PPP), a declared successor to TRT, received votes mainly from poor people in various parts of the country. From a political campaign point of view, the way to win elections is to come up with a policy platform in favour of the poor. Thus the Democrat Party extended TRT's 30 baht-per-visit medical programme to free medical care. One of the successes of TRT is that political parties are now more concerned with the plight of the poor. All parties in the 2007 general election came up with populist policies in various forms, without conceivable explanations of how those populist programmes could be financed.

The military coup revived the boom in defence spending.[9] As the budget is limited, higher spending for the military means less budget for other purposes (see Table 12.2). The share of the defence budget declined under the previous administration, as priority was given to social welfare and education. Budgets allocated to health and welfare have been rising over the last three years.[10] Education was given the highest priority, amounting to more than 4 per cent of GDP in 2007.

The military-installed government reversed the downward trend of military spending by increasing the defence budget in fiscal year 2008 by 24.3 per cent, including plans to purchase military hardware such as

Table 12.2
Budget Allocation by Fiscal Year
(per cent)

Ministry allocations (% share)	FY 2007	FY 2008	% Change in value
Defence	7.3	8.6	24.3
Education	18.0	18.1	6.7
Public health	4.0	3.9	4.7
Central fund	12.6	14.8	24.3
Agriculture	4.1	3.9	0.6
Transport	4.5	4.1	−4.7
Total amount (billion baht)	1566.0	1660.0	6.0

Source: Budget Bureau.

a submarine and jet fighters. One should remember the efficient rule of budget allocation that the marginal benefit of each baht must be equated so that the social welfare of the nation can be maximized. The 2008 budget was raised by 6 per cent in order to compensate for the fall in investment and consumption. The expansionary impact of the increased budget will be much less if the budget is geared towards imported goods, while the marginal propensity to consume remains subdued.

For the fiscal year 2008, the budget allocation to the Ministry of Science, ICT, and Transportation was curtailed by 14 per cent, 8.4 per cent, and 4.5 per cent respectively. The impact of reducing investment spending on these infrastructure resources will be felt in the long run. According to Easterly and Rebelo, transport and communication public investment has a positive impact on long-term growth, while private investment is complementary to public investment.[11]

CONCLUSION

According to Rodrik, institutions are linked to the quality of formal and informal socio-political arrangements — from legal systems to political institutions. Good institutions provide property rights, appropriate regulatory structures, quality and independence of the judiciary and bureaucratic capacity. Institutions that provide dependable property rights, manage conflict, maintain law and order, and align economic incentives with social costs and benefits are the foundation of long-term growth.[12]

The overthrow of the legitimate government by the military coup caused considerable damage in terms of economic losses. The rule of law, good governance and good institutions, both legal and democratic infrastructure are required to nurture an economic environment suitable for long-term development which raises living standards. Military coups in the past did not destroy the confidence of the business sector, thereby leaving intact economic strength. The latest coup, however, has destroyed the democratic underpinning of the stability of political and economic structures, and sapped the economic strength of the Thai economy. The long-term growth of the economy and social welfare are threatened as the government budget is allocated to non-productive spending. Infrastructure public investment and human capital-related spending have been curtailed for the sake of defence. The Thai economy has stepped backwards, losing an opportunity to grow when the world economy expanded in 2007. Alas, the September 2006 coup may not be the last one.

NOTES

1. For evidence of the favourable impact of growth on poverty reduction in Thailand, see Peter Warr, "Globalization, Growth, and Poverty Reduction in Thailand", *ASEAN Economic Bulletin* 21, no. 1 (2004): 1–18.
2. The unemployment rate in 2007 was 1.6 per cent — the lowest in the world. With 49 per cent of the labour force in agriculture, the official statistics ignores the bias caused by under-employment.
3. The potential growth path, 7.1 per cent per annum, is constructed from a non-linear time trend of real GDP from 1960 to 2005.
4. Blanchard argued that consumers expected a recession and reduced their spending during the 1990–91 Recession in the United States. See Oliver Blanchard, "Consumption and the Recession of 1990–91", *American Economic Review* 83, no. 2 (1993): 270–74.
5. Similarly, in the first eight month of 1998, automobile sales dropped by 71 per cent, while exports in dollar terms declined by 4 per cent.
6. The Security Exchange of Thailand Index dropped by 108 points within one day.
7. Elizabeth Asiedu and Donald Lien, "Capital Controls and Foreign Direct Investment", *World Development* 32, no. 3 (March 2004): 479–91.
8. The index accounts for 59 per cent of the manufacturing sector value added in 2000. The index is biased upwards since it does not sufficiently capture the utilized capacity of small and medium-sized firms.
9. For evidence that there are benefits from reducing military spending — the so-called peace dividend — see M.N. Knight, N. Loayza, and D. Villanueva, "The Peace Dividend: Military Spending Cuts and Economic Growth", *IMF Staff Papers* 43, no. 1 (March 1996): 1–37.
10. It has been accepted by the military-backed government that a populist policy has some merit, but the money should be spent on the type of populism policy that works.
11. William Easterly and Sergio Rebelo, "Fiscal Policy and Economic Growth: An Empirical Investigation", *Journal of Monetary Economics* 32, no. 3 (1997): 417–58.
12. Dani Rodrik, *In Search of Prosperity: Analytic Narratives on Economic Growth* (New Jersey: Princeton University Press, 2003).

13
The Impact of Political Uncertainty on Business

Glen Robinson

During the political turmoil of 2006–07, a great deal of media and other expert attention has focused on the effects political instability might have on the business community. This chapter is an attempt to provide insights into business perceptions, from a member of Thailand's foreign business community.

It is difficult to generalize because there are a range of experiences. Some businesses have been in Thailand thirty years or more, and seen such instability before, while others have been there for quite a short period of time, and could be fazed by the events. It was some time ago (perhaps twenty years) that I was with some very senior Thai business people, and as we drove past a military establishment, I made some comment about military coups. The response, after the initial deathly silence was: "Mr Robinson, we in Thailand have a coup on the first Tuesday of each month. It starts at 11 a.m. and must be finished by lunchtime." Such was the frequency of coups at that time, and the lack of gravity with which they were viewed.

However in the current life of most investors, they do not know of coups, nor that they have generally been conducted with gentlemanly observance of other peoples' rights. The most recent coup occurred over fifteen years ago, in February 1991. Moreover, a high level of political uncertainty and actual machinations surrounded the September 2006 coup, sufficient to make Machiavelli look almost amateurish. So it was with great relish and some enthusiasm that I thought I should undertake the project of trying to establish what the current view of the foreign business community has been.

I thought that I would take my lead from attitudes of Thailand's English language newspapers. These can be taken to reflect the perceptions of the local and foreign business community, including the foreign business chambers, and Australia and other Western governments.

The effects of those attitude changes are to be measured against the factors below which I have called the "reality":

- Inward foreign direct investment (FDI), which shows the actual funds being invested in (mainly) capital works, but certainly in ventures in which the capital is not liquid and not very mobile.
- Applications to the Board of Investment (BOI), which is very current and reflects the "up to the minute" thinking of potential investors.
- Actual tourist numbers from Australia.

WHAT WAS THE PERCEPTION?

If we take a timeline of the twenty months leading up to the December 2007 elections, there were some very significant events which warrant some discussion.

Figure 13.1
Timeline of Events

2 April '06	8 May '06	19 September '06	18 December '06	1 January '07
Thaksin 'won' the election.	Election deemed null and void.	A military junta overthrew the elected government.	Currency controls imposed; modified day later to exclude investment in FDI and stockmarket, but retained for bonds and currency.	Bangkok bombings

9 January '07	28 February '07	30 May '07	August '07	December '07
Cabinet approves amendment to Foreign Business Act, received with alarm by many in the foreign business community. Around same time Retail Business Act also mooted.	Cabinet Finance Minister MR Pridiyathorn Devakula resigned under controversial circumstances following earlier appointment then quick resignation of Thaksin's Finance Minister, Dr Somkid Jatusripitak, as a special envoy for promoting the Sufficiency Economy Theory to the international community.	Court decision: Thaksin and 110 TRT executives banned.	Draft constitution accepted at referendum.	General Elections

EARLY 2006 TO SEPTEMBER 2006

Leading up to the April election the country experienced some disquiet as the Bangkok-based opposition to Prime Minister Thaksin became more vocal. Thaksin's Thai Rak Thai (TRT) Party comfortably won the April election, which he called only twelve months into a parliamentary term because of increasing opposition to him following the sale of his family's Shin Corp to Singapore's Temasek. This election was, however, boycotted by the main opposition parties, and on 8 May deemed null and void by the Constitutional Court. Thaksin stayed on as caretaker prime minister, but conflict between his supporters and the opposition continued to grow.

It is clear that this period was unsettling, and domestic consumption began to decline. There was considerable speculation and comment about the Foreign Business Act (FBA) because it in fact had been the act which Thaksin's family flouted in the Temasek deal in order to maximize their own benefits, and which brought so much criticism on their heads. Such was the speculation that the newspapers were reporting changes were about to occur, and it became obvious that foreigners required some clarity and stability in the foreign investment climate. There was also much speculation that because of the uncertainty, foreign investment would decline.

The 19 September Coup

While Prime Minister Thaksin was in New York preparing to talk to the United Nations and to justify some of his actions, the military in Thailand led a coup against his government. The monarchy endorsed the coup, and within two or three days, newspaper polls claimed 80 per cent public acceptance of it. Coup leaders soon appointed General (Retired) Surayud Chulanont as prime minister, and set in process a series of steps to return Thailand to democratic rule in around twelve months.

After the coup, public discussion about the level of foreign ownership, and the form in which foreigners might invest, were widely discussed. A sense of nationalism was beginning to grow, strengthened in part by the Surayud government's promise to follow the king's proposal for a "sufficiency economy". Nationalism seemed to permeate the economy, and many foreigners started to get a little nervous. This persisted and accelerated right through to mid-December. Some of the newspaper headlines as shown below reflect the sentiment:

> "Foreign Ownership; Deal Flow Dries up on Policy Uncertainty" (*Bangkok Post*, 14 October 2006).

"Foreigners Want Policies to be Clear; Investor Confidence Needs to be Restored" (*Bangkok Post*, 20 October 2006).

"British Seek Clarification on Investments" (*The Nation*, 3 November 2006).

"Curbs on Expansion Worry French Envoy" (*The Nation*, 25 November 2006).

DECEMBER 2006–JANUARY 2007

Speculation and complaints reached a crescendo during December 2006 and January 2007. They were prompted initially by the introduction of tough capital controls on 18 December. Even though the controls were eased twenty-four hours later, great damage had been done. Cabinet approval of a revised FBA around three weeks later heightened foreign concerns. Other matters discussed at the time included a restrictive Retail Business Act (to address public concerns over the rapid expansion of international retail giants such as Tesco Lotus and Carrefour), further restrictions on foreign land ownership, and an attempt to import cheap generic versions of drugs for treating HIV and heart complaints, prompting U.S. complaints that Thailand did not provide adequate protection or enforcement of intellectual property rights.

By this time, the government and the administration were being increasingly criticized for their "anti-foreign" acts, and dire predictions were being made about the flight of foreign capital. Media reports claimed that foreign investment had stalled, the BOI had no work to do because there were no enquiries, and that the level of interest in Thailand was low. Such was the conventional wisdom, reflected in the following headlines:

"Foreign Business Act; Foreign Chambers Step up Lobbying" (*Bangkok Post*, 22 December 2006).

"Korn: New Rules could Hurt SET" (*Bangkok Post*, 29 December 2006).

"Foreigners Rip New Rules on Ownership" (*Bangkok Post*, 10 January 2006).

"Faith of Investors must be Restored" (*The Nation*, 10 January 2006).

"New Investment Rules are Impractical" (*Bangkok Post*, 11 January 2007).

"Pridiyathorn Tries to Ease Fears, but Foreigners Wary" (*Bangkok Post*, 11 January 2007).

"Investors may Look Elsewhere after Revision" (*Bangkok Post*, 11 January 2007).

"Joint Chambers Warn of Blow to Investment" (*Bangkok Post*, 11 January 2007).

"Overseas Investors Wary of Changes" (*The Nation*, 11 January 2007).

"Investors in a Pickle over New Foreign Business Law" (*The Nation*, 12 January 2007).

"FBA Changes Leave Big Credibility Gap" (*The Nation*, 16 January 2007).

"Japanese Investors are 'worried'" (*The Nation*, 24 January 2007).

"Foreigners Halt Expansion Plans" (*Bangkok Post*, 30 January 2007).

The underlying themes were that the new laws were anti-foreign, and changed the ownership and voting requirements so that foreigners could not gain or retain control of their businesses.

The Bombings

On New Year's Eve, a series of bombs went off in central Bangkok, killing three and injuring forty. It was widely speculated the bombings were not intended to injure people or property, but more to make a statement. The fact that the injury toll was so low probably supports that contention. However, the Australian government and other governments issued a travel warning aimed at discouraging their nationals from travelling to crowded spots in Thailand, which obviously included Bangkok.

To May 2007

The criticism of authorities increased in volume, frequency and vitriol, a fact which is surprising given the welcome the coup received in September. We must recognize, of course, that this criticism was concentrated in the English language press and from within the expatriate community in Bangkok. Even so, a considerable amount of criticism was coming from the Thai community, and some from well-placed individuals. The authorities had shown themselves to be slow-moving, inept, and insensitive to public needs. They played to nationalistic fervour, and anti-foreign commentary became widespread. The press and Bangkok's large foreign business community were strongly focused on the Foreign Business Act, the retail laws, capital controls and changes to the land ownership requirements. The following headlines demonstrate these points:

"FDI 'under Threat unless Govt Acts'" (*The Nation*, 17 February 2007).

"FBA Overhaul may Hit Retail" (*The Nation*, 24 February 2007).

"Editorial; FBA must Move with the Times" (*Bangkok Post*, 19 March 2007).

"US Envoy Tells of Investor Unease over Govt's Moves" (*The Nation*, 2 April 2007).

"Japanese Worry about FBA Changes; New Investments may Go Elsewhere" (*Bangkok Post*, 5 April 2007).

"Executives want FBA to be Liberalised; Thailand Falling behind Regional Rivals" (*Bangkok Post*, 10 April 2007).

"Foreign Business Act Amendments will still Steer Investors away" (*The Nation*, 13 April 2007).

"Finance Ministry's Research Body Pessimistic about Growth" (*Bangkok Post*, 18 April 2007).

"Investment in Thai Hotels is Stalled by FBA Moves" (*The Nation*, 3 May 2007).

WHAT WAS THE REALITY?

What was the reality in terms of the three measures mentioned earlier — FDI, applications to the BOI, and Australian tourist numbers?

Foreign Direct Investment

Actual statistics on FDI do not reflect the alarm expressed in the media. Figure 13.2 shows that monthly FDI has been relatively stable, apart from the month of September (when the coup occurred) when it took a significant dive. It recovered quite quickly thereafter, and has returned to almost normal. Claims of stalled investment are not supported by this information.

The annual rate of FDI in Figure 13.3 shows a decline between 2006 and 2007 (2007 is annualized from the first eight months information).

**Figure 13.2
FDI (US$ millions)
3 month moving average**

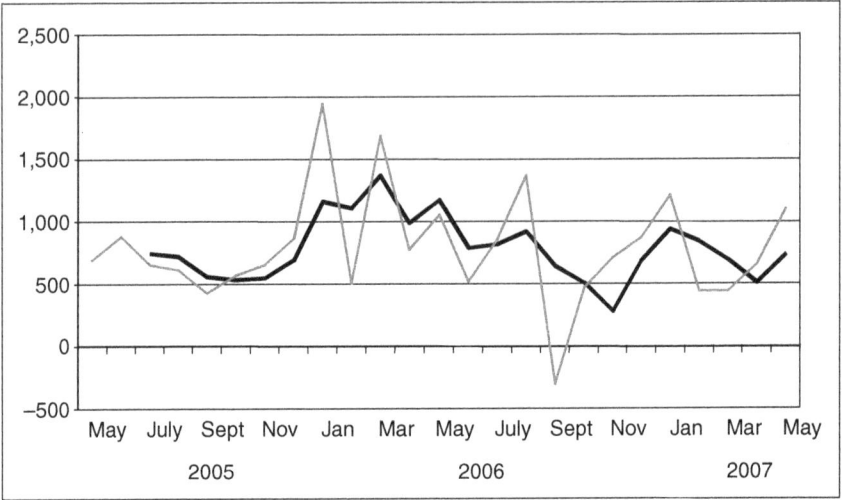

Source: Bank of Thailand.

**Figure 13.3
Thailand — Net FDI, US$ billions**

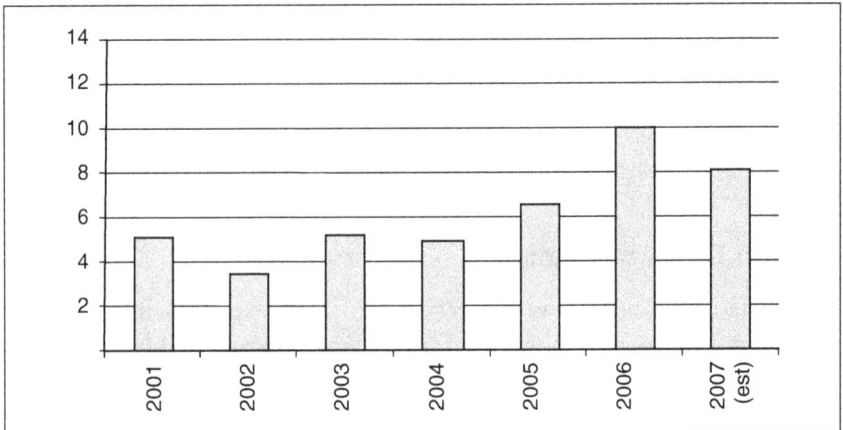

Source: Bank of Thailand.

Even so 2007 is still significantly higher than 2005, again contradicting the claim that foreign investment stalled.

Nonetheless there is probably sufficient evidence to say that had recent political difficulties not occurred, the level of foreign investment would have been higher. FDI going to Indonesia and Vietnam for the same period (see Figure 13.4) demonstrates significant increases for 2007.

Figure 13.4
FDI (US$ billions) in Indonesia and Vietnam

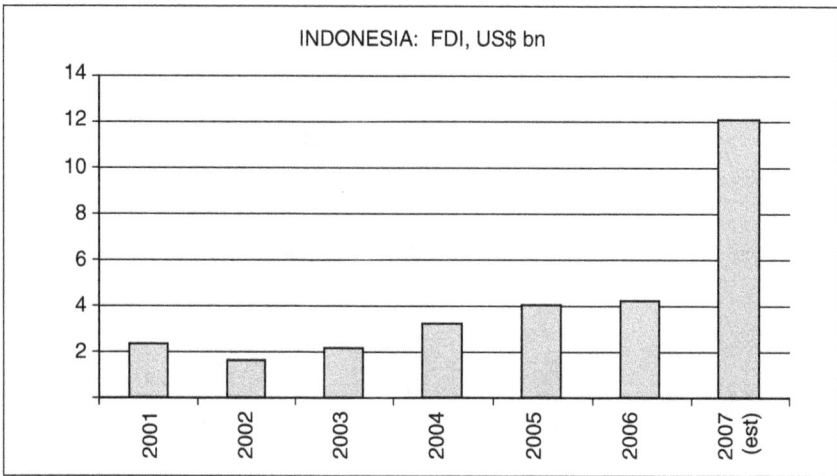

Source: BKPM (Indonesia Investment Coordinating Board).

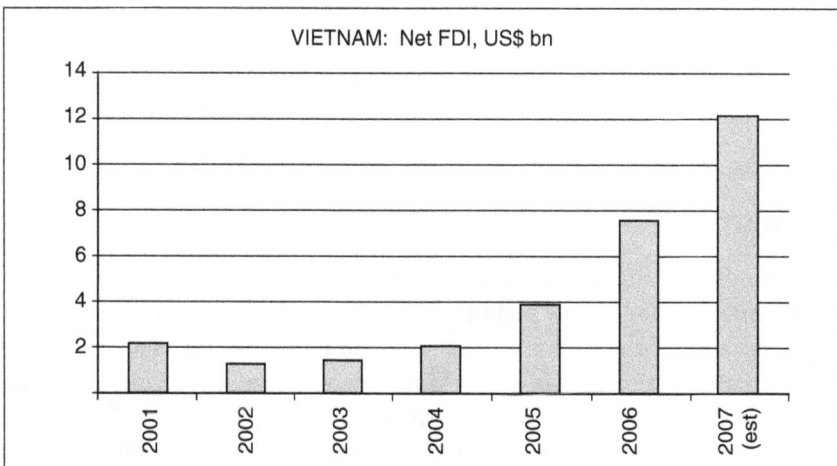

Source: CEIC Data.

BOI APPLICATIONS

BOI applications are a good measure of the intentions of the people at the time. It must be recognized that not every investment in Thailand requires registration at the BOI, however most local and many foreign organizations apply for registration as approved projects often receive government incentives.

The statistics in Figure 13.5 show a slight decline in applications between 2005 and the first half of 2006. However there was no decline in the latter half of 2006 or the first half of 2007 — rather, there was a small increase.

Figure 13.5
FDI — Number of Applications to BOI

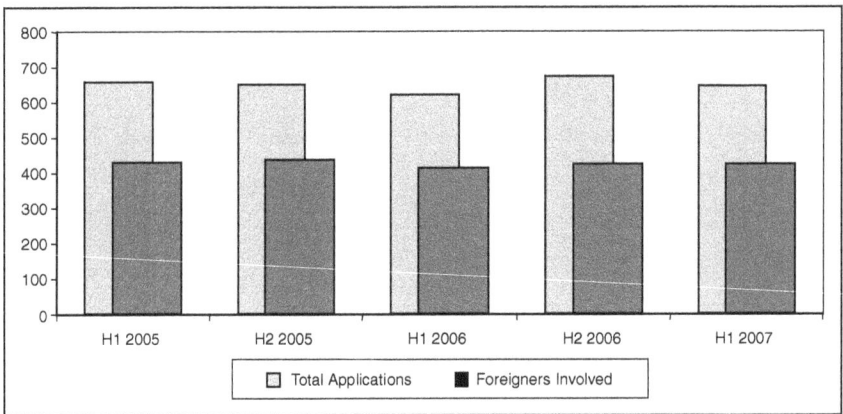

Source: Statistics from BOI website <http://www.boi.go.th/english/about/statistics.asp>.

TOURISTS

The number of Australian tourists visiting Thailand over the period is a clear demonstration of the feelings which Australians have for the country. Notwithstanding the military coup, and the bombings on New Year's Eve which made the front pages of world newspapers, the number of Australian tourists has continued to increase. In the eighteen months to September 2006, tourists arrived at an annual rate of 466,000. In the nine months after October 2006, the annual rate increased to 622,000.

CONCLUSION

When one reviews newspaper headlines since the beginning of 2006, along with pronouncements from foreign business chambers and government authorities, the perception is that foreign investment in Thailand has stalled, foreigners are withdrawing capital from the country, and Thailand is not a place to visit. In fact, FDI has remained stable, and since the coup investment applications to the BOI have crept up, while Australian tourist numbers have expanded rapidly. The conclusion then is that despite the extremely pessimistic perceptions of the media and governments, the business community has continued to invest at healthy levels. There is, however, every probability that investment would have been even higher without the political uncertainty.

Index